Designing Liners

A history of interior design afloat

Anne Wealleans

Routledge
Taylor & Francis Group

LONDON AND NEW YORK

Arts & Humanities
Research Council

 # S
i / 11

First published 2006
by Routledge
2 Park Square, Milton Park, Abingdon, Oxon OX14 4RN

Simultaneously published in the USA and Canada
by Routledge
270 Madison Ave, New York, NY 10016

Transferred to Digital Printing 2008

Routledge is an imprint of the Taylor & Francis Group, an informa business

Typeset in Charter ITC by Keystroke, 28 High Street, Tettenhall, Wolverhampton
Printed and bound in Great Britain by TJI Digital, Padstow, Cornwall

British Library Cataloguing in Publication Data
A catalogue record for this book is available from the British Library

Library of Congress Cataloging in Publication Data
Wealleans, Anne.
    Designing liners: a history of interior design afloat/Anne Wealleans.—1st ed.
        p. cm.
    Includes bibliographical references and index.
    ISBN 0–415–37466–9 (hb: alk. paper) — ISBN 0–415–37468–5 (pb: alk. paper)
    1. Ocean liners—Decoration—History. 2. Interior decoration—History. I. Title.
    VM382.W389 2006
    623.82'432—dc22   2006003834

ISBN10: 0–415–37466–9 (hbk)
ISBN10: 0–415–37468–5 (pbk)

ISBN13: 978–0–415–37466–8 (hbk)
ISBN13: 978–0–415–37468–2 (pbk)

Contents

Illustrations

Acknowledgements

I am grateful to a great many people who have helped bring this book to fruition. Kingston University allowed me the time and support for the project. I am also grateful to my colleagues there for their encouragement, most notably Jonathan Black, Stuart Durant, Emma Holloway, Chris Horrocks, Trevor Keeble, Fran Lloyd, Brenda Martin, Helen Potkin, Marq Smith, Penny Sparke, Dejan Sudjic and Pat Wheaton. Also the students on the *Design, Style and Luxury* course were an important sounding board. Thanks also to the AHRC for supporting the research with one of their Small Grants in the Creative and Performing Arts. Thank you to Caroline Mallinder from Routledge for commissioning the book, and Julia Mohm for help along the way. Thanks also to fellow design historians Ray Batchelor, Barbara Penner and Greg Votalato for encouragement and ideas. Michael Manser helped with aspects of the White Star Line, and Stephen Rabson, P&O's Historian and Archivist, was incredibly helpful and generous with his time. Shane Casey at the SS Great Britain Trust provided invaluable help, as did Kenneth Anderson at the Ulster Folk and Transport Museum and David Thompson at the Science Museum. John Graves and Rena Prentice at the National Maritime Museum, Greenwich, gave me some useful insights, as did Linda Parry from the V & A. Many thanks also to Maureen Watry and the staff at the Special Collections, Liverpool University, for access to the pivotal Cunard archives, and Lesley Richmond and the staff at Glasgow University's archives for help with John Brown's and Wylie and Lochhead in particular. Thanks to Amira Driscoll, Catherine Moriarty and Jonathan Woodham at Brighton University Design History Archive for help with QE2 material. W. Marcel Kroon at the Maritime Museum, Rotterdam, and Audrey Joly at the French Lines Archive in Le Havre provided me with exceptionally open and friendly access to their collections.

Most of all, thanks are due to my husband Bruce, who was always there to support and inspire, encourage and offer advice. This book is dedicated to him.

Picture credits: SS Great Britain Trust: 1.1, 1.3; Bruce Wealleans: 1.2; Science and Society Picture Library 1.5, 4.8; National Museums & Galleries of Northern Ireland, Ulster Folk and Transport Museum 2.1, 2.3, 3.3, 3.8, 4.6, 6.4; Liverpool University 2.2, P&O 2.4, 4.4, 4.5, 5.1, 5.4, 6.5, 6.6; Hapag-Lloyd AG 3.1, Tyne and Wear Museum Service 3.4, 3.5, National Maritime Museum 3.9, 3.10; Eco Museum, St Nazaire 3.11, 4.2, 4.12, 4.13; Canadian Pacific Railway Archives 4.9, 4.10; Glasgow University Archives Service 5.2, 5.3; Mariners' Museum, Newport News 6.1, Rotterdam Maritime Museum 6.3. The remainder are drawn from the author's collection.

Introduction

This book looks at the process of designing the interiors of ocean liners. This has never been attempted before, as histories of liners tend to celebrate the image of glamorous travel, on a trajectory of modernity viewed within the schemata of technological determinism. I consider the process of the design of the liners, from the commissioning of the designers, through to execution and reception. Key changes in design trends are illustrated by the analysis of representative examples. The work is situated within the developing field of the history of interior design, and as such, it considers the work of the designers in the context of the power and ownership of the shipping lines and the developing sense of national identities, the boundaries of social class and the challenge of modernity. The central theme is an exploration of the developing role of the interior designer, from local decorating firm to international designer heroes, which is mapped against the clearly demarcated social hierarchies of liner interior design.

Roland Barthes has written incisively about sea travel in his text, 'The *Nautilus* and the Drunken Boat': 'An inclination for ships always means the joy of perfectly enclosing oneself, of having at hand the greatest possible number of objects, and having at one's disposal an absolutely finite space. To like ships is first and foremost to like a house, a superlative one since it is unremittingly closed, and not at all vague sailings into the unknown: a ship is a habitat before being a means of transport' (1973: 66). The interior design of ocean liners exemplifies spaces carefully constructed to give a sense of security in an uncertain world, challenged by the forces of modernity. The ship interior offered a clear-cut representation of social distinctions and national identities, which lulled the passenger like the gentle motion of the waves, rocking you to sleep in a cosy bunk. The vagaries of etiquette and the threat of the 'other' were safely contained on board the ocean-going liner. The risk of the chance encounter with elements of society which were not like you were minimized within the confines of the ship, where steerage was kept below deck, women and men had their own social space and non-white crew were kept out of sight.

The concept of heterotopias described by Foucault in his lecture, 'Of Other Spaces', is useful when considering the history of the ocean liner:

> Brothels and colonies are two extreme types of heterotopia, and if we think, after all, that the boat is a floating piece of space, a place without a space, that exists by itself, that is closed in on itself and at the same time is given over to the infinity of the sea and that, from port to port, from tack

to tack, from brothel to brothel, it goes as far as the colonies in search of the most precious treasures they conceal in their gardens, you will understand why the boat has not only been for our civilization, from the sixteenth century until the present, the great instrument of economic development . . . but has been simultaneously the greatest reserve of the imagination. The ship is the heterotopia par excellence. In civilizations without boats, dreams dry up, espionage takes the place of adventure, and the police take the place of pirates.

(1967: 6)

The perfect and privileged space of the ship interior, this heterotopia of the high seas, symbolizes society and nations as they would like to see themselves. A perfect representation of how people should be organized, how the ruling elite located their place in the world in relation to others, and how others were defined through their identity and place on the ship.

The historiography of the ocean liners further reinforces this perception. The greatest volume of published work on the subject celebrates the development of the liner in terms of modernity and techno determinism. Maritime historians have produced some excellent work on the history of the ocean liner, which tends to focus on the technical marvels and national rivalries, as symbols of modernity. Of course this is pertinent to the history of the interior design of ocean liners, and has provided some excellent background material. However, the designers involved in the creation of the interiors are rarely, if ever mentioned. The focus is largely on the technical details of the ship, its construction and engines. When attention is paid to the interior design, it is the luxury end of the accommodation which receives the most attention (Miller 1985; Brinnin 1982). These popular books are based on uncritical reading of sources such as *The Shipbuilder*, which always contain glowing descriptions of the ships and their interiors, drawn largely from the prodigious press information produced by companies such as Cunard and P&O. Publications which focus more on the social and literary aspects of ocean liner travel are descriptive, enthusiastic and positive, rather than academic and critical (Brinnin 1972; Maxtone-Graham 1972).

Signalling the beginning of the cult of nostalgia which surrounds the ocean liner, these two classic texts were produced at the time when ocean liners had finally been eclipsed by the aeroplane for long-distance travel. John Maxtone-Graham described his regrets over this loss: 'As I complete this book, there is every indication that the airplane rather than the ship will shortly be the only way to cross. Liners still in service will presumably confine their activities to the Caribbean. Like so many other civilized delights, the elegance and enjoyment, the comfort and convenience of that legendary passenger service on the North Atlantic will pass into history' (1972: xiv). The cult of nostalgia continues to hold sway when considering the history of the liner, and informs the dominant discourse of contemporary cruising, a very different type of activity to travelling by liner. The liner offered transport by sea on various lines, between different ports, for a variety of passengers, whether business travellers or immigrants. Cruising is travel by ship for leisure purposes, but the notion of heterotopia also underpins the popular perception of cruising. *Berlitz Ocean Cruising and Cruise Ships 2005* allays potential passenger fears: 'Cruising is popular today because it takes you away from the pressures and strains of contemporary life by offering an escape from reality. Cruise ships are really self-contained resorts, without the crime, which can take you to several destinations in the space of just a few days. . . . The hassles of ordinary travel are almost eliminated in one pleasant little package' (Ward 2005: 7).

The special heterotopia of the ocean liner has inspired and informed architectural and design writing. Le Corbusier idolized the technology of the steamship. In 1923 he argued: 'A seriously-minded architect, looking at it as an architect (i.e. a creator of organisms), will find in a steamship his freedom from an age-long but contemptible enslavement to the past' (Le Corbusier 1987: 103). Le Corbusier used illustrations of the exterior of Cunard's *Aquitania* and C.G.T.'s *France* to illustrate his point. He did not choose to illustrate the luscious interiors. He urged architects to learn from the engineering of ships, from their rationality, unity of materials, powerful masses and solid forms. Le Corbusier's major point was that ship design liberated architects from using the styles of the past, and enabled them to embrace new technology and create a contemporary form of architecture which was essentialist and functional. It was also in the section devoted to steamships of *Vers une Architecture* that Le Corbusier argued that: 'The house is a machine for living in. Baths, sun, hot-water, cold-water, warmth at will, conservation of food, hygiene, beauty in the sense of a good sense of proportion. . . . Our modern life, when we are active and about . . . has created it own objects: its costume, its fountain pen, its eversharp pencil, its typewriter, its telephone, its admirable office furniture, its plate-glass and its "Innovation" trunks, the safety razor and the briar pipe, the bowler hat and the limousine, the steamship and the airplane' (Le Corbusier 1987: 95).

This modernist approach underpinned design writing about the interior design of ocean liners from the 1930s onwards. Designers and critics were of the opinion that using styles from the past was outdated and that a more modern, contemporary style was a more appropriate expression of the age. And this adoption of a modern look also carried with it overtones of class and gender distinctions. Just as the level of knowledge of historical styles revealed social class in the earlier part of the century, so rejection of revivalist design and adoption of modernism became a symbol of middle-class knowingness from the 1930s onwards. For example, the speech and article which guaranteed *Orion* a place in history as the pioneer of modern design, 'The Interior Design of Passenger Ships' was delivered by Sir Colin Anderson at the Royal Society of Arts in 1966 and published in its *Journal* in May of that year, when Anderson was also President of the Design and Industries Association (DIA) (Anderson 1966). By this point P&O had absorbed the Orient Line, and although Anderson was still a Director of P&O, the valorization of the past which permeates the article may have been prompted by this 1960 takeover by Orient's arch-rivals. Anderson reinforced the message of *Orion* as the pioneer of modern ship interior design in 1967 in an article entitled: 'Ship Interiors: When the Breakthrough Came' for *Architectural Review*, in which he stated: 'As a new ship, in 1935, the *Orion* was revolutionary as far as British ships were concerned. She not only influenced the interior design of passenger ships in general but also of hotels, including their furnishing, lighting and general equipment, and of other kinds of transport including train and aeroplane interiors' (Anderson 1967: 452). Anderson selected significant images of P&O ships to contrast with the modernist splendours of the *Orion*. For the *Journal of the Royal Society of the Arts* he chose the baronial smoking room of the *Viceroy of India* (Figure 4.4), and for the *Architectural Review*, the first class reading and writing room of the *Stratheden*.

Anderson's assertion that the *Orion* was the pioneer of modern design in ships entered circulation as accepted fact and informed all subsequent writing on the subject. For example, in the special edition of *Architectural Review* to mark the introduction of the *QE2* in 1969, it was proclaimed: 'Her company's design policy of full coordination, admirable as this is, represents a belated acceptance of a philosophy spelled out by the Modern Movement in architecture half a century ago and put into practice by a merchant shipping company (the Orient Line, when building the 'Orion') as long ago as 1935' (*Architectural Review* 1969: 397). More recently, Veronica Sekules, in an article on Sir Colin Anderson, argued: 'He was justifiably proud of the *Orion*, and its place as a landmark in the history of design has been long acknowledged' (Sekules 1985–6: 22).

However, such a modernist view of the history of design serves to reinforce existing hierarchies. Design history as a discipline had tended to pay more attention to the development of modernism, and its attendant pioneers, than other aspects of production and consumption or styles (Pevsner 1991). The case of the *Orion* focuses on one ship, designed by a male, modernist architect with overall control and support of a sympathetic client. Recent work in the fields of architectural and design history have challenged this type of hegemony by including the work of women and acknowledging the existence of other styles and other responses to modernity (Colomino 1994; Heynan 1999; Sparke 1995, 2004, 2005). When examining the history of the interior design of ocean liners, more avenues need to be explored than that of modernism. Using the concept of heterotopia, it is possible to see the first class smoking room on the *Viceroy of India* as an early example of a space designed by a woman, Elsie Mackay, for the exclusive use of male passengers. It is also an appropriation of British aristocratic tradition, created at a time when the powers of that particular elite were in severe decline and as an expression of British national identity (Cannadine 2005). So the consideration of a broader set of precepts, including identity, enriches our understanding of the history of the interior design of ocean liners.

Writing the history of ocean liner interior design is a challenging task. As Sir George Holmes lamented in 1906, in his Victoria and Albert Museum Science Handbook, *Ancient and Modern Ships*:

> An endeavour has been made in this handbook, as far as space and scant-
> iness of material would permit, to trace the history of the development of

wooden ships from the earliest times down to our own. Unfortunately, the task has been exceedingly difficult; for the annals of shipbuilding have been very badly kept down to a quite recent period, and the statements made by old writers concerning ships are not only meagre but often extremely inaccurate. Moreover, the drawings and paintings of vessels which have survived from the classical period are few and far between, and were made by artists who thought more of pictorial effect than of accuracy of detail.

(1906: vii)

This book is located within the field of design history, but the research has been a matter of piecing together fragments of information from maritime history, art history, industrial archaeology, local studies and travel history. The work uses primary sources wherever possible, most notably the excellent archives of Cunard held at Liverpool University, John Brown's held at Glasgow University, and the collection of the National Maritime Museum at Greenwich. But the work of the designers has remained the key constant, and their relationship with the line owners, passengers and professional maritime and design press has provided the thread. What has emerged from this study is a complex picture of industrial progress and innovation, balanced by a desire to lavishly decorate the interiors of ocean liners with as broad an appeal as possible. The history of design has concentrated on the history of modernism, of reform and the avant-garde. The history of the interior design of ocean liners presents a different story, as none of the great figures of design history were involved. Instead, the trajectory offers a sequence of designers who were popular in their day, whose work was attractive to customers, and whose contribution has been unacknowledged to date. Names such as T.E. Collcutt, Charles Mewès, and Arthur Davis, Peto and James Miller, Elsie Mackay, Jean Monro, Michael Inchbald, are relatively obscure in the history of design and in the history of shipping. This account offers an insight into their work and contribution to the creation of floating heterotopias.

Chapter 1

Decorating technology

The dominant discourse of ocean liner travel is one of luxury and glamour. Whilst this may have been the case for a certain class of passenger from the late nineteenth century onwards, travellers before this time did not enjoy such an experience. Indeed, to travel at all was a sign of prestige: 'Until the nineteenth century being able to travel, particularly for non-work reasons, was only available to a narrow elite and was itself a mark of status' (Urry 1995: 130). Travel by sea before and during most of the nineteenth century (and the advent of steam power and attempts to provide luxurious surroundings) was a very uncomfortable experience for the majority of travellers. The Industrial Revolution gave rise to exceptional, technological innovation in all areas of transport, beginning with train travel and then impacting upon sailing, but the design of the interiors mirrored social hierarchies and traditional forms of decoration. Indeed, the stimulus to provide liners came more from the need to transport mail and cargo more speedily, than the necessity to move passengers. Therefore, the interior design of the ships was considered less important than their safety and speed. This period witnessed the transformation of ship construction from timber to iron, as the impact of the Industrial Revolution and modernity was felt. This was paralleled by the transition from sail to steam power. It was also a period when the economic and political climate stimulated a growth in sea travel for the purposes of both trade and emigration, with the beginnings of the colonization of many parts of the world by Britain, France, Holland, Portugal and Spain. Before the era of mass passenger sea travel, ships were designed to carry the optimum cargo and often incorporated means of defence, and considerations of passenger comfort were not a high priority.

For the majority of the nineteenth century, responsibility for the interior design of the ships lay mainly with the shipbuilder, who would in turn delegate this work to the carpenters. As Adrian Forty argued in *Objects of Desire*: 'In every industry, design has become necessary as a separate activity in production once a single craftsman ceases to be responsible for every stage of manufacture from conception to sale' (1986: 29). The British modernist, John de la Valette, concurred, when he argued that this era was: 'The style of the "Foreman Joiner" developed from the fact that all the fittings and decoration of ships was at first carried out by the shipbuilders and consequently devolved upon their foreman joiner. The result was invariably suitable, thoroughly solid work. But where it came to working out a "high-class job", the tendency to "put a little more art" into it, usually meant adding extraneous ornament or using materials because they were expensive, often with garish result, albeit in the taste of the day' (1936: 706). The situation began to change during the second half of the nineteenth century, when the appearance of the interiors became an important commercial factor in attracting passengers, as the number of passenger lines and liners grew. This was paralleled by a marked escalation in the activity of the decorating firms, as upper and middle class taste in decoration blossomed. Decorating firms, such as the plasterers Jackson and Sons, were employed to add decorative plasterwork to the interiors of three significant ships, the SS *Great Western*; SS *Great Britain* and the SS *Great Eastern*. These ships were highly significant in terms of technological innovation, and nineteenth-century crowds marvelled at this spectacle of modernity; the huge machinery contrasting with the decoration on board. Just as the traditional skills of the shipwright/carpenter were perceived as being eroded by decorating firms, they were also eroded from a different direction, that of the replacement of wood by iron and sail by steam.

Sea voyages up until the early nineteenth century were still dominated by the traditional wooden sailing ship. Built from oak, with complex rigging and canvas sails, the cabins and public spaces were comparatively sparse and not purpose built for passengers. The most prestigious areas to be decorated at all were the captain's and officers' quarters, as exemplified in the extant battleship *Victory* or the *Cutty Sark*. For example, during the two/eight month voyage in 1620 of the *Mayflower* from Plymouth to North America, the 102 passengers lived primarily on the gun deck. This was the deck sandwiched between the hold and the top deck. It offered cramped living space, measuring 80 feet from stem to stern, of which about 12 feet at the back belonged to the gun room and would have been off-limits to the passengers. The width at the widest part was approximately 24 feet. An assortment of hatches provided access to the cargo hold below. The windlass and capstan, both used to haul heavy items by rope between the decks, also took up floor space, as did the main mast in the middle, and the sprit sail mast in the front. Many of the families custom built small 'cabins' for themselves, simple wooden dividers nailed together, to provide some privacy. Others, especially the single young men, slept where they could, some finding shelter in a shallop, a 30-foot sailing vessel that the passengers had brought with them, and which was stowed on the gun deck. There was barely room for all the passengers to lie down and sleep in the 1,800 square feet of deck space. There was no concept of the ship needing to be designed to meet passenger needs, only that of the senior crew.

The wealthiest travellers could ensure a comparatively comfortable passage by paying the captain to hire a private cabin, as it was within his gift to do so. As the majority of these passengers were emigrating, they brought their own furniture and furnishings with which to fill the cabin. This would usually include a bed and trunk. But the majority of those who travelled had few possessions, and endured the cramped and dark conditions of steerage, where you were responsible for cooking your own food and the only sleeping accommodation was on the deck. The majority of emigrants in the nineteenth century travelled steerage class on sailing packets, transported more as cargo than human beings. The smell and noise on these ships was notoriously bad, from the constant creaking of the timbers and stench of so many human beings travelling in such close proximity for so long.

The sailing times of the sailing ships were completely unpredictable, and relied solely on the weather. As the Industrial Revolution gathered pace in Britain during the early nineteenth century, so the impetus to apply steam power to sailing grew, and the innovations of the railways were applied to ships. Also, the desire to make ships larger and more robust was a further pressing need as the volume of cargo and distances travelled proliferated. Hence, work began on applying steam power to sailing vessels. The immediate challenge was to make the engines efficient, so that the amount of coal that needed to be carried was not prohibitive. At first, steam power was applied to small vessels undertaking short trips. For example, the *Comet* was a wooden paddle-steamer, the first to offer a regular service between Glasgow, Greenock and Helensburgh on the Clyde from 1812. The ship was only 40 feet long and offered sparse accommodation. There were several wooden benches on deck, and a small cabin aft, which passengers paid the premium fare of four shillings to use; this contained a table and benches either side. There was also limited accommodation in a small forecastle, reached by a wooden ladder, for the fare of three shillings. The *Comet* ran ashore in 1820, but proved that offering a regular steam-powered service was a possibility, her small size restraining the possible profits. Steamers were launched on the Thames and were pioneered en route between Britain and Ireland during the early nineteenth century. In America small-scale steamers were introduced in the late eighteenth century, with the introduction of a steamboat service on the Delaware River by John Fitch. In 1807 Robert Fulton's *North River Steam Boat* (later renamed the *Clermont*) began operating on the Hudson River, from New York to Albany. The longer route from North America to Britain was first successfully completed with steam power by the American boat *Savannah* in 1819; however, the majority of the 30 day journey was made under sail and it carried no cargo or passengers. The ship had the appearance of a traditional square-rigger, complete with three masts and sails, but with the addition of a funnel, paddle wheels either side and an engine below. The interior was reportedly sumptuous, the state cabin had mahogany wainscoting, rosewood and brass decorations and full-length mirrors carefully placed to create the illusion of space and contained berths for 32 passengers. This was the style of the traditional river boat. The first voyage with paying passengers for the ship had been the short trip from Savannah to Charleston in April 1819, just before *Savannah* sailed for Liverpool.

Apart from naval battles and travel to America and Australia, it was India which was the other major destination for British ships. The expansion of trade with the East India Company, and the deployment of the British in India to maintain the Empire, meant a significant increase in sea travel. The growth in trade by sea in the nineteenth century was immense; in 1801 British mercantile shipping totalled 1,726,000 tons and by 1846 it had reached 3,220,685 tons (Holmes 1906: 205). The most prevalent shipping company in Britain was the East India Company, which traded mainly with India and, through coercive action, completely controlled the country by the late eighteenth century. The 1784 India Act had established the East India Company as the major trading arm of the British government. By the middle of the nineteenth century, the company's rule extended across most of India, Burma, Singapore and Hong Kong, and a fifth of the world's population was under its authority. In 1858 the company lost its adminstrative function to the Crown, and India became a formal Crown Colony. The company was formally disbanded in 1874. By this stage, the East India Company had been eclipsed by P&O.

The Peninsular and Oriental Steam Navigation Company (renamed P&O in 1840) originated in 1837 and was founded to sail regular services to Portugal, Spain and Gibraltar, based on a mail contract from the Royal Navy. This important source of income allowed the line owners, Arthur Anderson, Brodie McGhie Willcox and Richard Bourne, to build up a successful fleet for the transport of mail, cargo, passengers and cruising to the Mediterranean, India and Australia. The interiors of P&O ships differed from those designed for the transatlantic trade or as mammoth symbols of modernity. The ships needed to be reliable and provide comfortable accommodation in tropical climates. The company bought two ships in 1840 for the newly won mail contract to Alexandria in Egypt, the *Oriental* and the *Great Liverpool*, both steamers originally intended for sailing the Atlantic. In 1842 the company won an important contract from the British government to offer sailings between the Suez and India. For this they needed to commission two new ships, the *Hindostan* launched in 1842, and the *Bentick* launched one year later. The two ships were wooden hybrid steam paddles with the addition of sails and iron bulkheads and provision for 102 first class and 50 second class passengers.

Traditional in design, with striking windows at the stern like traditional warships, they were more radical in their interior layout. The convention was to lay the cabins either side of the saloon, as was the case with the *Great Britain*. This layout was reversed, with the saloon spanning the full width of the ship across the stern, with two corridors leading from it on either side of the ship, with a double set of cabins either side, totally 60 in all. The theory was that the passengers would not be so close to the noises of the sea and the passages would provide extra ventilation during the heat of tropical journeys. The saloon, at the rear of the ship beneath the upper deck, was decorated with painted panels. One passenger who travelled on the *Hindostan* in 1844 complained that: 'She had a superb saloon, every panel of which is decorated with an elegant and costly painting on papier mache by an artist of taste and skill. Perhaps too much money has been lavished on mere embellishments. Pictures and finely carved woodwork are on the whole of that part of the ship which is fitted up for passengers, most of whom would be glad to go in vessels with less costly decorations at a lower charge. All this finery makes the ship look as if she were meant rather for holiday pleasure-trips on a smooth lake, than to brave the dangers of the wide ocean' (P&O 1844: 2–3). The saloon was the only public room for use by all first class passengers, and so it was used for dining, reading, writing, playing cards or board games and musical soirées. It was furnished with one central table with benches, a sideboard at the forward end and settee situated beneath the stern windows. Another contemporary commentator, a 'Madras Officer', published his reflections on travelling on the *Hindostan* in 1846 with a more favourable view of the Grand Saloon: 'The cuddy is a magnificent room, running as far aft as the stern posts, and as far forward as the situation of the engine room would permit. I forget the dimensions of this spacious apartment: suffice to say, that is large enough to hold four tables, with sufficient latitude to admit of the perambulations and running to and fro of the waiters, and a nice walk up and down of a rainy day. The sides, (or to be more explicit, the walls) of the *sale a manger*, are decorated with gaudy *papier mache* colourings, descriptive of various subjects: the stanchions and rudder-head, as well as the mast, (which was in the center of the cabin) are all painted with flowers in the most Beautifully arranged groups I ever saw, tastefully embellished with fountains and *jetties d'eau*, and other ornaments' (a Madras Officer 1846: 11–12). The cabins were similar in dimensions to those occupied by Charles Dickens, measuring a paltry seven by seven foot with two to four bunks and rudimentary washing facilties in a small sink. It gained a very similar response from passengers: 'Her accommodations for passengers are poor, cramped, and badly ventilated, built with the intentions, evidently, of cramming as many living souls into as small a space as possible. The number of people between decks, to say nothing of the fires in the engine room, renders the heat insufferable, in spite of the wind-sails down each hatchway' (a Madras Officer 1846: 8).

Despite making the cabins uncomfortably hot, the addition of steam power speeded up the journey to Calcutta and greater freedom to pick routes according to distance and convenience, rather than being at the whim of the weather conditions. By the time of the collapse of the East India Company in 1874, P&O was the established company for travel to the British Empire in India. The ships were a microcosm of the Empire, with the first class occupied by the privileged, white senior administrators or civil servants of the Raj and their families. In second class were the servants of the first class passengers, including batmen for the army officers and the Indian ayahs, plus poorer passengers including priests and missionaries. Emigrants to India, who would be few in number compared to the transatlantic route, would not travel by P&O ships, but cheaper, emigrant ships. P&O were occasionally obliged to carry third class passengers as part of the mail contract, who were usually low ranking soldiers and sailors. These passengers were normally upgraded to second class (P&O circular 23.7.1889).

The emigrant trade from Ireland and Great Britain, Germany, Norway, Sweden, Italy, Austria-Hungary, Russia, Poland, Estonia and Lithuania, Greece, Albania, Serbia, Bulgaria, Syria and Armenia to North America was also booming at this time. From 1820 to 1920 35 million emigrants made the daunting journey across the Atlantic in desperate search of a better life. Although the new technology of steam was used to pack more passengers into larger, faster boats, the conditions for most emigrants were appalling. Packed into tiny spaces, with little or no privacy, they were prey to diseases such as cholera and typhus. On the return journey from America to Europe as late as the 1890s, the space used for human traffic was used to transport cattle.

But the volume of the emigrant trade made it highly profitable, and it lay at the foundations of many companies which sailed the Atlantic. Cunard continued to service the mail contract, and, in response to competition from the Collins Line, built the *Persia* in 1855, the first iron paddle-steamer to service the Atlantic route. The largest ship afloat at that time, it carried 200 first class and 50 second class passengers. Cunard were slow to meet the needs of the emigrant trade and the company suffered, resulting in a financial crisis in 1878, which forced Cunard to review its approach to passenger accommodation, given the increased competition. The Dutch firm Holland America Line was founded in 1873 to provide sailings from Holland to America; sailings from Germany to America were provided by Norddeutscher Lloyd (N.D.L.) or North German Lloyd, founded in 1856, and the Hamburg-Amerikanische Packetfahrt Actien-Gessellschaft (HAPAG), or Hamburg-Amerika Line as it is better known, was founded in 1847. The French founded the Compagnie Generale Transatlantique (C.G.T.) in 1864. Conditions for the emigrants improved steadily, with measures such as the 1855 British Passengers Act. The profitable possibilities for providing mass emigrant travel were realized by William Inman, who founded the Inman Line and provided transport between Liverpool and Philadelphia from 1850. It targeted the Irish market and was one of the first lines to provide cooked food for steerage class passengers, providing improved facilities in advance of the 1855 Act.

It was Isambard Kingdom Brunel and his circle who pioneered the technology for global travel by steam, and were the first to replace the paddle, placed either side of the vessel, with the screw at the stern of the ship. The first voyage entirely under steam power across the Atlantic from Britain to New York and Boston took place in 1838 by the *Sirius*, the *Great Western*, the Canadian *Royal William* and the *Liverpool*. It was the *Great Western* which was specifically designed for the Atlantic passage by Brunel. The ship was 236 feet long and 35 feet wide, discounting the paddle boxes. It was constructed from an oak frame with iron trussing on the hull and wooden diagonals to withstand the challenges of the Atlantic, a route it traversed from 1838 to 1843. It carried an average of 90 passengers west and 79 east per voyage, although it had berths for 240 passengers, with six round trips made annually. There were 128 staterooms which were all one class. The main public room, the saloon, was 75 feet long and decorated with voguish Gothic arches and painted murals representing bucolic scenes in the style of Watteau by Royal Academician and fashionable portrait painter, Edmund Thomas Parris (1793–1873). The room was lit by one skylight with decorative plasterwork ceilings. But it was the rival *British Queen* which was most highly regarded from the perspective of interior design. It was larger than the *Great Western*, measuring 275 feet in length and 40 feet wide and had been launched in 1838 by Junius Smith. Contemporary accounts praised her: '. . . "spacious saloon or dining room", the length of which was "upwards of 60 ft; the width 30 ft; and in the narrowest part 20 ft; height to ceiling 8ft." The ladies' cabin was about 16 ft square' (Holmes 1906: 20).

The interiors of ships were now taking the needs of the passengers into account, as competition grew to attract paying customers and expectations were raised. The lucrative mail contract was offered by the British Admiralty in 1838 for travel between Britain and Canada. This was won, not by the *Great Western* or Junius Smith, but by Samuel Cunard of Halifax, Canada, who specialized in providing reliable but not highly decorated shipping. The lucrative mail contract meant there was less need to attract and impress the passenger part of the transatlantic trade, as part of the contract with the Admiralty was that the ship also had to be easily converted for wartime use. The first ship to be launched by Cunard, or the British & North American Royal Mail Steam Packet Company, to give the precise title of the company, was the *Britannia*. A comparatively small, wooden paddle-steamer which could carry the all-important mail, 600 tons of coal, 89 crew and 115 first class passengers – the emigrant traveller or steerage was restricted to the more unreliable sailing ships. The passengers' cabins were situated on the main deck with two dining saloons. On the upper deck were the officers' cabins, galley, bakery and cow house. Three more ships were built in Britain to augment the fleet – the *Acadia* and *Caledonia* launched in 1840, and the *Columbia* in 1841 to similar designs. One passenger summarized the experience of crossing the Atlantic on the *Britannia* thus: 'Despite the spartan aspects of the voyage, the saving of time and the reliability of arrival augurs well for steam propelled trans-Atlantic travel' (Wills 2004: 12). Charles Dickens travelled on the *Britannia* in 1842 and complained that his room had the dimensions of a coffin with:

> . . . a very thin mattress, spread like a surgical plaster on a most inaccessible shelf. But that this was the state-room concerning which Charles Dickens, Esquire, and Lady, had held daily and nightly conferences for at least four months preceding: that this could by any possibility be that small snug chamber of the imagination, which Charles Dickens Esquire, with the spirit of prophecy strong upon him, had always foretold would contain at least one little sofa, and which his lady, with the modest yet most magnificent sense of its limited dimensions, had from the first opined would not hold more than two enormous portmanteaus in some odd corner out of sight (portmanteaus which could now no more be got in at the door, not to say stowed away, than a giraffe could be persuaded or forced into a flower-pot): that this utterly impracticable, thoroughly hopeless, and profoundly preposterous box, had the remotest reference to, or connection with, those chaste and pretty, not to say gorgeous little bowers, sketched by a masterly hand, in the highly varnished lithographic plan hanging up

in the agent's counting-house in the city of London: that this room of state, in short, could be anything but a pleasant fiction and cheerful hest of the captain's, invented and put in practice for the better relish and enjoyment of the real state-room presently to be disclosed: – these were truths which I really could not, for the moment, bring my mind at all to bear upon or comprehend. And I sat down upon a kind of horsehair slab, or perch, of which there were two within; and looked, without any expression of countenance whatever, at some friends who had come on board with us, and who were crushing their faces into all manner of shapes by endeavouring to squeeze them through the small doorway.

(Dickens 1842: 53–4)

Dickens was seriously seasick for most of the journey, managing to go up on deck intermittently and seeking solace in the ladies' cabin, which was adjacent to his own. This was occupied by Dickens and his wife, one woman sailing out to America to join her husband, and two other couples. Hence, the ladies' cabin or saloon existed on ships of this period to allow women travelling alone to sit with other women or with couples. This cabin was usually located near the captain's quarters for added security, and was the case with Brunel's second ship, built with the engineer, Thomas Guppy, the SS *Great Britain*.

Now located at Great Western Dockyard, Bristol, the *Great Britain* was the first ship to be constructed from iron rather than wood, driven by an Archimedes screw propellor. The ship was a potent symbol of the achievements of modernity, and was celebrated as such during its first five years of existence. It was launched

1.1
Joseph Walter,
The Launch of the
SS Great Britain,
1843, courtesy of
the SS Great
Britain Trust
Source: SS Great
Britain Trust

without interior fittings, apart from the carpet, which had been laid in preparation for the royal visit. Launched by Prince Albert in July 1843, it was 322 feet long, 50 feet 6 inches wide, 1,016 tonnes, 252 passengers with berths, 26 single cabins, 113 two-berth cabins and required 120 crew to sail it. Steam was the primary source of power, with auxiliary sail to save coal in favourable winds. The arrival of Prince Albert in Bristol was a significant event in the history of modernity, as he travelled from London by means of the new railroad, constructed by the Great Western Railway between 1835 and 1841. *The Illustrated London News* described the Consort's journey and the new railway line in adulatory tone:

> The vastness of construction throughout the line entitles it to the rank of 'grand', and even 'gigantic' – as in the Box tunnel, in constructing which, for two and a half years, 1100 men and 250 horses were employed, 30,000,000 bricks were consumed, and a ton of gunpowder and a ton of candles every week – . . . Many other works on this gigantic line, especially in the very difficult country towards the Bristol end, might be referred to; but we can only here notice one other – the magnificent bridge by which the line crosses the Thames at Maidenhead: it consists of ten brick arches, of which the two principal are the largest and flattest brick arches ever built, being of 128 feet span'.
>
> (22 July 1843: 52)

The *Illustrated London News* contrasts these achievements of modernity with the interior of the carriage of the royal train:

> The royal carriage, fitted up for the accommodation of her Majesty and Prince Albert, and that in which his Royal Highness travelled on Wednesday, is 21 feet in length and 9 feet in width and is divided into three compartments, two end ones 4 feet 6 in. long; while the centre forms a noble saloon, 12 feet long, and 6½ feet high, and is fitted up in the style of Louis Quatorze, panelled with crimson and white silk, relieved by paintings of the four elements, by Parris. The sofas, &c., are of richly-carved oak; and at each end of the carriage is a large, plate-glass window, affording a view of the railway line. Of this truly sumptuous interior the annexed engraving is a correct presentation.
>
> (22 July 1843: 52)

The same contrast between traditional, luxurious interior decoration and the might of modernity is evident in contemporary descriptions of the SS *Great Britain*. The ship was divided into five levels, with the upper deck which carried the six, towering masts. The mighty engines and boilers were situated right at the heart of the ship. The principal promenade saloon lay at the rear or stern of the ship, just beneath the upper deck. Lit by ten skylights and one dome, it was an impressive 110 feet long, 48 feet wide and 7 feet tall. There were two staircases at either end and 24 single-berth cabins were fitted to either side of the space.

**Restored Grand
Saloon**, *Great
Britain.*
Source: Bruce
Wealleans, 2005

Contemporary accounts described, in glowing terms, the appearance and layout of this space, which concealed more than it revealed, reinforcing the notion that the private was associated with the feminine and public with the masculine:

> The door to each state room is carved and gilded, it is also surmounted with carved work, and the whole of the fittings present a most elegant and luxurious appearance. In this part of the ship there are twenty eight state bedrooms, all single, and these possess an advantage over those in any other vessel inasmuch as ladies pass from their own private saloon to their bedrooms without passing through the promenade, or being seen by those who are there.
>
> (*Bristol Gazette and Public Advertiser*, 20 July 1843: 1)

The promenade saloon was where saloon or first class passengers strolled when rough weather precluded the upper deck. The Ladies' Boudoirs or Saloons were just off the promenade deck, two tiny rooms, one of which was recreated with two sofas and one table for women wishing to exclude themselves from male passengers. Three doorways led from the Boudoirs into the cabins and another to the water closet. The captain's stateroom was situated between the two Boudoirs for extra reassurance.

Directly beneath the promenade saloon was the 100 foot long first class saloon or dining room, which was 50 foot wide and 8 foot high and lit by skylights from the promenade saloon. This was the most decorative of the ship's interiors, and its appearance was documented by a watercolourist in 1845, following the final fitting out at Blackwall. The space has now been restored to its original state, with help from the original decorating firm, Jacksons. Felix Farley's *Bristol Journal* records his impressions:

> The principle saloon is a noble apartment upwards 100 ft. in length looking in fact like a slice cut out of a ballroom. Three rows of pillars with gilded capitals support the overlying door, and the appearance of the whole viewed through the vistas of white and gold columns, with side doors covered with carving, and the whole brilliantly adorned with white and gold is both chaste and magnificent.
>
> (Farley 22 July 1843)

The colour scheme was a 'delicate lemon-tinted drab hue, relieved with blue, white and gold' (Claxton 1845: 17). The work on the panelling was undertaken by the leading plasterwork company, Jackson and Sons. The firm had been founded in 1780 and described itself as 'ornamental composition manufacturers' by this time. Jackson and Sons were involved in a range of prestigious commissions for domestic interiors, including Aspley House (1819) and Londonderry House (1825) plus public interiors such as the Ironmongers' Hall, London (1840).

Three hundred passengers could dine simultaneously in the space, at three lines of tables and upholstered bench seating. During the final fitting out, special crockery was ordered from Charles Mason of Mason's Ironstone, which included 250

1.3
Artist unknown, contemporary watercolour of first class dining saloon, 1845.
Source: SS Great Britain Trust

plates, 200 tea cups and 100 soap trays and the same number of chambers, totalling 5,125 pieces. Gilt framed mirrors at either end of the room enhanced the sensation of spaciousness, and suggests the influence of ballroom design, alluded to in Felix Farley's *Bristol Journal*. A variety of single and family cabins flanked the first class saloon, with narrow corridors dividing the cabins to assure privacy. The floor was covered by a luxurious Brussels carpet, custom made by the Bristol manufacturers, Messrs C. and F. Mogg. It was scarlet and purple and decorated in a small dice pattern and measured 1,200 yards.

Beneath the first class saloon was the cargo deck which lay next to the vital fresh water tanks. On the other side of the boilers and engines were situated the fore or second class saloon, which was 84 foot long with a ceiling height of 7 foot 9 inches and containing approximately 40 bed-places on each side. These cabins were larger, with only four on each floor designed for single occupation. Beneath was the lower fore saloon which was of the same dimensions with the same number of berths. Beneath these were two cargo decks. The crew's accommodation was situated right at the front of the ship, with officers placed on the top deck, the sailors' mess room beneath and the crew's quarters on the level beneath that. The water closets were situated below that. Hence, the desire to keep the two classes separate and the first class passengers nearest the captain's cabin had been established by 1845.

The SS *Great Britain* first sailed from Bristol in 1843 and in 1845 to the Thames to complete the fitting out stage; it was moored off Blackwall for five months and visited by an average of 1,500 people daily, including the Royal Family. June 12 1845 was the date of the maiden voyage, when 70 passengers sailed to Cowes, Plymouth, Dublin and Liverpool. On July 26 1845 the ship sailed for New York with 50 passengers. In New York 12,000 people paid to visit her, with an extra charge to see the engines. There was an element of inter-continental rivalry underpinning much of the contemporary American reactions. The commentator from the *Brooklyn Eagle* remarked:

> Upon the whole, we do not think the arrangements for comfort exceed those in our North River boats – the staterooms are certainly no larger or more commodious; and, as there is no accounting for taste, we would prefer a sojourn upon the Columbia or Niagara to one on board the Great Britain. The bed linen looks uninviting, and the whole appearance of the cabins, whatever may have been their original splendor, was, to us, greasy and smirchy. . . . The *tout ensemble* is very imposing, from the gigantic size of the different parts, and fills you with peculiar sensations of the mighty power of the great lever of the world – steam. One principle feature here is the grease and dirt with which everything is covered; and we would say to ladies who are emulous of visiting this monster steamer, do not be particular about putting on a nice dress to appear in, if you do it will, we fancy, be the last time you wear it.
>
> (*Brooklyn Eagle* 12 August 1845)

This is a measure of the attraction of modernity and new technology so characteristic of the Victorian era. Indeed, in the popular machine section of the Great Exhibition, Nasmyth's steam hammer, invented to forge the originally planned paddle shafts of the ship, was on show.

The SS *Great Britain*'s career as a cross-Atlantic steamship was short-lived, however, and it was sold in 1850 to Gibbs, Bright and Company of Liverpool for the burgeoning Australia run with the gold rush which had begun. The changes in the ship's interior design, overseen by Mackay and Miller, reflect important distinctions between the Atlantic and other global routes. For Atlantic travel, the spaces needed to be warm and enclosed, whilst the opposite was the case when travelling through the tropics. Similarly, there was less call for first class accommodation, and more for the lower classes as this was now to serve as an emigrant ship. The ship was changed from a steam ship with sails to a sailing ship with steaming capacity and could now take 730 passengers, with only 50 first class, as a new deck was created for second class passengers as part of the new deckhouse. The passengers were provided with food and eating utensils, but had to bring their own bed, bedding, linen and soap. Passengers travelling first class, or 'Fore-Saloon' and 'After-Saloon' enjoyed the luxury of '. . . every requisite will be provided, including Beds, Berths, Plate, Bedding, Linen' ('Steam from Melbourne to Liverpool' 1852). The distinction between Fore-Saloon and After-Saloon came in the provision of 'Provisions, Live Stock, Luxuries and Delicacies' (ibid.) for the latter, who paid a premium fare of between 80 and 90 guineas, in contrast to 40 to 45 guineas for second class. The first class passengers ate in the new dining saloon, located in the new deckhouse. Again, two tables ran lengthways down the 75 foot long space with benches either side. There were fixed gas lamps, bookcases and glassware situated in racks above the seating. Decoration was provided by '. . . paintings on glass of the armorial shields of all nations' (*Illustrated London News*, 12 June 1852: 462). Leading off from the saloon was the small boudoir, for use as a music room or makeshift chapel; the captain and chief officers' staterooms; smoking room and wheelhouse. The saloon cabins were situated on the promenade deck, but were comparatively cramped measuring 9.5 feet by 6 feet with double bunks, a sofa and a shelf. Further down the social hierarchy, the third class or intermediate fare was £18 and steerage £16. These passengers not only had to supply their own bedding, but also eating and drinking utensils. They suffered the long and hot journey beneath deck, beside the engine room, in the space previously occupied by the grandiose first class dining saloon. Deck space was similarly divided, with the After-Saloon passengers having exclusive access to the Poop aft; the Spar deck amidships was devoted to the After-Saloon and Fore-Saloon and forward to the Second Cabin. The promenade deck was covered with an awning to protect the passengers from the tropical sunlight.

From 1852 until 1876 the *Great Britain* sailed between Australia and Britain, carrying emigrants to Australia and bringing wool and cotton back to Britain in a journey averaging two months. In 1876 she ceased the Australia run and was put up for sale. In 1882 she was bought by Antony Gibbs, Son and Co. for conversion

to a sailing ship to carry coal from Cardiff round the Horn to San Francisco, returning with wheat. She ran into trouble rounding Cape Horn and ended up in the Falkland Islands as storage for wool and later to store coal. In 1937 she was towed out of the harbour and beached at Sparrow Cove and in 1970 towed back to Bristol where she is undergoing extensive restoration and conservation.

Improvements to accommodation on the transatlantic passenger route came about through the participation of America. Standards of comfort and decoration had been established with the development of small steamers for the inland water routes, particularly on the Hudson and the Mississippi. By 1833 there were 300 steamers on inland waterways and coastal routes in America, with a large, central saloon, usually the length of the vessel, richly decorated: 'Steamboats in North America retained this central compartment until far into the century, as they retained also an early established tradition of baroque opulence, over-decorated and sumptuous in their public apartments' (Greenhill and Giffard 1972: 35). The Collins Line was established in 1850 by Edward Knight Collins with a United States government subsidy of $858,000 which enabled him to commission four ships, including the *Atlantic*, which reached Liverpool in May 1850. The *Illustrated London News* was effusive about the décor of the ship, which included the novelty of carpeted cabins: 'Her saloon is 67 feet long by 20 feet wide. Her interior fittings are truly elegant, the woodwork being of white holly, satinwood, rosewood, &c., so combined and diversified as to present an exceedingly rich and costly appearance. In the drawing room the ornaments consist of costly mirrors, bronze-work, stained glass, paintings, &c. Between the panels connecting the staterooms are the arms of the different states of the confederacy painted in the highest style of art, and framed with bronze-work. . . . It would occupy more space than can be spared to detail the magnificence of the furniture of the *Atlantic*; the carpets are of the richest description; the table-slabs are of Brocatelli marble. Each stateroom has an elegant sofa; the berths are of satinwood, and the curtains of rich damask' (1850). Despite the opulence of the Collins Line fleet, its success was short-lived. Beset by disaster and eventual bankruptcy in 1858, the transatlantic trade became a European monopoly, with America concentrating on the internal development of an industrialized, transport system.

Meanwhile, the fascination with modernity continued in Britain. The last ship to be conceived by Brunel was even bigger than the *Great Western* and *Great Britain*. The *Great Eastern* exceeded all preceding records for the size of an ocean-going vessel, leading contemporary commentators to draw parallels between 'The Great Iron Ship' (Dugan 1953) and Noah's ark, and it has entered the history of shipbuilding as the symbol of the thwarted engineering genius of Brunel. Eventually launched in 1860 after a myriad of technical problems, the ship was 692 feet long, the longest vessel afloat at that time. Spurred by the possibilities of modernity to promote the needs of the British Empire, promulgated at the Crystal Palace Exhibition in 1851, Brunel pushed back the boundaries of technology to produce this mammoth ship. Indeed, *Great Eastern* was named 'The Crystal Palace of the Sea' (Dugan 1953: 15).

It was envisaged by the new Eastern Steam Navigation Company, established by Henry Thomas Hope in 1851, with Brunel and supported by the shipbuilder and naval architect, John Scott Russell, that the ship would carry 4,000 passengers (double that of the *Queen Mary*) and 15,000 tons of coal for rapid travel around the Cape of Good Hope to India and Australia. The massive amount of coal on board solved the problem of stopping at coaling stations en route. The ambition was to win the Royal Mail contract to carry mail eastwards, but the company lost this bid to the newly formed P&O Company and was undermined by Royal Navy subsidies for the building of White Star's *Teutonic* in 1889 and *Oceanic* in 1899.

The *Great Eastern* was constructed from iron with two massive paddle wheels and screw powered by two steam engines and was a popular attraction of the Victorian era. The progress of construction at the Isle of Dogs was recorded photographically week by week by Joseph Cundall. Further evidence of the design and construction of the ship exists in the hand-coloured lithographs by Scott Russell, copies of which were produced in the drawing offices at Milwall for the Patent Museum (now the Science Museum) and for publication in Scott Russell's *The Modern System of Naval Architecture* (1864) and *Great Ship Drawings* (1860) as well as to persuade the Eastern Steam Navigation Company board that it should continue to support the ship to completion. The images of the ship are therefore idealized, particularly the interiors, with mid-Victorian balloon back chairs, settees, round tables with wooden panelling and chandeliers in orderly layout. This representation is simplified and idealized, when compared to photographs of the interiors as they were furnished. There is far more surface pattern and rich decoration in asymmetrical layout. This may suggest that the control of the design and construction process did

1.4
J. Scott Russell, longitudinal section of the SS Great Eastern, 1853.
Source: Science and Society Picture Library

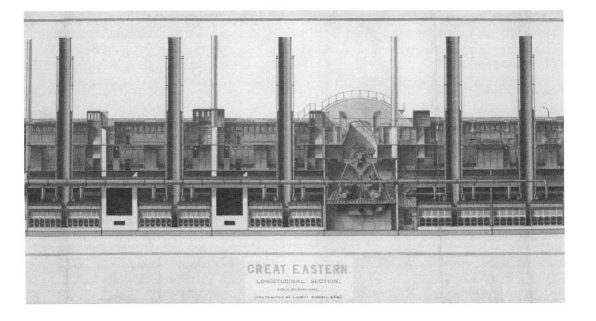

GREAT EASTERN.
LONGITUDINAL SECTION.

1.5
**Photograph of
Grand Saloon,**
Great Eastern
Source: NMM, Marine
Institute of Ireland

not extend to the interior decoration, which was executed by Jacksons and locally based decorating firms.

The process of the construction of the *Great Eastern* has been singled out as an important moment in the transition in working practices from handcrafted wooden construction to the more controlled and precise management of construction in iron (Baynes and Pugh 1981: 131–2). Brunel added the total control of the railway engineer to the working practices of the traditional shipyard, which led to conflict. Russell attempted to gain control of the construction process through the use of detailed engineering drawings. Scott Russell commented: 'I have made it a rule from the first that no part of the work should be commenced until it had been specially considered and determined upon and working drawings in full detail prepared, and, after due deliberation, formally settled and signed' (Scott 1865 as quoted in Baynes and Pugh 1981: 132). The shipyard drawing office now gained ascendancy over the shipyard foreman, much to the relief of Scott Russell: '. . . the great docility of the rising race of educated mechanics, the more intelligent skill of modern craftsmen . . . will enable even greater progress to be made in future' (Scott 1865 as quoted in Baynes and Pugh 1981: 132). With the full impact of the Industrial Revolution, working practices for the production of all forms of manufacturing became more controlled by the engineer and the manager.

When the ship was completed in 1858 the company took £5,000 in one week from visitors paying to marvel at the technology of the construction. Queen Victoria paid a visit by royal steam yacht. However, the financial challenges of building such a beast were too great for the original company to bear, and they folded, to be replaced by the new Great Ship Company, which bought the ship for £160,000 and financed the finishing off. The new company changed strategy, and completed the ship for service on the route to America, for which she had not been designed. The company began by completing the high end passenger accommodation, so vital for this particular route. The Grand Saloon was decorated and the staterooms furnished for 300 first class passengers at the stern of the ship.

The Grand Saloon was a stately 63 feet long, 47 feet wide and an impressive 14 foot high. The addition of a balcony also added to the feeling of spaciousness providing the first double height saloon on board. The walls were decorated with a heavy cloth of gold and silver and were panelled with imitation, oxidized silver pilasters, in white and gilt with oxidized ornamental ironwork. One of the vessel's five funnels passed through the Grand Saloon, and this was encased with mirrors and panels, decorated with delicate arabesque ornament with representations of the arts and sciences. Compared to the *Great Britain*, the principal passenger accommodation was plushly upholstered with extensive pattern and ornament by the local decorating firm of Messrs Crace of Wigmore Street, London. The frames of the sofas and chairs were carved teak and upholstered in claret, set against a maroon carpet and dark red velvet portieres. The dark and sumptuous, high Victorian interior was further enhanced by walnut buffets with green marble tops. The room was lit by huge gilt, gas chandeliers which illuminated ceiling beams which were also gilt with the panels between gold. The staterooms had removable panels to accommodate 2, 4, 6, or 8 passengers. Each cabin had a washbasin, dressing table, rocking chair and Turkey rug. A fitted settee concealed a bath which had hot fresh or cold salt water. The ship was fitted out with gas lighting and chandeliers hung from the ceiling of the Grand Saloon (see Figure 1.5). On the ship's first voyage to America a rosewood piano was placed in the Grand Saloon to provide entertainment on the 17 day voyage, and to provide accompaniment by a six piece band. Second and third class passengers were to be accommodated on the lower decks, but these were not fitted out for a further nine years.

The fitting out of the ship was celebrated in August 1859 and the ship undertook its maiden voyage from Southampton to New York during the following year with 300 passengers. The ship was again dogged by technical problems, and did not leave for America until June 1860 with only 35 paying passengers, 418 crew and a cargo of 500 gross of 'London Club' sauce. Upon arrival in New York, this monster of modernity was visited by 143,764 curious New Yorkers during the first week, who paid 50¢ each for the privilege. *Great Eastern* proved to be unprofitable for the transatlantic route, particularly as there was increased competition from Cunard, the Inman Line and, from Germany, the Hamburg-Amerika and Norddeutscher Lloyd Lines. *Great Eastern* was then employed as a cable-laying ship, and was the first vessel to lay a transatlantic cable, one unfortunate result being that the plush decorations from the Grand Saloon and cabins were replaced with giant tanks to hold the cables.

But the *Great Eastern* was to gain another lease of life in 1867, when it was chartered by Louis Napoleon Bonaparte to bring visitors to the Paris Exposition. The ship was extensively refurbished at a cost of £50,000 in order to impress potential visitors. This included three new dining rooms on the main deck, finished in gilt and silver with light yellow panelling. However, the ship did not have the magnetic power that the Emperor had hoped, and only 191 travelled from New York in 1867 rather than the planned 4,000. The luxurious fittings were ripped out once again in 1869, when the ship returned to cable-laying work for Reuters. However, the draw of the ship for the public was to be exploited one more time in 1886 as part of the Liverpool International Exhibition of Navigation, Commerce and Industry, which was opened by Queen Victoria on 11 May 1886. *Great Eastern* was chartered by the northern clothes and draper's chain, Lewis's, to carry advertising for the stores, and particularly the store at Ranelagh Street in Liverpool. This was the main success of the exhibition, attracting nearly half a million visitors, with the ship decorated externally with advertising for Lewis's. The ship was then dismantled, her fittings and fixtures auctioned off and she was towed away to be broken up in 1889. Some of the walnut panelling was bought by a pub at New Ferry for the bar buffet.

By the time of the *Great Eastern*'s demise in 1889, the construction and interior decoration of ocean liners had progressed beyond the early attempts to impose industrial working practices in the shipyard at Milwall. The stimulus for the provision of more ships and more lines came from increased trade and communication globally. With the growth of the imperial powers of Britain, Germany, Holland, Italy and France came the need to support this with speedy and efficient naval transport for passengers, mail and cargo. Coupled with this was the burgeoning need to express competing national identities as part of the interior design of the ships. The need to attract passengers was also paramount, particularly on the transatlantic route and the emigrant trade. The pioneering struggles of Brunel and Scott Russell had been superseded by a more industrially organized and mechanically based shipbuilding industry. The interiors of the ships were left less and less to the joiner and more and more to decorating firms, designers and architects.

Chapter 2

Luxury interiors and Arts and Crafts architects

Travel by ocean liner in the latter part of the nineteenth century grew more commonplace, and also more prestigious, as an increasing number of lines offered global travel by means of a greater number of ships. This growth in the passenger trade was matched by the need for lines to compete to attract the most affluent travellers. 'Status distinctions came to be drawn less between those who could and those who could not travel but between different classes of passengers' (Urry 1995: 130). Whilst the vast majority of passengers travelled in steerage, the design of liners served to attract the wealthy minority and make clear distinctions between the various social strata. Hence, the internal layouts of ships were radically altered to accommodate the passengers' needs, and more sophisticated interior decorations were employed. By the 1880s the trend of shipping lines to commission fashionable architects to design the interiors of ships had begun, paralleling the growth in status of the ocean liner as a design type, which also saw the development of the profession of naval architecture. Whereas previously, only a tiny number of the social elite would undertake travel of any great distance by sea, and they travelled at the behest of the captain in accommodation which was rarely specially decorated, now, the elite travelled in accommodation which usually reflected the upper-middle class taste of the line owners. The wealth generated by a new breed of Victorian shipping magnate and industrialist was reflected in the creation of new, prestigious Arts and Crafts houses. And it was the same architects, the same patrons and the same money which instigated the first phase of the professional interior design of ocean liners. By the late nineteenth century at least three British shipping lines had used an architect to design the interiors of their ships. All were from an Arts and Crafts background – J.J. Stevenson (1831–1908) at the Orient Line; Richard Norman Shaw (1831–1912) for the White Star Line; and T.E. Collcutt (1840–1924) for P&O – and all three managed to decorate modernity using the vocabulary of a romanticized English past with hints of the exotic 'Orient' (Said 2003).

The market leader in terms of providing luscious interiors for Atlantic travel by the latter part of the nineteenth century was the White Star Line, the official name of which was the Oceanic Steam Navigation Company. Founded in 1869 by Thomas Ismay and the Belfast-based shipbuilding company of Harland & Wolff, it formed an exclusive partnership, whereby all White Star ships would be built by that company for the total cost plus 4%. The possibilities offered by more reliable steam power for the Atlantic crossing were realized, and the emphasis was placed on the needs of the passengers by this new company. The White Star ships were characterized by their elaborate interior fittings, which were informed by a special tour made by the Harland & Wolff gentleman apprentice, William James Pirie (1847–1924), to English and Continental hotels (Moss and Hume 1986: 31). Pirie was to become one of the four partners in Harland & Wolff in 1874 and Chairman in 1896, and made frequent visits to European hotels to find what was fashionable and appealing in the interior decoration of the transient, public space. The first ship of the new fleet to offer a service to New York was the *Oceanic* in 1871, which could accommodate 1,166 passengers and was 3,707 gross tons and offered sailings between Liverpool and New York. The vast majority of passengers who sailed on the *Oceanic* did so in

2.1
W. L. Wylie,
***Oceanic*, 1895.**
Source: Ulster Folk &
Transport Museum

steerage class, with 1,000 cramped spaces available at six guineas each, one way. The saloon class, so called because passengers had access to the saloon for meals and entertainment, could accommodate a comparatively small number at 166, but the publicity and interior design effort was devoted to this social elite. In 1872 White Star publicity emphasized that the fleet was first class, fully powered, iron-screw steamships and that travel by Saloon Passage, at 18 and 21 guineas one way: '. . . according to accommodation in State Rooms, all having equal privileges in Saloon' (Cunard D42/PR3/1/23/10 1872: 1). The *Oceanic* signalled a significant transition from the traditional design of the ship's structure, with an upper deck, enclosed by iron railings rather than the traditional bulwarks, beneath which was a complete deck devoted to passenger accommodation. The same innovative structure was used for the five subsequent liners to be built by Harland & Wolff in the 1870s for the burgeoning fleet. Hence, seawater which had formerly been trapped and took time to drain away through the scuppers, could wash away by means of the railings. On the top deck was placed various freestanding structures including the Gentleman's Deck Smoking Saloon, the Companion and Ladies' Deck Saloon, Galley, Engineers, Officers' and Captain's accommodation. Shelter was provided to create one of the first promenade decks. The smoking accommodation was an improvement on previous arrangements, which had been a case of standing on deck. Because steam engines were becoming more efficient and compact, so the mechanics of the ship did not dominate the heart of the ship to the extent that they had done with the *Great Britain*. And the height of the ship began to migrate to the centre, rather than the stern.

Traditionally, the most important passenger accommodation was located to the stern of the ship; this derived from the days of sailing ships, when the captain needed to be at the stern to oversee all the sails and to steer, hence the best accommodation was situated there. The engines and paddles of the early steamships were located in the centre of the ship, so the design and layout of the accommodation did not need to alter. However, with the adoption of the screw propeller, the rear of the ship became far more noisy and prone to vibration compared to the centre of the ship. Also, the proliferation of decks meant that the engines were much further down in the ship, and also, no longer a source of attraction for passengers to view, as had been the case with the *Great Britain*. As George Holmes observed in 1906: 'As a relic of the olden days – probably handed down from remote classical times – when the position of importance was near the rudder, or "steer-board" – the place of honour was at the after end of the ship. It is at the ends, however, that the motion due to the waves is greatest, and in screw steamers there also the jar and vibration produced by the propellers is most felt. Passengers, therefore, prefer to be in the middle of the vessel and, as it was one of Mr. Ismay's cardinal principles to do as much as he possibly could for the passengers, it was in the middle of the ship and forward of the machinery that he placed the main saloon' (Holmes: 58–9). The first class saloon of the *Oceanic* was on the deck directly beneath the promenade deck, and could be reached by a decorative stairway. The saloon spanned the breadth of the ship at 40 feet and was 80 feet long and situated amidship, just aft of the funnel. The saloon included cushioned settees at either side of the room with dining tables. Seating was also provided on innovative, individual, swivelling chairs. There were a further two dining tables in the centre to facilitate dining in smaller groups, rather than the traditional method, as exemplified on the *Great Britain*, of two long tables with benches at either side, which made joining and leaving the table awkward. There was also a piano and space for books which could be borrowed. The dimensions of the space made it possible for all the saloon class passengers to eat together at the same time. Adjacent to the saloon was the ladies' boudoir, a pantry and bar. The first class cabins were placed either side of the saloon and were larger than was customary, with enlarged portholes with the added luxury of bells which could be pressed to summon stewards or stewardesses, and running water. There were also two honeymoon suites, complete with double beds – the norm was to provide two singles. The toilets were also situated on this deck, near the cabins, rather than up on the top deck, as had been customary. Passengers still relied on candle power for illumination, although the transfer to gas lighting was introduced on White Star's *Adriatic* of 1872, as was the practice in railway carriages. The Inman liner, *City of Berlin*, was the first to use electric lighting in 1878 with six bulbs in the saloon and engine room. It was not until the 1880s that electrical lighting became more commonplace, which was well in advance in its use on shore, when the London *Savoy* was the first public theatre to be lit by electricity in 1887. Three other ships of similar design were constructed by Harland & Wolff for White Star: the *Atlantic*, *Baltic* and *Republic*, to support their reputation for comfort as opposed to speed. The larger *Teutonic* and *Majestic* were delivered by Harland & Wolff for White Star in 1889 and 1890 respectively. Henry Fry commented in 1896:

> The fittings throughout are really superb, and the decorations highly artistic, indeed, they must be seen to be fully appreciated. In each ship the midship-saloon is 60 × 57 feet, the full width of the ship, 10 feet in height, with a crystal dome in the roof. The decorations in this splendid banqueting hall are in the Renaissance style. Bas-relief figures of tritons and nymphs in gold and ivory gambol around, and the ceiling is decorated in a corresponding style . . . The smoking-room is a cosy and handsome apartment. The woodwork is of dark mahogany; the walls are covered with embossed leather of the same tone, richly gilt. The panels are oil-paintings representing the ships of the Middle Ages . . . On the promenade deck and supper decks there are a number of spacious state-rooms, luxuriously fitted up, some of them have double bedsteads, wardrobes, armchairs, writing tables, and couches . . . There are numerous bathrooms and lavatories in the charge of special attendants, and a barber's shop fitted with electric motors to drive revolving hairbrushes.
>
> (Fry 1896: 175–7)

The ships could carry 855 steerage passengers, 175 second class and 300 saloon or first class.

P&O were under pressure to respond to the increased expectations of the public for comfort whilst at sea, established by White Star, and so the *Kaisar-i-Hind* (Empress of India) was launched in 1878 with a gross tonnage of 4,019, the largest yet built for the company. *The Home News* reported the launch and the upgrade of passenger comfort: 'In her internal decorations the directors of the company have aimed at something different and more artistic than the usual style of cabin work. It has been considered that the improvements affected in our domestic arrangement by the revival of a taste for genuine art could be adapted to the fitting out of a first class ship . . . The refined and unobtrusive richness of decoration will be the characteristic of saloons and cabins, while in the more important essentials of substantial comfort such as bathrooms, remarkable elaboration has been bestowed. We are informed that this expensive type of vessel is viewed by the P&O company in the light of an experiment to test whether the Indian public really care to encourage a luxurious and, of course, somewhat costly mode of traveling, rather than run after cheapness irrespective of comfort' (10 May 1878). The ship contained a saloon of far larger dimensions than was usual, illuminated by oil lamps, a smoking room on the upper deck with settees, more bathrooms, decorated with coloured tiles, electric bells in all cabins and refrigeration to keep the ice rooms at the appropriate temperature. But it was to be 1895 before P&O were to employ a professional architect to oversee the design of public rooms; it was the new Orient Line which introduced the practice in 1877.

The newly formed Orient Line commissioned J.J. Stevenson (1831–1908) to design the public rooms for its first ship, the SS *Orient* in 1877. The line did not have government subsidies for the transportation of mail, and so relied on making the accommodation appealing for potential passengers. It is likely that Stevenson obtained the commission through his family connections. He was married to Elisa

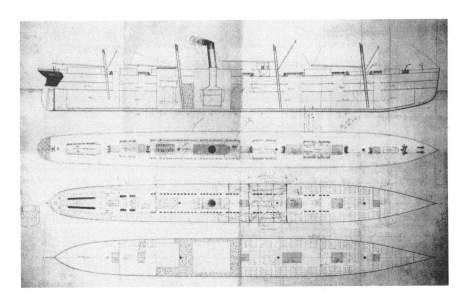

2.2
**Deck plan
of Oceanic**
Source: Liverpool
University

Anderson, the cousin of Skelton Anderson who was one of the founders of the Orient Line. The couple formed part of the Garrett circle, as Skelton Anderson was married to the feminist and first British woman doctor, Elizabeth Garrett Anderson (1836–1917). Elizabeth's sister was an interior and furniture designer. J.J. Stevenson's brother, Archibald Stevenson, married Skelton's sister, Margaret Jane. By the time of the commission from Orient line, J.J. Stevenson had worked in the offices of Sir Gilbert Scott in London and had just designed the Jamaican High Commission in South Kensington. He is best known for the Queen Anne revival designs of houses, schools and university buildings. His important published work, *House Architecture*, of 1880, is a treatise on new technology in the home, including discussions of water closets, electric bells, speaking tubes and service lifts. Given that he was an Arts and Crafts architect and friend of William Morris, it may seem incongruous for him to work on a modern steamship, but he relished the challenge that modernity presented and his connections with the Garrett circle provided a context of radical political views linked with radical principles in design.

The ship was launched in 1879, for the new Australia run for passengers and mail. It was built by John Elder & Co. of Govan, and at 5,386 gross tons it was the biggest ship to be built on the Clyde at that time. Stevenson designed an oval drawing room for the ship and a well to look down on the dining room below. He also designed the card room and smoking room. Stevenson went on to design the interiors of the *Ormuz* (1886), *Austral* (1881), *Ophir* (1891) and *Orontes* (1902) in similar style. The designs for the dining saloon of the *Ormuz* were exhibited at the Royal Academy in 1887. The dining saloon of the *Ophir* was a double-storey space with barrel-vaulted, glazed ceiling. The first level had decorated pillars and heavily carved panelling, which was echoed on the level above. The drawing room was decorated with wall panels inlaid with rosewood and satinwood by Messrs Knox and Webb, a local decorating firm, with 16 panels showing landscapes and allegorical figures by Napier Hemy and aesthetic movement artist and illustrator, Walter Crane. Stevenson was succeeded as architect for Orient Line ships by Andrew N. Prentice, a pupil of T.E. Collcutt, who employed the fashionable Beaux Arts style introduced by Mewès and Davis in the early twentieth century.

Another Arts and Crafts architect to work with the challenge of modernity was Richard Norman Shaw. An early contributor to ship interior design, he was the most fashionable architect to employ for the design of family homes in late Victorian Britain. He designed Grims Dyke in Harrow for W.S. Gilbert, the lyricist of the Savoy Opera's Gilbert and Sullivan fame, and Cragside for the great Victorian inventor and industrialist, Lord Armstrong (1810–1900) from 1869. This fairytale castle in half-timbering with soaring chimneys and stone arches was the first to be lit by hydro-electricity. It was lit by Joseph Swann's incandescent lamps and had numerous labour saving devices. J. Aldam Heaton, '. . . Shaw's favourite decorator of the 1880s, . . . was probably responsible for much of the Drawing Room's original appearance' (The National Trust, 2003: 69). The firm of A. Heaton & Co. was later to play a major role in the interior decoration of liners from the *Olympic* and *Titanic* onwards.

In 1882 Shaw was commissioned to design another house for a Victorian industrial entrepreneur, this time for Thomas and Margaret Ismay of the White Star Line. Situated on the Wirral, near Liverpool, the house, Dawpool Manor, was again in rustic, half-timbered Queen Anne style, complete with banqueting hall and worked as a backdrop to entertaining, rather than a family home. But Shaw also designed commercial properties, and in 1896 he was commissioned to design the new head-quarters for the Oceanic Steam Navigation Company which ran the White Star Line. Using his successful design for New Scotland Yard in London, Shaw employed red and cream stone facing and again, revived the Queen Anne style. Typically of this group of architects, the interior of the building belied its historicist exterior. The offices were open plan and the floors supported on cross girders, with upright iron stanchions running as pillars through the storey, almost like a warehouse. Such exposed structure would normally be concealed behind plasterwork.

There was a distinct nautical flavour to the interior of the building, and in 1897 Thomas Ismay invited Shaw to design the interior of the new White Star ship, *Oceanic* of 1899. 'In 1897 Ismay was unhappy with proposed interiors for one of his new liners, and asked Shaw to take it on' (Saint 1983: 357). Shaw acted as consultant designer for the library, smoking-rooms, drawing-room and other spaces for the first class passengers. The first class dining saloon definitely bears the stamp of Shaw. It was 80 feet long by 64 feet wide and was designed to seat 350. The space was lit from above by a huge, circular skylight, the dome of which extended into the promenade deck. The walls were panelled in dark wood, with oriel windows with heavily carved surrounds and with coffered ceilings along the edges of the space. The central dome was supported by carved, fluted pillars and the walls beneath the skylight were richly painted with renaissance style decoration and central murals depicting New York on one wall, America on the next complemented by Liverpool and Great Britain on the other two sides. The main figures were surrounded by appropriate names of famous associates – New York's roll call of fame included Abraham Lincoln, Longfellow and Henry Clay; America was represented by the names of Franklin, Columbus and William Penn; Liverpool rather strangely by Lord Nelson, James Watt and the Duke of Wellington; whilst the names chosen for Great Britain included William Caxton, Shakespeare, Sir Walter Raleigh and Isaac Newton. The decoration was carried out to the designs of Shaw by the decorating firm Messrs Trollope & Sons, and the total cost for the decoration work was £30,000 (Cunard 14.3.1905), (Holmes 1906: 81). The stairs to the library also reveal the involvement of Shaw in the dark oak, classical balustrade and the Queen Anne style, white pillars. However, the interior of the library is panelled in Louis XIV, rococo style carved wood with white and gold ceiling, which appears to be more of the work of Trollope & Sons than of Shaw. The one feature of the room which reveals Shaw's involvement could be the octagonal central table and glazed dome (Belfast H309). The dome is octagonal with oriel windows at its base and solid, white supports which fan into the smaller octagonal in the centre, which is punctuated by 16 bare lightbulbs – still enough of a novelty to be included without shades. The dome above the first class entrance aft also uses painted white

**Dome and
Decorated Panels
of the First Class
Dining Saloon
during outfitting,
Oceanic, 1st June
1899.**
Source: Ulster Folk &
Transport Museum

wooden supports, this time in simple panelling surmounting a simple carved frieze. The entrance is simply panelled in oak with pillars without lavish decoration and simple coffered ceiling. The first class smoke room is conventionally dark in treatment, with boldly patterned wallpaper, carved columns and leather covered settees and chairs. The ceiling is richly decorated plasterwork with acanthus leaves and scrolls. The glazed dome of this room, however, is decorated with a standard Roman scene which is used repeatedly in Harland & Wolff ships built at this time, so perhaps this is rather more the design of Trollope and Sons than Shaw. The painted panels in the room echo the theme of the dome in the first class dining saloon, with depictions of Columbus and sailing ships on voyages of discovery. Although it is difficult to disentangle who was responsible for what on the *Oceanic*, it seems clear that Shaw did influence aspects of the dining saloon, library and entrance hall. Subsequently dismissed as an unfortunate part of his design career, there was much of interest in the interior design of this ship (Saint 1983: 358).

The third Victorian Arts and Crafts architect to design early ship interiors was Thomas Edward Collcutt. Like many of the Arts and Crafts architects, he had been apprenticed to G.E. Street, and had established his own practice in 1873. He was experienced at designing not only buildings but also exhibition stands and furniture. He designed ebonized furniture for Collinson and Lock in Aesthetic Style. In total he designed 12 interiors for P&O, from 1896 to 1903 and was the first architect to be employed by the shipping line to upgrade their interiors emulating the White Star Line and Orient Line. He had just finished designing the Holborn Restaurant (1894) and his designs for the extensions to the Savoy Hotel in 1889 were just underway; he also designed the P&O Headquarters in Leadenhall Street. Collcutt first worked for P&O in 1891, when he designed the exotic pavilion for the company at the Royal Naval Exhibition. Held in the grounds of the Royal Hospital, Chelsea in London in the same vein as the Army show of the previous year, the show reinforced British national identity (Van der Merwe, 2001). There was a 40-ton Yarmouth sailing trawler with full-scale replicas of the new Eddystone Lighthouse and the hull of HMS *Victory* for the 2,351,683 visitors to marvel at. The P&O pavilion stood adjacent to the National Panorama pavilion and placed the company at the centre of the British Empire.

The first commission for ship interior design for Collcutt consisted of a group of five ships: the SS *India* (1896); SS *China* (1896); SS *Egypt* (1897); SS *Arabia* (1897) and SS *Persia* (1900) known collectively as the Egypt class. The ships followed the same basic layout, which emulated the deck plan of the *Oceanic*, with six decks in total. The first to be launched, the SS *India*, was built by Caird & Co. of Greenock and was 7,911 gross tons, over 3,000 more than the *Kaiser-i-Hind*. It was 500 feet in length and 54 feet in width, and could accommodate 314 passengers in first saloon class and 212 in second. The first class passengers were situated amidship, and the second class accommodation was placed towards the front of the ship (Longworth 2002). The interiors were decorated to Collcutt's designs by a specialist firm; in the case of SS *Egypt* it was Jacksons with the shipbuilders' Caird & Co.'s carpenters. The first class dining room of the *Egypt* was in fashionable taste and bears striking similarity to the Holborn Restaurant. It was furnished with mahogany furniture with long tables and carpet runners, to ease floor cleaning. The dining chairs had solid, carved wooden backs and arms with decorative, patterned squab. The chairs were also fixed to the floor to avoid movement during rough weather, but rotated around for passenger convenience. The pattern on the textiles was reflected in the swirling, decorative plasterwork on the ceiling and the walls were panelled in wood to dado rail height by the shipbuilders, with decorative plasterwork friezes above by Jacksons. The room was lit on either side by windows, dressed with plain, dark curtains. The overall colour scheme was white and gold for the wood and plasterwork. Despite the colour scheme, designed to create a feeling of spaciousness, the room appeared cramped, given the low ceiling height, the punctuation of the space by a central row of columns and the heavy decoration on the ceiling and beams. The second class dining room was similar in style, only the plasterwork decoration on the walls was replaced by Tynecastle tapestry panels. Tynecastle tapestry was a special, heavy wallpaper produced by the firm of Scott Morgan, which was cheaper than Jacksons' alternative of plasterwork.

Both the *Egypt* and *Arabia* had a hurricane deck above the first class dining room and the first class lounge/music room which enabled a stained glass skylight

to add more illumination and decoration. The lounge/music room had a capacious bookshelf running along one wall and the woodwork was African mahogany with ceiling decoration again by Jacksons. There were built-in sofas, freestanding sumptuous armchairs and a piano stool upholstered in heavily patterned moquette with heavily patterned carpet to match. Collcutt subcontracted a range of decorative tiles from the up-market Arts and Crafts ceramicist, William Frend De Morgan (1839–1917). De Morgan tiles were more expensive than the mass produced, transfer printed variety, but Collcutt obviously thought the extra cost was worth it for the added kudos and quality of appearance (Catleugh 1983: 114). He used lustreware to create a shimmering surface for the tiles, derived from Italian majolica and Hispano-Moresque examples. His colour range was distinctive and inspired by that of fifteenth- and sixteenth-century Isnik ware, or Persian ware as De Morgan called it. This consisted of dark blue, turquoise, manganese purple, green, Indian red and lemon yellow. This formal inspiration, coupled with the depiction of near Eastern scenes in ceramic made De Morgan's work a perfect match for P&O ships, destined for the East in the service of the British Empire – an appropriation of Eastern decorative styles to decorate vehicles of Western modernity. It is worth stressing that the tiles were used for passageways and smoking rooms, not first class sitting rooms or saloons, which were decorated in historicist, Western styles.

By this date De Morgan had undertaken some prestigious commissions, including the supply of Islamic tiles for the Arab Hall at Leighton House for the Victorian painter, Frederick (later Lord) Leighton, and supplied panels of tiles for the Czar of Russia's yacht, *Livadia*, both in 1879. He had supplied tiles for other P&O ships before Collcutt's commissions, possibly due to the publicity which the Czar's luxury yacht attracted: the *Sutlej* (1882); *Britannia* (1887); *Oceana* (1888); *Nubia* (1895); *Malta* (1895); *Palawam* (1895) and *Sumatra* (1895). The tiling provided cool and robust wall decoration, essential for the tropical heat and to withstand the wear and tear of passenger use – plus they ensured cleanable surfaces for areas such as the smoking saloon. For companionways on the *India* De Morgan provided two 11″ by 32″ panels and 88 9″ frieze tiles. The smoking saloon, situated on the hurricane deck aft, was decorated by De Morgan tiles in panels of 41″ by 32″and 42″ by 32″, drawn from designs already used on the *Sumatra* and *Palawam*. Described by *The Glasgow Herald* as: 'The first-saloon smoking room is perhaps the prettiest room in the vessel. It is fitted up with oak panels, stained green, and art decoration in the shape of handsome seascapes and landscapes are placed all around' (14.10.1896). De Morgan's tilework provided a utilitarian and fittingly exotic decoration for the walls of the public spaces. However, De Morgan found the experience of working with P&O to be very different from the client–designer relationship he was accustomed to for land based design. He wrote to his business partner Halsey Ricardo describing the P&O Chairman and Board as: '. . . a highly meddlesome pragmatic body' (18.2.1895). No records can be traced of P&O's opinion of De Morgan, but the system whereby the commissioning architect responsible for the interior design of the ship would present design ideas to the board in great detail for approval was a pattern which characterized the interior design of ships from this period and throughout most of the following century.

The shipping lines had amassed great wealth through the provision of reliable and increasingly comfortable sea travel. This invested them with immense political and economic power. The business of building ships is also one which requires utmost care and attention to detail, given the disastrous consequences of ocean travel if a collision took place, or technical faults or fires at sea. Hence, De Morgan's sentiments were to be reiterated throughout the next hundred years. However, his and Collcutt's work, along with that of Shaw and Stevenson were important markers as the beginning of the professional design of ships. This process was to take on increased significance, as the hegemony of Britain as provider of ocean travel for passengers was challenged by the ascendancy of Germany and the close relationship that existed between the architect and the line owner, with Hamburg-Amerika line working with Blohm & Voss/Waring & Gillow and North German Lloyd with Johannes Georg Poppe.

Chapter 3

Beaux Arts luxury on board

The designer and national identity

From the end of the nineteenth century until the outbreak of the First World War, there was a mammoth escalation in the building and refitting of ocean liners. This was interlinked with the burgeoning employment of designers to ensure that the ships expressed the appropriate visual national identity to serve official needs, and also attract the most prestigious customers. America, Britain, France, Germany and Italy vied for domination of the oceans, the North Atlantic in particular. The tangible symbol of hegemony was the acquisition of the Blue Riband prize, awarded annually for the fastest transatlantic crossing, which was a potent attraction for passengers. The editor of the Shipping Section of the *Magazine of Commerce and British Explorer*, R.A. Fletcher, commented: 'The public demand for speed and safety in vessels of great size entails the provision of expensive luxuries as an inducement to the public to patronise the vessels in which the demand is met' (Fletcher 1913: 239). But what style was most appropriate? The vogue for the Arts and Crafts had passed, and the fashion for the French Beaux Arts was prevalent for the interior design of hotels and country houses. The years leading up to the First World War witnessed a marked increase in German activity, with innovative liners in Rococo revivalist style by Poppe; Beaux Arts interiors by Mewès and Davis and more modern designs by Bruno Paul and Alexander Schroder. In response, Cunard employed designers for the first time for their prestigious ships, *Lusitania, Mauritania* and *Aquitania*, in largely Beaux Arts style. This was closely followed by the launch of White Star's *Olympic* and *Titanic* in 1911 with even more grandiose fittings by the decorating firm of Aldam Heaton & Co. with help from Mutters & Co. What all the interiors shared, beyond their French inspiration, was a denial of their nautical function; just as the: '. . . nineteenth-century bourgeoisie turned the home into a palace of illusions, which encouraged total dissociation from the world immediately outside', so liner interiors of this period were modelled on palaces, country houses or luxury hotels (Forty 1986: 101).

National rivalries and global dominance were played out by the design and construction of larger, faster and more lavishly decorated ships; this was reinforced through international exhibitions and events. Existing accounts tend to highlight technological determinism and the progress of modernity. However, as Paul Atkinson has argued, this is a simplistic model and the history of technology needs to take the social and political context into account (2005: 194). Hence in this part of the history ocean liner interior design served the needs of a burgeoning crisis in competing national identities at the turn of the nineteenth and twentieth centuries, accompanied by the escalating wealth of the social elite (Veblen 1899). National identity is a nineteenth-century concept, rooted in global travel and empire building and reinforced in the media. Benedict Anderson has defined nation as: '. . . an imagined political community – and imagined as both inherently limited and sovereign . . . National identity is visual evidence of how this is made manifest' (Anderson 1991: 6). And this drive towards expressing national identity and social distinction was witnessed in supporting events and the media. For example, the 1889 Spithead Review was attended by Germany's new ruler and grandson of Queen Victoria, Kaiser Wilhelm II, at the invitation of the Prince of Wales. The Kaiser was impressed by the general display, but particularly by White Star's latest addition to the fleet, the *Teutonic* and took design ideas back to Germany. His leadership supported the massive expansion in German shipbuilding leading up to the First World War. German ships dominated the Atlantic from 1897 until the introduction of the *Mauretania* and *Lusitania* in 1907. Whilst the competition between the shipbuilding nations was to dominate the Atlantic route, signalled by the Blue Riband competition, the most prestigious ships were built to convert easily for war use, with reinforced decks to take guns and massive passenger space, which could be used to transport troops and cargo quickly. The interior design of these ships, like the British *Mauretania, Lusitania* and *Aquitania* reflected an increased awareness of visual national identity in their interior décor.

The designer of the *Aquitania*, Arthur Davis (1878–1951), wrote a seminal article on ship design for the British architectural periodical, *Architectural Review*, in 1914. This is the first extensive article in English to appear in the press on ship design, signalling its growing status as an activity. In the article Davis was critical, as were most British commentators, of German design: 'Another temptation to be avoided is to overcrowd a room with heavy ornament and meretricious decoration. This fault has been very apparent on some of the earlier German liners, where refinement of detail has been often sacrificed to tawdry magnificence and over-elaboration' (Davis 1914: 89).

Part of the reason for the British dislike of German ships may have been their dominance of the North Atlantic. The *Kaiser Wilhelm der Grosse*, built by the Bremen-based North German Lloyd Line, wrested the Blue Riband from Britain's

Lucania in 1898. This was the first liner to have four funnels, paired fore and aft, to service the boilers. This enabled the builders to place broad, high ceilinged public rooms amidships, lit from above with huge skylights. The ship was designed to carry 332 first class, 343 second and 1,074 third class or steerage passengers. The interiors were designed by Johannes Poppe. There was a heavy, dark smoking room at the aft end of the promenade deck, decorated in German, Baroque revival style. There was a heavily carved ceiling, with dark brown, stamped leather, and some panels were decorated with representations of naval history. The chairs were dark wood and the oblong tables of the same material, which faced banquettes covered in dark brown, patterned textile. This contrasted with the ladies' drawing room, in light, French Rococo revival style, decorated in white and gold panelling and light blue, upholstered settees and chairs. The library was further forward on the promenade deck and was decorated in Baroque style, with swirling lines and floral decoration on the ceiling and plush seating, upholstered in strongly patterned fabric. The ship was a great success, as the largest and fastest of its time, and set the scene for prolonged German domination of the Atlantic. The main competition at the turn of the century for the Blue Riband came from North German Lloyd Line's German rival, the Hamburg-Amerika Line, which took the Blue Riband in 1900 with their new

3.1
Johannes Poppe, First Class Smoking Room, *Kaiser Wilhelm der Grosse*, 1897.
Source: North German Lloyd

ship, the *Deutschland*. The ship was fast, with the same four funnel arrangement as the *Kaiser Wilhelm der Grosse*, but uncomfortable to travel in, and so was transferred to the cruise market in 1910. The Hamburg-Amerika line was under the directorship of Albert Ballin (1857–1918), who had begun working at the company in 1886 as Head of the Passenger Department, and so understood the demands of the customer and the importance of marketing. The *Deutschland* was built to rival the *Kaiser Wilhelm der Grosse*, and so was longer at 686 feet and larger overall at 16,502 tons, with accommodation for 467 first, 300 second and 280 third class passengers. The first class dining room was three decks high, lit by a dome of ground glass with light reflected in the huge mirrors around the room. The room could seat 425 first class passengers at once. There was an intimate grill room for those who missed a meal and wished to order a quick dinner. The combination drawing room and music room was dominated by a huge, full-length portrait of Kaiser Wilhelm II. The smoking room had a medieval doorway, flanked by Gothic style carved figures and surmounted by a painting of Hamburg harbour. In 1904 the Hamburg-Amerika Line lost the Blue Riband back to the North German Lloyd Line's *Kaiser Wilhelm II*.

Built for the North German Lloyd Company by the Vulcan Works in Stettin, the *Kaiser Wilhelm II* was approximately the same length as White Star's *Oceanic* (II) but was a broader and deeper vessel with a much more powerful engine. The interiors by Poppe were in German Baroque revival style, the main dining saloon (Holmes 1906: 85) had three levels with balconies richly decorated with festooned carved shields. The room was lit by a domed skylight and was situated on the main deck, spanning the full width of the ship, with seating for 554. Arthur Davis, working with his senior partner, Strasburg-born Charles Mewès (1860–1914), succeeded in introducing a refined Beaux Arts elegance to the German ship interior. The Hamburg-Amerika Line had decided to follow the example of the White Star Company, and privilege comfort over speed, resulting in the *Amerika* of 1905, built at the same shipyard of Harland & Wolff with a gross tonnage of 22,225.

With this ship, interiors began to be closely modelled on luxury hotels, rather than palaces or castles; on public spaces rather than private. This was the approach of Harland & Wolff, who won the contract to build the ship after offering an irresistibly low cost to the managing director of the Hamburg-Amerika line, Albert Ballin (1857–1918). Harland & Wolff's first passenger ships built for the Hamburg-Amerika line were the *Prussia* and *Persia* of 1894, at a tonnage of 5,840 and 5,857 respectively, at cost to the yard, returning a profit of less than 1%. The public interiors of the *Amerika* were designed by Mewès, based on the success of his design of the Ritz Hotel in Paris, built in 1898 in fashionable Beaux Arts style, which Mewès had studied at the École des Beaux Arts in the 1880s. Mewès had also remodelled London's Carlton Hotel in partnership with his recently appointed junior partner, Arthur Davis. Davis had worked with Mewès whilst still a student at the École des Beaux Arts on designs for the Grand Palais and Petit Palais for the Paris 1900 exhibition. The pair were unsuccessful in that competition, but Mewès was impressed by Davis and established him as his London based partner in 1900. Mewès and Davis remodelled

3.2
**Johannes Poppe,
First Class Main
Saloon,** *Kaiser
Wilhelm II,* **1904.**
Source: North
German Lloyd

the restaurant and palm court of the Carlton Hotel in Haymarket in 1901. As Charles Reilly recalled in 1931: 'I can well remember the time, just about thirty years ago, when Arthur Davis and his work first began to make a stir in architectural circles in London. He was then a young man of twenty-one, having been born in 1878. I think he first appeared on the scene over the Carlton Hotel, where he was employed with the well-known French architect, Monsieur Charles Mewès, to alter the restaurant and palm court in order to bring this part of the hotel more into line with that international standard of taste which good feeding on the whole seems to inculcate. In place of rather stuffy Victorianism, London was surprised by a sudden intrusion of French elegance' (1931: 67).

On a return visit from Harland & Wolff in Belfast to discuss the building of the *Amerika*, Ballin dined in the newly fitted out Ritz-Carlton Grill at the Carlton Hotel, and was impressed by the interior decoration and clientele which were attracted to the ostentatious, Louis XVI interiors. He discovered that the architect, Mewès, had also acted as architect for the Warburgs, who were old friends of Ballin and were based in Hamburg. As director of the company, Ballin was able to move quickly, and Mewès was commissioned to design the interiors of *Amerika*. To under-take the German based work, Mewès engaged another partner, Cologne based Alphonse Bischoff – but Mewès was the dominant designer in his German and British based companies. Waring & Gillow gained the contract to decorate the main public rooms of the *Amerika*. This was the first major ship fitting contract for this traditional, decorating firm, which had been formed in 1903 out of a merger of two furnishing companies, the most prominent being Gillows of Lancaster which began in the 1730s supplying mahogany furniture to the West Indies and importing rum and sugar. In 1764 a London branch was opened at 176 Oxford Road (now Street) to supply high quality furniture to the wealthy. The Liverpool based firm of Waring had begun as a cabinet-making business in 1835, which expanded during the 1880s to a decorating company with contracts to furnish hotels and public buildings throughout Europe. Waring & Gillow continued to flourish as a high class, decorating firm and contributed to the decoration of the *Lusitania, Heliopolis, Cairo, Queen Mary* and *Queen Elizabeth*. Waring & Gillow recognized that the days of the foreman-joiner were over as far as ship interior decoration was concerned. In a brochure dating from *c.*1907, the company outlined this change:

> Shipyard fittings and decorations, thought excellent in their strength and durability, have served their day, and many owners are now awakening to the fact that there should be some relation between design and power in their ships. As the sail had to give place to steam, and even the triple expansion engine is in turn making room for the turbine, so the old shipyard design and execution of internal and domestic arrangement must inevitably make room for more artistic and up-to-date designs. Some of the more advanced among the great steamship owners, when placing orders for new vessels, now keep the specification for the construction free from all question of artistic taste and high-class cabinet work and upholstery. At first sight this new order of things appears prejudicial to the interest of the builder, but it is not so. Some of the most enlightened and experienced are themselves going to firms outside the shipbuilding trade for the design and execution of fitments, furniture, &c., the reason being that any step in the direction of making their boats attractive enhances their reputation and increases their business.
>
> (Waring and Gillow *c.*1907:108)

The overall decorating style was French Beaux Arts, popular in Paris and London for luxury hotels, office buildings and exclusive residences. It was also the fashionable style for the elite on the east coast of America, where it was used by firms, particularly McKim, Mead and White to design imposing public buildings, mansion houses and luxury hotels for America's elite (White and Wallen 1998; White and White 2003). The model of the luxury hotel rather than the palace also prevailed in the creation of an à la carte restaurant on board the *Amerika*, based on the model of the Ritz-Carlton Grill at the Carlton Hotel in London. In 1903 Mewès and Davis received the prestigious commission to design the London Ritz, based on the success of the Paris predecessor. This was the first steel-framed building in London, faced with Norwegian granite with Rue de Rivoli arcades and Mansard roofline, it is '. . . the finest Edwardian hotel interior I know, with an imaginative use of space and a splendour of decoration that represents the grand architecture of the period at its best' (Service 1975: 40). It seems likely that Mewès designed the exterior with Davis designing the interior, including the Winter Garden with Corinthian columns, elegant Louis XVI friezes and porticos. The dining room is impressive, with Corinthian columns linked by a ring of hanging garlands. Waring & Gillow's was again the decorating firm to work with Mewès and Davis.

The *Amerika* was the first liner to carry an electric passenger lift, and this introduction of new technology as an attractive novelty for first class passengers mirrored the practice of hotels rather than palaces. The dining facilities were also novel. Up until this date, dining saloons had served meals on board liners to all passengers at set times. The new style restaurant was run by Cesar Ritz, who trained the staff, with the food created under the management of Auguste Éscoffier. The maître d'hotel of the Ritz-Carlton Grill, Nagel, ran the restaurant for the first year. Mewès designed the interior for this new venture, recreating the Ritz-Carlton Grill ambience for the passengers at 25 separate tables. The space had windows on three sides. Cream and gold walls were lit by ormolu sconces and subtle table lights. The furniture was mahogany, and stood on a dark blue carpet, and the linen and crockery displayed the Carlton crest. Aft of the restaurant was the lounge, decorated in the Adam style, from where was the first class ladies drawing room, in similar style. The room was furnished with elegant, Georgian furniture and patterned carpet. A portrait of the Kaiser hung over the mantelpiece. Delicate floral garlands twisted around the white pillars, to create the ambience of lightness and feminity. This was one of the first ocean liners to include a range of different period rooms as part of its interior design. There were two Imperial State Rooms, decorated with the most expensive materials; both suites were panelled in enamelled whitewood, one in the Adam style with satinwood furniture and one in the Empire style with furniture in mahogany with gilt ormolu decoration. The 13 *chambes de luxe* were decorated by Waring & Gillow in a range of eighteenth-century French and English styles, but not German. There were Queen Anne rooms furnished in oak with walnut inlay; Georgian furnished in walnut with boxwood inlay; Adam in inlaid satinwood; Sheraton in inlaid mahogany; Louis XVI rooms had painted green furniture and Empire mahogany, decorated with ormolu. There was also a main grand staircase, vital for making an impressive public entrance, particularly in the evening. This was in Beaux Arts style, a subtle blend of Adamesque and Louise XVI with wrought iron balustrade with gilt-brass handrail. The wall panelling, like that of all the first class spaces, was white. The exception to this was the two-storey smoking room. Connected by an oak, double flight internal staircase, this male preserve was lined in oak, with the lower room recreating a great hall or hunting room in an Elizabethan house, complete with beamed ceiling on the lower floor. On the upper floor the panelling was surmounted by a carved wood frieze

which illustrated hunting and the life of St Huburt, patron saint of the hunter. To complete the dark, masculine mood, the seating was upholstered in brown cowhide. The elegance and informality of these public rooms set a new trend in ocean liner interior design. Mewès & Davis and Waring & Gillow were also responsible for the design of the *Kaiserin Auguste Victoria* for the Hamburg-Amerika Line in the same year of 1905.

Germany's new-found success in transatlantic travel challenged Britain's dominance as a maritime nation, an important facet of British national identity. Germany was now equipped and able to build enormous passenger liners, and so usurped the traditional hegemony of Britain as the prime, shipbuilding nation. As long ago as May 1901 the Cunard Board had discussed the possibility of building 'New, Fast Steamers' for the Atlantic trade in response to Germany's success in the Blue Riband competition (Buxton 1996: 55). Cunard were also aware of new ships under construction for North German Lloyd at Harland & Wolff, which would sustain German dominance. Cunard exerted pressure on the British government, playing on its fear of an imminent American takeover of Cunard, after J. Pierpoint Morgan's new shipping combine, International Mercantile Marine (IMM) had taken financial control of White Star in December 1902. White Star was Cunard's main rival and had a hold over the market with *Celtic* and *Nordic*. Morgan also had financial interests

3.3
Mewès and Davis, First Class Ladies Drawing Room, *Amerika*, Hamburg-America Line, September 1905.
Source: Ulster Folk & Transport Museum

in both German lines, with the full support of the Kaiser. It was also advantageous for the government to have two potential armed merchant cruisers for possible requisition by the Admiralty, and American ownership of cruise ships might jeopardize this. Therefore, on 30 September 1902 the Prime Minister, Arthur Balfour, announced that Cunard would be granted a government loan of £2.6 million on very favourable terms to build the two new ships as long as the company remained British. The ships also had to have the capacity to be converted to auxiliary cruisers in time of war. Cunard prepared detailed specifications for the two ships, referred to as the 'New Fast Steamers' on Cunard correspondence throughout 1902–5, known as No. 367 (*Lusitania*) and No. 735 (*Mauretania*). The Clydeside shipbuilders, John Brown, were contracted to build No. 367 and Tyneside based Swan Hunter & Wigham Richardson Ltd to build No. 735.

The main aim was to build two ships which would be faster and larger than the German rivals, to regain the Blue Riband for Britain, which had been won by the *Kaiser Wilhelm der Grosse* in 1899, the first time that the coveted prize had been lost by Britain. It was decided in March 1904 that the two ships should be driven by quadruple screw turbine machinery, to reach the desired top speed of 24 and one half knots. The two ships were the largest ever to be built at that time, at some 31,000 tons and 790 feet in length. There was a visit by Cunard to the North German Lloyd liners, *Kaiser Wilhelm der Grosse* and *Kronprintz Wilhelm* in 1903 and the visit was subsequently reported upon (Cunard: 1903). Cunard were particularly impressed by the general atmosphere of airiness, obtained by the use of white paintwork, gilding, and windows on the staircases and cafes on sundecks. However, Cunard found the general layout inferior to their own ships: 'Our arrangements for the individual comfort and convenience of the passengers are better, more compact, more economical in space and in every way more comfortable' (1903: 1–2). The style of the interiors was particularly unappealing to the Cunard visitors. The Baroque revival interiors were heavily criticized by Cunard: 'They are of a type particularly unsuitable to the situation, which demands an absence of restless forms and refined richness of style. These decorations are bizarre, extravagant and crude, loud in colour and restless in form, obviously costly, and showy to the most extreme degree' (1903: 2).

Cunard had a different approach to what was appropriate decoration for the interiors of its liners. This was underpinned by a perception that an appropriate style was simple, elegant and unobtrusive, perhaps based on Mewès & Davis's work with the Hamburg-Amerika Line, bearing in mind that the *Amerika* was being built at Harland & Wolff in Belfast. For the first time in the company's history, Cunard began a hunt for suitable architects late in 1903. Compared to the ease of appointment for Mewès & Davis by Ballin, the Cunard Board moved ponderously, taking two years to select and appoint the two architects. The decision to appoint architects for the first time may have been prompted by the government or may have come as a result of competition from the other lines. By this date P&O, Union Castle, Orient Line, North German Lloyd and Hamburg-Amerika Line had all used architects to design the interiors of their ships, which added a certain cachet and element of prestige. A preliminary list was drawn up by Cunard's Chairman, Lord Inverclyde who was the direct descendant of George Burns, Samuel Cunard's partner, and the first Chairman of Cunard. The list consisted of all the architects known to have worked on British ship interior design. The list comprised T.E. Collcutt, William Flockhart, Dunn and Watson, Niven and Wigglesworth and J.J. Stevenson (Cunard 3.9.1903). This initial trawl was unsuccessful; architects such as Stevenson and Collcutt felt a certain loyalty to their employing shipping lines. William Flockhart replied on 21 September 1903, that he did not want to be in competition with cabinet-makers, and Dunn and Watson demanded that they be paid for any preliminary work. James Miller (1860–1947), who was eventually appointed to design the *Lusitania*, was initially suggested by the Glasgow based Inverclyde in a letter of 14 April 1904 to the Cunard Company Secretary, A.D. Mearns:

> I may say that one of the principal architects in Glasgow, Mr James Miller, has spoken to me with reference to being allowed to submit designs for steamer decoration. Mr Miller is quite a young man and has not yet done any steamer work. He was made Architect of the Glasgow Exhibition after severe competition, and ever since then has had a very large amount of work of all kinds to do.

The Chairman of Swan Hunter, G.B. Hunter, suggested using the decorating firm of Messrs Trollope plus one other firm, for the same competitive tendering in a letter of 14 November 1904. However, the idea was rebuffed by Bains on 18 November 1904: '. . . the Directors are not prepared to go into the question of the decorations at present', signalling that it was architects which Cunard was seeking to appoint first to oversee these high status projects and the work of the decorators, although Messrs G. Trollope & Sons did decorate the port side of the promenade and boat decks including the 'Regal Suites' aft. A letter from Lord Inverclyde to Mearns on the 6 February 1905 recounts a telephone conversation with Mr Sam Waring of Waring & Gillow, which reveals that the firm was anxious to undertake the design and decorating work for the new ships: 'Mr Waring would prefer that they should have the designing as well as the carrying out of the work, and this I am very strongly against, because we would have no protection between them and ourselves in regard to the quality of the work' (p.1). However, Inverclyde was vaguely encouraging, as he: '. . . asked Mr Waring to see the *Caronia* and he will probably be in Liverpool this week and arrange to do so' (p.2). Waring & Gillow, who were eventually contracted to decorate the starboard side of the boat and promenade decks, from and including the 'Regal Suites' aft on the *Lusitania*, wrote again to Cunard on 1 November 1906 explaining the importance of fashion to the design of cabins:

> Waring and Gillow have experience of fitting ships – SS Amerika and SS Kaiserin August Victoria (the work on the latter being remarked upon

by Herr Ballin as being the 'best in the ship'), we have the necessary knowledge and experience in the essentials for combining elegance and comfort in the limited area occupied by these cabins, and we have met the demand made by passengers for increased accommodation owing to the stricter requirements of dress, in consequence of the greater facilities for fashionable gatherings in ships.

We also have the necessary experience in dealing with these rooms for combining the effect of simplicity and good taste in style, which is necessary to attract the best type of passengers (Cunard 1.12.1906: 1–2).

Mearns also received an expression of interest from the decorating firm of White Allom in a letter of 10 March 1905:

Our Chas. Allom has for some time been travelling to and from New York on various ships, and last Saturday arrived on your 'Campania'.

As an expert in decorative work, he has been struck with the loss of opportunities which is taking place, to bring ship decoration up to the standard of the improved taste of the last few years.

We have had a very wide experience in the highest class of work, both in this country and in America, and we should have pleasure in laying designs and photographs before you of work we have carried out, and if it interests you, would free of charge make you some designs for consideration.

We have recently completed the re-decorating of the State Rooms and Staircases at St James' Palace for His Majesty The King, and the whole of Marlborough House for HRH the Prince of Wales . . .'

Hunter's recommendation, Trollope and Sons, also approached Cunard direct in a letter of 27 February 1905, offering to visit the Cunard offices in Liverpool to consult on any new designs, pointing out that the firm was already undertaking work for the Royal Mail Company. Inverclyde met with H.J. Burgess of Trollope and Sons, and a letter to Mearns of 14 March 1905 reports on meeting Burgess and showing Inverclyde the designs for a new steamer, the *Arragon* for the Royal Mail:

I cannot say that I thought there was anything wonderful in them, but the firm's name can be considered along with others who are wishful to do our New Fast Ships. There is this to be said in their favour that they are not new to Ship Work as they did the whole of the internal decoration and Fittings in the Public Rooms of the Majestic and Teutonic and most of the work in the Oceanic. The saloon of the Oceanic was of course designed by Mr Norman Shaw but carried out by Messrs. Trollope & Sons, and Mr Burgess informs me it alone cost £30,000. I have given Mr Burgess an order to see over the *Caronia* and have told him that I will arrange for his having an opportunity later on of submitting his Plan to the Board.

(pp.1–2).

Whilst Cunard kept the decorating firms on hold, the quest for suitable architects received a higher priority. They needed to be appointed first, in order perhaps that they could be consulted about the appointment of decorators. James Miller was eager to win the contract, and wrote to Mearns on 30 January 1905 putting himself forward, citing his work for the 1901 Glasgow International Exhibition as his major achievement. Cunard still had not reached a decision, and in a letter to Mearns of 18 April 1905, Inverclyde reveals that he would take up the Company Secretary's suggestion to approach various architect's associations, and singles out the RIBA as the most important, suggesting that Cunard meet with the President, Aston Webb before Easter. Inverclyde also suggests, for the first time, employing different architects for the two ships: 'It would bring about competition and it does not seem to me necessary that the two ships should be designed and decorated alike'. This suggestion was agreed at the meeting of the Shipbuilding Committee on 19 April 1905.

Ernest Cunard and Lord Inverclyde met with Arthur Davis in late April or early May 1905 (Cunard 3. 5.1905). Davis undertook to approach the Hamburg-Amerika Line about working for a rival. However, Inverclyde reported in a letter of 11 May 1905 that Mewès & Davis could not undertake the work. However, Davis was to design Cunard's new headquarters before the First World War, into which the company moved in 1916. Cunard and Inverclyde also interviewed T.E. Colcutt who: 'need not be considered', possibly due to his involvement with P&O (Cunard 3.5.1905). Probably on the recommendation of Aston Webb, Cunard and Inverclyde met with the country house architect, Harold A. Peto (1854–1933) on 24 May 1905, and discovered that Peto had recently left his previous architectural practice (in 1892) a wealthy man, but with the understanding that he would not design any more buildings. He was now concentrating on interior decoration and garden design, and during the period he was working on the Italianate water garden for Alexander Henderson, created Lord Faringdon in 1916, at Buscot Park, Berkshire. The design of ships was new to Peto, but he was positive about working on the project, with the proviso that he did not have to work with the entire Cunard Board (Cunard 25.5.1905). A letter of 3 June 1905 to Mearns outlines Inverclyde's disquiet at the risk of employing an architect with no experience of ships. He was nervous about using Peto and Miller, but also aware that the Cunard Board wished to use an architect and not: '. . . leave it in the hands of the (ship) builders as we have done in the past'. However, Cunard decided to proceed and invite Peto to submit designs for the *Mauretania* and Miller for the *Lusitania*.

As an established architect, Peto had the confidence and experience to query the terms of his engagement with Cunard, who had never hired a professional architect. When Peto had been in partnership with Ernest George (1839–1922) it was Peto who handled the commercial aspects of the architectural business. His family background as son of Victorian railway contractor, Samuel Morton Peto Bt (1809–1889) meant he had excellent business connections (Ottewill 1989: 147). Due to the efforts of the RIBA, the practice of architecture was becoming more formalized and professionalized. Therefore, when Cunard offered Peto an initial flat fee of 1,500 guineas, rising to 2,000 guineas plus expenses on 30 June 1905, Peto retorted with a request for £4,000 which he calculated to be 5% of the total cost of the interior design work of £80,000 (Peto 3.7.1905). On July 11 1905 he included the RIBA form 'The Professional Practice as to the Charges of Architects' to give Cunard further guidance. However, this only added to Inverclyde's anxieties, and he expressed a desire to dispense with Peto, particularly in contrast to Miller, who will be happy with a fee of £1,000: 'My own feeling is to drop Mr Peto and try and find somebody else. Either as you say the matter will have to stand over until I return or if the Directors think this is leaving it too long I shall not stand in the way if they desire to settle it' (Cunard 12.7.1905). The matter was finally resolved in August 1905, when Peto accepted Mearns's offer of 5% of total costs, with the proviso that there should be an agreed minimum of £3,500 and that a Clerk of Works be appointed to oversee the project on Tyneside, as Peto planned to work from his offices in London (Peto 28.8.1905). The younger, less established Miller proved a lot easier to deal with and accepted a fee of 1,000 guineas to act as Advisory Architect and prepare designs for the public rooms (Miller 30.8.1905).

Before embarking on their design work, both architects arranged to examine the competition, with Peto visiting Southampton to see the *Kaiser Wilhelm* and Miller making plans to visit Belfast, Bremen and Hamburg (Miller 13.9.1905). Cunard outlined their design philosophy to Peto in a letter from Mearns in September 1905:

> Everything in connection with the designing and decorating of the First Class accommodation is to be of the best character, workmanship and material, but the Directors do not desire anything of an extravagant nature. The simpler the work, so long as it is good, the better, and the more the cost can be kept down, the more satisfactory it will be to the Cunard Company, provided the general effect is tasteful and pleasing.
>
> (Cunard 13.9.1905)

The structural designs of the two ships were very similar, so their interior design would serve to distinguish them. From the very beginning, given the contrasting attitudes towards fees already described, the *Mauretania* was far more costly and luxurious than the *Lusitania*. The final cost of the former was £1,812,252 which was £186,789 or 15% more than the latter. The sum spent on interior decoration for the public rooms was £130,000 for the *Mauretania* and £82,000 for the *Lusitania* (Cunard File D42/S7/1/9). This was largely due to higher labour costs and more lavish work undertaken on Tyneside (Buxton: 1996: 68). Peto's background was in upper class, country house design, and this was the experience he brought to the design of the interiors of the *Mauretania*. Domestic design, albeit it the top end of the market, was his model, rather than that of the luxury hotel. George and Peto's practice had been one of the most fashionable in London, with Edwin Lutyens working there as an assistant. Peto was also well aware of fashion in interior decoration in America, as he travelled there in 1887.

Initially, Peto was given greater autonomy, designing the interiors for all first class accommodation and also having the authority to approve designs and supervise the work of Swan Hunter and Wigham Richardson for the second class spaces. When work began on the interiors, Swan Hunter became frustrated at Peto's slow rate of response; the shipbuilders may also have been disappointed not to have total control of the interior decoration. In October 1905 Hunter wrote to Mearns: 'With regard to the second-class Public Rooms etc and to your desire that the designs for these should be approved by Mr Peto, we have sent out outline designs to Mr Peto and are unable to proceed with the work until we know that they have been approved by him. We are glad if you will kindly urge on Mr Peto to take heed of timings with delivery set for Autumn 1907' (Cunard 27.10.1905). This prompted Mearns to contact Peto, urging him to take heed of the timings with delivery set for late 1907. Peto did respond on the same day, observing that he agreed the timings, but that Swan Hunter's need for control over his designs was: 'An unusual and complicated arrangement' (Cunard 8.12.05). Cunard resolved the situation with advice from their solicitors, to accept Swan Hunter's point that they had overall responsibility for the ship, so that Peto remained responsible for the first class public rooms, stairways, first class staterooms and the overall decoration and furnishing, whilst Swan Hunter kept control of the finances and technical details. Hence, this was a complex arrangement, with the shipyard, architect and line owners involved to the minutest level of detail. Employing an architect ensured that the interior styling of the first class areas was of an impressive and fashionable standard, but the price to be paid was the addition of an extra loop in the communication and decision making process. Peto rarely travelled to Tyneside, delegating responsibility for the fitting out work to a clerk of works, and completing the design work in London.

Peto chose from a range of historic French style for the interiors of the first class rooms, as was fashionable in the early twentieth century in Britain and North America. This approach was castigated by naval experts in the early twentieth century. For example, Edward Keble Chatterton (1878–1944) commented:

> There are some characteristics of the *Mauretania* and *Lusitania*, with their lifts, their marbles, curtains, ceilings, trees, and other expressions of twentieth century luxury, which, while appreciated by the landsman and his wife, are nauseating to the man who loves the sea and its ships for their own sakes, and not for the chance of enjoying self-indulgence in some new form.
>
> (as quoted in Brinnin 1986: 336).

However, country houses at that time were decorated in this manner to signal taste and social status, as shown by the New York based decorator and author of *The House in Good Taste*, Elsie de Wolfe, and the domestic interior design work of Mewès & Davis, for example Polesden Lacey, begun in 1906. So knowledge of French interior decorating style was a sign of education or belonging to the upper class (Veblen 1899; Bourdieu 1984). Peto worked with the decorating firm of Turner Lord

& Co. on the majority of his designs, with the exception of the lounge and library, which were undertaken by Charles Mellier & Co. The first class accommodation was situated amidship and spanned five decks, from A to E, or boat to main decks and built to accommodate 560 passengers. This space was connected centrally by means of a grand staircase, which encased two electric lifts. The panelling was in French walnut, and *The Shipbuilder* recognized the domestic background of Peto's designing career when they described: 'The grand staircase is unequalled in size and beauty in any vessel afloat, and indeed it is worthy of any mansion ashore' (as quoted in Smith 1997: 27). The other professional shipbuilding magazine, *The Engineer*, echoed this view: 'In visiting this colossal ship one has need to be prepared for surprises everywhere, and one of these surprises will be the grandeur of the stairways and approaches. Except in Mauretania's sister-ship, never has there been in a vessel a stairway of such size, and resembling so nearly that of a private mansion; . . .' (Warren 1987: 16). The carpets on the stairs were dark green to complement the walnut. In two of the entrances to the first class area were recessed settees, richly upholstered and set in a carved, walnut surround.

The largest and most complex interior from the *Mauretania* was the first class dining room, situated in the centre of decks C, upper and D, saloon. It was designed by Peto in French sixteenth-century or François I style, mainly inspired by the Château du Chambord, with comparatively simply carved features in dark, Austrian oak, decorating the balcony of the second storey of this two storey space. The main storey had richer carving, which was cut back from the solid oak. The ceiling was a graceful, groined dome in cream and gold, which was decorated with the signs of the zodiac in small spheres at the cross-sections of the groins. The dome was lit by hidden electric lamps, concealed by the octagonal balustrade at the top. The lights were reflected against a gilded, convex disc at the very top, given a soft and muted illumination below. The chairs were upholstered in a patterned, deep pink. The lower dining room could seat 333 passengers and the à la carte restaurant on the upper storey, 152, making a total of 485. The lower dining room had an Austrian oak parquet floor with carpet runners between the tables, and the restaurant a fitted carpet in cerise, copied by Taylor from an Italian velvet original. The arrangement of the furniture and floor coverings was selected by Cunard's upholstery and furnishing department, and sent to the Shipbuilding Committee for approval, before being sent on to Peto. The arrangement of the dining room furniture was innovative, as the established norm had been to provide long tables, with rows of seating either side. The *Mauretania* used the layout adopted on Cunard's *Caronia* and *Carmania*, with smaller, more intimate dining groupings provided by small, circular tables (Cunard 31.10.1906).

The remainder of the saloon deck was occupied by cabins and bathing and toilet facilities. On the upper deck there was a small bar, just off the dining room. At the other end was the children's room, lined in white enamelled wood panelling with pictures by Newcastle based artist J.E. Mitchell on the theme of 'Four and Twenty Blackbirds'. The promenade deck above was populated mainly by cabins,

including the two 'Regal Suites', comprising dining room, drawing room, two bed-rooms, bath and toilet. There were very few first class cabins with en suite facilities, as this was considered an extra luxury. The 'Regal Suites' were the most expensive to hire on the ship, at £400 in peak season for a return trip. The suites were in Adam style and panelled with East India satinwood and fitted with marble mantelpieces. One suite was decorated with striped, green silk wall panels and the other rose, with

3.4
Harold Peto, First Class Restaurant, *Mauretania,* **Cunard, 1907.**
Source: Tyne and Wear Museum Service

carpets in the same colourways. There were also 64 special state and en suite rooms, complete with fine wooden panelling and onyx washstands, and 109 first class staterooms without facilities. Shared bathrooms and toilets were provided for the majority of first class passengers, plus second and third. The ratio of passengers to bathing facilities is indicative of their status – in first class there was one bath for every 15 passengers; one for every 30 in second class and only four for the 1,400 third class, the expectation being that they would not bathe at all.

The main public rooms for the first class passengers were situated on the top deck, or boat deck. At the rear of the ship was the veranda café, an innovation modelled on the open air café on the *Kaiser Wilhelm II*. Cunard's upholstery and furnishing department wanted to emulate the success of North German Lloyd's latest ship, and a memo from the department to the Cunard Secretary outlined their suggestion for cane furniture:

> It is submitted that seats be fitted after the type shown in Messrs White & Co's catalogue submitted herewith, and that chairs & tables of similar character be fitted in the centre under the dome.
>
> In the 'Kaiser Wilhelm II' seats, chairs & tables after the types above suggested were fitted in the small outdoor café on board that ship. The effect was very good and showed that some thought had been expended on it to get away from the ordinary ship style of fitting.
>
> (Cunard 19.3.1907)

However, the department were overruled by the General Superintendent, Bain, on 27 March 1907 who had estimated the purchase of such furniture would add £147 to the cost of the ship, and was unnecessary. Instead, heavy restaurant chairs were used, which detracted from the *al fresco* appeal of this space. It was covered by a glazed dome and was open to the promenade along one side. A door led from this open space, through a hallway with stairs down to B deck, and into the sixteenth-century, Italian smoke room. There were recesses in the room for added seclusion, complete with writing tables. *The Shipbuilder* again commented positively on the similarity between the ship and a house: 'The windows in these recesses are of unusual size for ship-work, and have been most successfully treated with semicircular arches, giving every appearance of the windows of a private house' (Warren 1987: 17). A complete vista of almost 350 feet was created through the public rooms, as Peto chose to use glazed doors to connect the rooms. Leading from the smoke room was the lounge and music room. Peto worked with the decorating firm, Charles Mellier & Co. on this room and the writing room and library beyond it. The lounge was decorated in Louis XVI style, with *acajou mouchete* mahogany panelling, and *fleur-de-peche* marble and ormolu was used for the 16 pilasters and chimneypiece. Three large, French Aubusson tapestries depicting a floral arrangement decorated the walls. The room was lit by a wrought-iron, oval skylight and electric chandeliers. The writing room and library was also in fashionable, eighteenth-century taste, with sycamore panelling stained silver grey. The mouldings were gilt and a huge bookcase covered one entire wall. The carpet and curtains were a dusky pink and the furniture was made from mahogany. The spaces designed by Peto succeeded in creating a fantasy of travel in time rather than space, as one contemporary commentator noted:

> The lounge and the library have been decorated by Messrs. Ch. Mellier and Co., Albermarle-street, London, and upon entering them one is transported in a moment from the cold realities of a modern steamship to the exquisite taste of a French *salon* of the eighteenth century. Thick carpets, comfortable chairs, soft colourings, and bright, but carefully shaded, electric lights, all combine to give an atmosphere of luxury and beauty hitherto considered impossible even in modern steamships. The style is influenced by the revived appreciation of the beauties of the Louis Seize period, but the colouring is original in its charming blending of harmonising tints.
>
> (Warren 1987: 18).

But what of the other classes of passenger on the ship? Sources for these interiors are scarce, with publications rarely mentioning them (Forsyth 1985; Brinnin 1986). The ship carried 475 second class and 1,300 third class passengers. The accommodation for the second class passengers was overseen by Swan Hunter with the approval of Peto. The dining room was in Georgian style, decorated with oak and lit by a central dome. It had been planned to use stained glass in the dome, but as costs escalated, this decorative feature was abandoned by Cunard during a visit in January 1907 (Cunard 30.1.1907). 'Stained Glass Domes for 2nd Class Smoke Room, Ladies room and 2nd Class Lounge. The designs submitted for these domes were too elaborate and the builders were informed that the domes were to be simplified and glazed with Ground glass. Messrs Swan & Hunter promised to communicate with Messrs Holler & Co. who are making this iron work and procure their amended estimate, and submit same to Directors' (1907: 2). A decorative, electrical light hung from the centre of the dome. The flooring was parquet with green runners and at each end of the room there was a large, carved oak sideboard and piano.

The second class drawing room returned to the French, eighteenth-century theme, with maple wood and gilt ornaments, lit by a glass dome. The furniture was upholstered in red velvet. The smoking room was in late-Georgian style, with deep blue velvet upholstery. The lounge on the boat deck was upholstered in blue with matching carpet runners. The staterooms were panelled in white enamelled pine with mahogany furniture. For the third class, accommodation was basic. Photographs exist in the Cunard archives of the accommodation, but it is indicative of the importance with which they were held that they are labelled 'Lusitania and Mauretania', with nothing to distinguish the third class on either ship. The dining room was spartan, with long wooden tables and lines of revolving, balloon back chairs. The walls were panelled with polished ash with teak mouldings. The space was the entire width of the ship and 330 could eat at one sitting. The low ceiling was painted white in attempt to add a feeling of spaciousness. The saloon, smoking room and ladies' room were of similar design. The floor of the smoking room consisted of bare floorboards, with

3.5
**Swan Hunters,
Third Class
Restaurant,
Mauretania,
Cunard, 1907.**
Source: Tyne and
Wear Museum
Service

whitewashed wall panelling and simple chairs and benches. The room was dark, with globe pendant lights in white and sloped wall to one side, indicating how low down the room was in the ship's structure.

If the third class accommodation was the same on the *Mauretania* and *Lusitania*, the first class public rooms were certainly not. Cunard were anxious that the two ships would not be unfavourably compared. As Denman, head of the upholstery and furnishing department, wrote to the Secretary in 1906: 'I would point out that when these vessels are in commission the "Lusitania" will suffer seriously by comparison with her sister ship the "Mauretania" on account of the uninteresting treatment of her Public Rooms generally, and a really serious effort is necessary to lift this ship above the level of the "Caronia" and "Carmania"' (Cunard 14.8.1906). And indeed, according to archival sources, Cunard devoted far more effort to overseeing the *Lusitania* than the *Mauretania*, implementing many changes to the architect's initial proposals. This may have been due to Miller's comparative lack of experience, having mainly designed public buildings, including stations and hotels in the west of Scotland whilst staff architect for the Caledonian Railway Company from 1888. In 1896 he designed the St Enoch Square Underground Station and in

1898 won the competition for the Industrial Hall at the 1901 Glasgow International Exhibition, through which he attracted the attention of Lord Inverclyde. His design style was comparatively simple compared to that of Peto, and when Cunard suggestions were added, the outcome lacked the unity of the *Mauretania*'s interiors.

The layout of the *Lusitania* was identical to that of the *Mauretania*, with the first class accommodation spanning five decks, but they differed in terms of interior design. Miller was responsible for acting as an advisor to Cunard, so this might explain why his designs were often altered. Miller decided to decorate the first class dining room with enamelled, white panelling in Louis XVI style, with gilded, carved detail. The carving was by John Crawford of Glasgow, and gilding by Waring & Gillow. The balcony on the upper storey was surrounded by a metal banister, and surmounted by a white and gilt plaster dome. The effect was perhaps marred by the insistence of Cunard on traditional, swivel chairs, upholstered in Edwardian, rather than period style textile (Forsyth 1985: 2035). On the boat deck, the veranda café was very similar to that of the *Mauretania*, and appeared to be within the control of Cunard. Miller's designs for the first class, public rooms were reviewed at a meeting

3.6
**James Miller,
First Class
Restaurant,
Lusitania, Cunard,
1907.**
Source: Merseyside
Maritime Museum

between Miller, the Chairman, and Mr Maxwell on 7 May 1906 at the Cunard head-quarters in Liverpool. Miller proposed that the smoke room be panelled in Austrian oak. However, Cunard felt that Italian walnut would be preferable, as it was lighter in tone. A letter from Miller to Mearns, the Secretary of Cunard, of 1 June 1906, proposed an alternative design: 'I . . . note that your Directors prefer Italian walnut in the Smoke Room instead of oak. I will accordingly see that a design is prepared which will be suitable for Italian walnut. The one which is being prepared for oak would not be suitable' (Cunard 1.6.1906). Miller submitted new designs, but these were rejected by Cunard. Denham, the head of the upholstery and furnishing department, wrote to Mearns on 14 August 1906: 'I beg to state that I do not consider the design submitted to be sufficiently attractive for the Smoke Room of this ship. It is much too simple in treatment and the builders appear to rely on the figure of the wood for their decoration' (Cunard 14.8.1906). Miller responded on 16 August 1906: '. . . your Directors would like something not quite so severe. I am having a new drawing prepared . . . giving effect to what I think will be your Directors ideas' (Cunard 16.8.1906). Miller was clearly dissatisfied with the double rejection of his scheme, and on 22 August 1906 he submitted the third set of plans. These were . . . 'less severe treatment than the design previously submitted, but still keeping to the Georgian period of architecture with the large veneered walnut panels' (Cunard 22.8.1906). Miller replaced the flat pilasters surrounding the fireplace with fluted columns; he also added decoration to the frieze above the chimneypiece, soffits, cupola and door surrounds. Peskett, of Cunard's Superintendent and Engineer's office, remarked: 'Without wishing to criticise the designs submitted by Mr. Miller, I would like to remark that the fireplace does not appear to stand out in sufficient relief, when compared with the adjacent decorative work and the dimensions of the room, also the windows at the sides appear flat and would have a better appearance if they were fitted with bold architraves as shown on sketch No.491 attached' (Cunard 28.8.1906). The design for the smoke room was finally agreed, and the Leeds firm of Marsh Jones & Cribb was selected by Miller during a meeting on the ship between six Cunard directors, Bain, Peskett and Denman and Miller on 9 February 1907 to decorate the space (Cunard 13.2.1907). It was in Queen Anne style and panelled in walnut with a dramatic barrel vaulted skylight.

There was more conflict between Cunard and Miller over the first class lounge. After a visit to the ship, Lord Inverclyde observed that: '. . . I am not sure that the large marble fireplaces are in keeping with the rest of the decoration . . .' (Cunard 20.5.1907). In response, Bain wrote an internal memo to Mearns:

> With reference to the extract from the letter received from Lord Inverclyde, stating that his Lordship is not very sure that the large marble mantelpieces are in keeping with the rest of the Lounge in the 'Lusitania', it is submitted that the decision in this matter be left until the room is completed and the furnishings in place, as the marble mantelpieces are now fixed and to alter them would cause additional expense and considerable delay in the

completion of this room. It is quite possible that when the whole decorative scheme is complete that the effect of these mantelpieces may appear more in keeping with the general surroundings.

(Cunard 23.5.1907)

Because of Mearns's points regarding delay and expense, the marble mantelpieces remained, but discussion of what was to be placed above them then developed. During a visit by Mearns to the *Lusitania* during the following month: 'The Writer had an interview with Mr. Miller, Architect, regarding the arched Overmantels in the lounge . . . Mr Miller stated that he had written to the Directors on the subject strongly recommending that nothing should be done until the carpet is laid and the furniture uncovered in the Lounge and the whole of the work completed . . . Nothing is therefore being done until the Directors give their decision' (Cunard 21.6.1907). The arched overmantels stayed, and John Brown suggested in a letter of 6.7.1907 that they commission a bronze relief of the Cunard crest from the Bromsgrove Guild of Applied Arts above each fireplace. The suggestion was rejected by Cunard, and John Brown responded on 24 July 1907:

> We duly received your letter of the 11th instant, which came to hand during our holidays, and note that you do not quite approve of the Company's crest being fitted in the space above the fireplace in the forward end of the Lounge in SS Lusitania, and we now learn from Mr Miller, Architect, that it has been arranged to fit a green marble centre piece over forward fireplace in the first class lounge, in corresponding position to electric clock fitted over fireplace in after end. We shall be pleased to have confirmation of this.
>
> (Cunard 6.7.1907)

Miller was to select two hand-painted, enamel panels by Alex Fisher of London, framed in silver, for a total of £275 to decorate the mantelpieces. The other problem the Directors had with the design of the use of marble: 'The Directors were unanimous in the opinion that something should be done to take away the sepulchral look of the marble work included in the decorations and suggested that the columns should either by painted or covered with wood veneer' (Cunard 15.6.1907). The columns were covered in wood veneer, and the room was decorated by Waring & Gillow at a cost of £1,905. The style generally was early Georgian, with inlaid mahogany panelling and furniture, upholstered in green. There was a large, barrel vault section which rose 20 feet above the room, the base was decorated with white plasterwork, and the skylight consisted of 12 sections of stained glass by Oscar Patterson, each representing a different month of the year. The floor was covered by a fitted carpet, also in green, with a bold pattern. The overall effect was incoherent, with jarring bold patterns on every surface.

Adjacent to the first class lounge was the writing room. Once again, Cunard and Miller disagreed about its decoration. Miller proposed the use of carton-pierre, a form of plaster produced by Jacksons, which could be used to replace the traditional wood. Miller wrote to Mearns on 9 July 1906, reassuring him that the material is safe to use and bits would not drop off during voyages. Interestingly he reflects on the ephemeral nature of ship interior design:

> Had the work been intended for some monumental building or mansion built to last for ages I would not think of doing it in anything else but carved wood. A ship however is essentially a commercial enterprise and its life is limited to some 20 or 30 years at most.
>
> (Cunard 9.7.1906)

Which is particularly poignant in the case of the *Lusitania*, sunk by a German U-boat on 7 May 1915 with considerable loss of life, which triggered the entry of America into the First World War.

Miller won this particular disagreement with Cunard, perhaps because his suggestion was inspired by practice already established on the German liners, or perhaps because it saved a substantial amount of money. Miller proposed that the ceiling of the room be constructed out of plaster, as opposed to the traditional wood:

> In the latest German Boats, namely the 'Kaiserin Auguste Victoria' and the 'Amerika', fibre plaster has been used in the ceilings, and it is really these plain ceilings, with ornament introduced at parts, which impart to the rooms of these boats the character they possess and make them appear so different from the cross beamed and panelled ceiling so common in boat work.
>
> (Cunard 22.12.1906)

The room was decorated by Messrs Trollope in white, enamelled panelling with delicate, Georgian decoration as fitted a traditionally feminine space.

Exactly like the *Mauretania*, the second and third classes on the *Lusitania* received comparatively scant attention. The second class accommodation was the responsibility of John Brown, with the approval of Miller. The specifications for the dining saloon reveal that standards of finish had certainly improved, as it was specified that the work should be similar to the first class dining saloon on the 'Caronia'. The third class spaces were equipped in similar fashion to the *Mauretania*. Adjustments had to be made to the promenade area for third class, when it was decided to have clear glass in the first class restaurant: '. . . as it would be more cheerful for passengers dining to be able to see outside. The 3rd class have plenty of promenade at the fire side of the Restaurant, a collapsible gate to be fitted in an approved position to mark the boundary of the deck area allotted to them for promenade' (Cunard 13.2.1907: 5). The inference being that the first class passengers would not like to gaze upon the third class passengers whilst dining!

The ships were launched with great imperialist vigour and the *Lusitania* won the Blue Riband on her second outward voyage, from the German *Deutschland*. The ship made the journey in 4 days 19 hours and 52 minutes. The *Mauretania* won the Blue Riband for its eastward journey in 1907, and westward in 1909, which was retained until 1929, when it was won by the *Bremen*.

Whilst Britain foregrounded the achievements of modernity to lead the technological revolution of speed, with interiors decorated with French and British historic styles, Germany led innovation in terms of using modernism rather than historicism. Germany's modernist design culture was developing as part of the country's new national identity and J.G. Poppe was still employed by North German Lloyd, designing the interiors of *Prinz Ludwig* of 1906, with the decorating firm of A. Bembé, in the usual luxurious, historicist style. However, the appointment of a new General Director to North German Lloyd, Dr Heinrich Wiegand in 1899 heralded a new era for modern design. He was keen to involve the modern designer, Bruno Paul (1874–1968), in his line's ships, but Paul had just been appointed Director of the Berlin Museum of Art School and could not devote sufficient time to the project. Paul was also one of the co-founders of the Deutscher Werkbund, established to further modern design in Germany, and his design for a hunting-room at the Exposition Universelle in Paris in 1900 and a study at the St Louis World's Fair four years later won him the Grand Prix award for his spare and simple interiors.

Wiegand therefore launched a competition for the interior design of the *Kronprinzessin Cecilie*, which first sailed in August 1907. Poppe was by now 70 years old, but still oversaw the decoration of the main public rooms: 'For him the basis of his decorative art remains sacrosanct, the imitation of old stylistic forms, emanating from ornament' (Schaefer 1907: 296). But 40 of the first class cabins were designed by a new generation, including the Bremen based designers Runge and Scotland plus Richard Riemerschmid, Olbrich and Bruno Paul. In the following year North German Lloyd launched the *Prinz Friedrich Wilhelm* with first class dining room and saloon, and for the *George Washington* he designed the majority of the first class accommodation with Rudolf Schröder and the Vereinigte Werkstätten. Paul strove to make the most of the confined space on board the ship by using simplified forms and smooth surfaces. For instance, in the first class lounge designed by Paul and executed by the Vereinigte Werkstätten, the walls were plain white with only spare, black linear decoration; the floor covered in a geometrically decorated carpet, the furniture simple in form and the glazed dome decorated with a repeated, abstract pattern. Bruno Paul was a pragmatist, and understood the constraints of designing interiors for liners. Writing in the third Deutscher Werkbund Yearbook in 1914, in an article entitled 'Passagierdampfer und Ihre Einrichtungen' (Passenger steamships and their mechanisms) he explained: 'The spaces should not only appear comfortable and elegant, but rich too, and should have something special to say to those accustomed to a stay in splendid surroundings' (Paul 1914: 57–8). North German Lloyd continued with its strategy of employing modern architects, and used Paul Ludwig Troost (1878–1934), a devotee of German classicism, and Schinkel; he designed interiors for the *Columbus*, which entered service in 1914, in a style which was simple but harked back to earlier examples from Germany's past. Troost was to become Hitler's first, official architect, designing buildings for him in Munich; he was replaced

3.7
Bruno Paul, First Class Lounge, *George Washington,* **North German Lloyd, 1908.**
Source: Author's collection

by Albert Speer. Hence, the designers associated with the Deutscher Werkbund and more contemporary forms of design were no longer favoured in the expression of German national identity.

Back in Britain, the launch of the two Cunarders had regained the Blue Riband for Britain. However, the British based shipping line of White Star continued to maintain that the transatlantic passenger trade was more receptive to luxurious ships, where the journey could be enjoyed in comfort and the speed of the trip was less of a consideration. Hence, the decision was taken to build the *Olympic, Titanic* and *Britannic* in 1907, partly in response to the Cunard challenge. These were mammoth ships, at 45,000 tons, and one and a half times longer than the *Mauretania* and *Lusitania*. The investment which made the building of this trio possible came from J. Pierpoint Morgan's International Mercantile Marine Company (IMM), which had bought out White Star in 1902. Despite the buyout, White Star remained under the control of the son of the founder, Bruce Ismay, and the ships sailed under a British flag with British crew. Much has been written on the *Titanic*, and history of her first Atlantic voyage and sinking has reached epic proportions, which has become known as Titanicism (Gronberg 1999; McCaughan 1998: 3). The most recent film devoted to the tragedy, the blockbuster *Titanic*, included attempts to authentically reproduce the interiors in the film sets (Hammond and Massey 1999) and there are a myriad of books, websites, fanclubs and events devoted to the phenomenon. From the perspective of the history of interior design, *Titanic* was designed using the same plans as *Olympic*, which was built four to six months ahead of *Titanic* at the Harland & Wolff shipyard in Belfast. As such, lessons learnt from the design of the *Olympic* were applied to the *Titanic*, and extra effort applied to the design of the first class accommodation. The publicity for the two liners, released to mark *Olympic*'s launch, reveals the strong national and racial identities associated with the ships: 'The *Olympic* and *Titanic* are not only the largest vessels in the World; they represent the highest attainments in Naval Architecture and Marine Engineering; they stand for the pre-eminence of the Anglo-Saxon race on the Ocean; for the "Command of the Seas"' . . . (White Star 1911).

There was a close working relationship between White Star and Harland & Wolff. The shipyard was given a free hand with the design and cost of the ships, to which they added a percentage at the end of construction as a fee. This is in marked contrast to the Cunard process, which featured tight controls over finance and design. This also led to Harland & Wolff building ships for the Holland America Line up until 1929, as J.P. Morgan owned 25% of the company as part of his International Mercantile Marine. Harland & Wolff also entered into a lucrative contract with the Royal Mail Steam Packet Company in 1903, and built and decorated ships for the South American route in lavish style, starting with the 9,441 gross tons *Aragon* of 1905. The partnership with the Holland America Line brought in Mutters & Co., a Dutch based decorating firm that had been founded in 1795. This was a similar company to Waring & Gillow, with many prestigious contracts to their name by this stage, including furniture making and decorating for the Dutch Royal Family. The firm also were producing more modern furniture, including work by Henrick Petrus Berlage (1856–1934). The firm decorated the Holland America Line ship, *Nieuw Amsterdam*, which was 16,913 gross tons and built by Harland & Wolff at Belfast. The style was distinctively modern and much simpler than the historicist, French norm. For example, the first class ladies' tea room was Japanese in inspiration with dark wood panelling and fretwork on the ceiling and walls, punctuated by mirrors with Japanese decoration. The fireplace was decorated with Japanese figures in kimonos, exotic birds, dragons and a representation of Mount Fuji. The furniture was simple, with a boxlike construction for the chairs, simple, open structured tables and upholstered banquettes. The carpet was also plain, with an unobtrusive pattern of repeating squares. The lighting consisted of bare, electric bulbs and Japanese lanterns.

But this simplicity was not emulated by the partnership of White Star and Harland & Wolff, who attempted to emulate the lavish style of Cunard's *Mauretania*, but did not employ a professional architect, using decorating firms instead, and so the effect was one of uncoordinated but luxurious, period styles. The technical might and gargantuan proportions of the ships were matched by the lavishness of interiors, and sheer quantity of styles employed. The underlying desire to create ships to surpass the *Mauretania* and *Lusitania* in terms of quantity and size dictated the choices made in interior design. Ideas about the Cunard ships' interiors would have come through the White Star and Harland & Wolff officials visiting the ships plus the media coverage. This largely focused on the technical might of the ships and their historic interiors, so the builders of the *Olympic, Titanic* and *Britannic* wanted to emulate this success, but on a grander scale (Warren 1987). The original design drawings for the *Olympic* and *Titanic* were presented by Harland & Wolff to the White Star Line directors and Bruce Ismay and approved on 29 July 1908. The interior decorating firm appointed for the ships was A. Heaton & Co. of London, a decorating firm founded as a limited company in 1895, which had worked with Norman Shaw in the 1880s. Indeed, such was the imperative to decorate the ships to the standard of Cunard, that an offshoot of Harland & Wolff, the Ocean Transport Company, took over A. Heaton & Co. to ensure that the required number of skilled decorators would be available for the fitting out of the two White Star liners, as pressure mounted to complete the ships as quickly as possible (Moss and Hume 1986: 144). The Dutch firm of Mutters & Co. were enlisted to decorate 12 of the cabins on both the *Olympic* and the *Titanic*.

A contemporary English interior designer, John Aldam Heaton (1828–97) was probably the founder and namesake of the firm, A. Heaton & Co. He established a partnership with Richard Norman Shaw, an erstwhile employee of White Star, and acted as consultant decorator for Bedford Park in London and was a member of the William Morris circle. He was friends with Dante Gabriele Rossetti, and designed a wallpaper, which he named after the Pre-Raphaelite painter. Aldam Heaton was also knowledgeable about the history of furniture and decoration; he edited a four volume set which reproduced facsimiles of work by key eighteenth-century furniture designers, including Adam and Sheraton, in 1889. He published his critical views of contemporary taste in *Beauty and Art* in 1897. A. Heaton & Co. supplied furnishing fabrics to retailers, including Morris & Co. well into the twentieth century (Parry 1988: 128). They had offices and workshops located at Harland & Wolff's Belfast site and also in London and Liverpool. The 'Ship Decorators and Furnishers' were renamed Heaton Tabb & Company Ltd in the 1930s, when Ashby Tabb took over responsibility for design (Harland & Wolff: 5.12.1961: 1). By 1930 they were a wholly owned subsidiary of Harland & Wolff, and the shipbuilding company was represented on the board by Henry P. Harland until his death in 1945, when his place was taken by Sir Frederick Rebbeck. Rebbeck was regularly invited to the Heaton & Tabb Directors' Meetings at the Adelphi Works, Willesden, London NW10, but never attended. The company was eventually sold off in 1963 by Harland & Wolff as part of an economy drive, to Ashby Tabb Limited for £199, 250. Heaton & Co. were considered by P&O for the decoration of the *Viceroy of India* of 1927, but Waring & Gillow were chosen instead (P&O/ 60/12:105).

On the first ship to be built, the *Olympic*, the range of period styles used ran the gamut of possibilities – from Louis XIV, XV and XVI to Empire, Italian Renaissance, Queen Anne and 'Old Dutch'. The White Star publicity boasted: 'The finish and decoration of the first class staterooms are well in keeping with the excellence of the public rooms; the staterooms are also exceptionally large and beautifully furnished. Perhaps the most striking are the suite rooms of which there is an unusually large number, decorated in different styles and periods including the following: Louis Seize, Empire, Adams, Italian Renaissance, Louis Quinze, Louis

Quatorze, Georgian, Regency, Queen Anne, Modern Dutch, Old Dutch' (White Star 1911: 45, 47). As one contemporary commentator noted:

> In regard to the styles of interior decoration, there may be enumerated Louis Seize, Empire, Adams, Italian Renaissance, Louis Quinze, Louis Quartorze, Georgian, Old Dutch, Modern Dutch, Colonial, two or three Georgian and Jacobean, the Regency, and Queen Anne. There are also several combinations. Any or all of these may be found on modern liners in the North Atlantic. All social classes of passengers and all tastes in surroundings and furniture are catered for. If a good democratic citizen of the United States thinks he can enjoy his voyage better in an Empire suite of rooms – in a more comfortable bed than the Emperor ever had – or a French republican likes a royal suite of one of the Louis monarchs; or an ardent German Socialist suddenly evinces a desire to travel in luxury in an Imperial suite or in one named after some Tueton hero or ruler; whatever the taste, the steamship company will welcome and make them comfortable, as long as they can pay the fare in advance.
>
> (Fletcher 1913: 257)

Cunard's Naval Architect, Leonard Peskett, sailed on the *Olympic* from New York to Liverpool in August 1911. As part of his mission to check out the opposition, he made a detailed 6,000 word report on the construction and decoration of the ship. He noted: 'The First Class en suite and special cabins are overdone in detail and garish in decoration . . .' (Cunard 1911). Peskett was also unimpressed by the Jacobean-inspired, first class dining room, which lacked adequate ventilation and was prone to overheating, due to the myriad of electric ceiling lights. The dimensions of the room were certainly awe-inspiring, at 114 feet long and 92 feet in width, which could sit 532 diners at once on C deck. The Jacobean inspiration came from a close study of Hatfield and Haddon Hall, according to the White Star publicity. However, the room was painted white throughout, which was not authentically sixteenth century, but did add a sense of spaciousness. The first class lounge of the *Olympic* was decorated in Louis XV style, with carved boiseries and ceiling. The first class smoking room was decorated in Georgian style, with mahogany carved panelling, inlaid with mother of pearl and interspersed with large mirrors. The white fireplace was surmounted by a painting of *The Approach of the New World* by Norman Wilkinson. This theme was echoed in the painted windows, which showed various ports of the world and sailing ships. From the smoking room it was possible to step onto the Palm Court through a revolving door. The publicity boasted: '. . . we emerge upon a gay little veranda, over whose green trellis grow climbing plants, which foster the illusion that we are still on the fair firm earth; but one glance through the windows, with their beautifully-chased bronze framing, adds to the charm, and we realise that we're still surrounded by the restless sea, once so dreaded a barrier to national intercourse' (White Star 1911: 41). Complete with white, wicker furniture and potted palms and white panelled ceiling decorated with light bulbs, the first class restaurant provided a more intimate space than the dining saloon. It was decorated in Louis XVI style in French walnut panelling with gilt mouldings and decorations. The large bay windows were dressed with fawn silk curtains with floral borders and embroidered pelmets. The ceiling was decorated with plasterwork flowers with garlands in the bays. The chairs were constructed from the same French walnut as the wall panelling. The reading and writing room was in white: 'The pure white walls and the light and elegant furniture show us that this is essentially a ladies' room' (White Star 1911: 45). The first class rooms were connected by lifts and also the grand, main staircase in oak with iron scrollwork infills to the balcony and balustrade. On the main landing of the staircase was a richly carved panel encasing a clock, supported by two female figures representing Honour and Glory. The staircase was lit by an iron and glass dome.

Whilst the all white reading and writing room was provided for female, first class passengers, the Turkish bath was provided for first class, male passengers. The first Turkish bath had been introduced to London in 1862 by David Urquhart (1805–77) as an Orientally decorated space for middle class, male sociability (Potvin 2005). On the *Olympic* and *Titanic* this was located on Deck F, adjacent to the swimming bath, which was decorated in a very utilitarian style, with plain white tiles, basic wooden changing facilities beneath the exposed structure of the ship. More ornate was the fashionable Turkish bath with cooling room in seventeenth-century, Turkish style, shampoo rooms and hot room. The cooling room was the largest, with portholes covered with a carved, Oriental screen: '. . . through which the light fitfully reveals something of the grandeur of the mysterious East' (White Star 1911: 43). The walls were tiled in blue and green from the dado upwards. The dado, doors and panelling were in teak. Lighting was provided by bronze Arab lamps and a marble drinking fountain was provided. In addition there was a gymnasium.

The first class suites on board the *Olympic* were furnished in a huge range of historic styles. There was Modern Dutch and Old Dutch. The latter, with beamed ceiling, oak four-poster with velvet curtains and marble topped washstand. Linda Parry has identified the wallcovering 'Utrecht Velvet', as by Morris & Co., who may not have had the capacity to produce it at that time. Therefore, it was manufactured by Heaton & Co. in Halifax (Parry 1983: 45). There was also Queen Anne, Italian Renaissance with gaudily figured panelling and beds to match, Georgian parlour suite, with adjoining sitting room panelled in white, and Louis XVI style sitting room for parlour suite number 1,388. The Empire style first class suite bedroom had white panelled walls with gilded decoration in suitable style, complete with sphinxes above the doorway and Empire style black and gilt single beds. The Regency style sitting room had dark panelling. The Holland America Line decorating firm, Messrs H.P. Mutters & Zoom were responsible for the decoration of 24 staterooms on the *Olympic* and *Titanic* (Cunard D42/S7/3/35).

The second class accommodation was far plainer, but still comfortable by contemporary standards. For example, a library was provided with sycamore panelling and mahogany dado and tapestry upholstered chairs and settees. The smoke room followed the historic styling of the first class rooms, and was in Louis XVI style and had carved oak panelling and furniture, upholstered in dark green leather. The second class staterooms were finished in white enamel, with mahogany furniture upholstered in hard wearing moquette and lino tiles on the floor.

Lessons were learnt from the first voyages of the *Olympic*, and changes made to the *Titanic* before it joined the White Star service between Southampton and New York. The number of staterooms was increased, and the premium parlour suite rooms on Deck B were extended into the promenade deck. These elite passengers had their own private promenade deck which was half-timbered in mock Tudor style further aft. On the same deck, the former promenade deck for second class passengers was converted into a Café Parisien for first class passengers. The space was decorated in trellis work with climbing ivy and plants, much in the same vein as the veranda cafés on the *Mauretania* and *Lusitania*. The main dining room was converted to take the additional first class passengers to a maximum of 550. Also in imitation of the Hamburg-Amerika ships, the *Oceanic* and *Titanic* had an à la carte restaurant on Deck C, just beside the Café Parisien.

3.8
**A. Heaton & Co.,
First-class Parlour
Suite B59, *Titanic*,
White Star Line,
March 1912.**
Source: Ulster Folk &
Transport Museum

The first class private accommodation also featured the full repertoire of period styles. The parlour suites ranged from Georgian, Louis XIV, Adams and Empire periods plus an Arts and Crafts room, to the Dutch Suite, with beamed ceiling and oak four-poster with velvet curtains. The second class staterooms were finished in white enamel, with mahogany furniture upholstered in hard wearing moquette and lino tiles on the floor. The 1,788 beds provided for third class were basic, with the provision of a larger proportion of two and four berth cabins than was normal for ocean liners. The third class saloon could sit 594 of the passengers at any one time, compared to the full complement for first class of 600 and 80% of the 716 second class.

The history of the *Titanic* and its first, tragic crossing of the Atlantic has reached mythical proportions. The *Olympic* is overshadowed by the myth, but it did successfully offer a transatlantic service until the outbreak of the First World War. From then its lavish interiors were removed and it was used as a troop ship, along with the third of the White Star ships to be built, the *Britannic*. The *Britannic* was too late to enter civilian service, and entered service straight away as part of the fleet of requisitioned ocean liners, which included the *Olympic*, *Mauretania* and *Lusitania*.

In the lead up to the First World War, the competition between western European nations heightened, with the ocean liner, particularly for the north Atlantic run, the focus. Germany's Hamburg-Amerika Line continued to build bigger and faster ships, with historic interiors by Charles Mewès, working with his German partner, Bischoff for the design of the *Imperator*, which entered service in 1913. At 51,969 tons the ship could carry 5,500 people, with 908 first class; 592 second and 1,772 in steerage. National pride was now running at such a height that Hamburg-Amerika added a vast eagle to the bow of the ship, to add extra length, ensuring that they beat the Cunard competition statistically. The interiors displayed a similar celebration of German national identity, with a full-length portrait of the Kaiser (who launched the ship) adorning the wall of the top flight of the 55 foot, first class staircase. However, Mewès and Bischoff designed the first class interiors, and injected British and French styles into the mix, which may have been the cause of the criticism of the ship's interiors. The smoking room was Tudor in appearance, with dark wooden pillars and white ceiling, decorated with heavy carving. The room also had an open fireplace and the decorating work was carried out by Messrs W. & E. Thornton-Smith of London. There was the familiar Ritz-Carlton restaurant, designed by the Parisian based firm of P.H. Rémon & Sons. The swimming pool, the first to appear on a giant liner, was modelled on the remarkable Pompeian bath designed by Mewès and Davis for the Royal Automobile Club in Pall Mall, London, built 1908–11. The water area was 39 feet by 21 feet, and it was surrounded by Doric order, mosaic columns. At the foot of the stairs was a fountain, replicated from an example in the Louvre, which stood on a mosaic floor with a representation of the signs of the zodiac (which had also been seen as decoration for the domed ceiling in the first class dining saloon on the *Mauretania*). Like the RAC Club, there was also a Turkish bath. The two Imperial

Suites were situated on the lower promenade deck, complete with their own private veranda, breakfast room, and two bedrooms with two bathrooms.

One year later, the 54,282 ton *Vaterland* was launched, with interiors by Mewès. However, the days of the Mewès and Davis historicist interiors were over for the German ships. According to Heskett, there was widespread criticism of the revivalist styles of the *Imperator* in particular, and Albert Ballin approached Hermann Muthesius, the powerful civil servant responsible for art education at the Prussian Ministry of Trade and Commerce for advice (Heskett 1986: 65, 103–4). Muthesius had spent time in England and was a keen supporter of the Arts and Crafts Movement and simplicity in design. He recommended Riemerschmid, Karl Bertsch and Adalbert Niemayer to propose designs for new ship *Burckhard*, eventually completed in 1917. These were German designers, who ushered in a new era for ship interiors, which eschewed the French inspired, revivalist style of Mewès in favour of a more Germanic, modern style and used only German workshops for the decorative work.

The rejection from Hamburg-Amerika could have made it possible for Mewès and Davis to work for Cunard, as the shipping line continued to value the historicist approach. Mewès and Davis wrote to Cunard on 24 August 1910, responding to a telegraph from Cunard of the previous week in which they asked: '. . . us whether we were at liberty to design decorations for ships belonging to your company. You will, no doubt, remember that there was some difficulty raised by the Hamburg American Line when this question was last discussed. We beg to inform you that this matter has now been satisfactorily settled, and that we are at liberty to undertake any work you may feel disposed to favour us with' (Cunard D42/S7/3/51 24.8.1910: 1) A letter from E.H. Cunard to the Cunard Chairman, Sir Alfred Booth, of 27 August 1910 outlined the reasons for wishing to appoint Arthur Davis as the architect for the *Aquitania*:

> Although I presume we shall not spend nearly so much money on the decoration of the new ship, as compared with the 'Mauretania', on the other hand she must be more or less a ship 'de luxe', and as such I think it would be an advantage to employ an architect who thoroughly understands the requirements of the class of passengers we will necessarily carry, and in this respect Mr. Davis would appear to be well qualified, seeing that his firm have had the entire decorating and furnishing of the Paris and London 'Ritz' and also the Carlton Hotel, and the experience gained in fitting up the German ships should also be of considerable value to us.
>
> (Cunard D42/S7/3/51/ 27.8.1910: 1)

Mewès and Davis were officially appointed in October 1910, and this was the last ship to be designed by the firm, although undertaken entirely by London based Davis. It was launched in 1914 and successfully challenged German hegemony and provided the first, three-ship service across the Atlantic. Arthur Davis wrote an article for *The Architectural Review*, just after the ship had been fitted out, in which he proudly declared '. . . the decorative equipment of the *Aquitania* is of a character which challenges comparison with the best modern work in hotel or other buildings on land' (Davis 1914: 96). Therefore, Mewès and Davis were still designing within the public, hotel frame of references rather than that of the grand domestic interior, as exemplified by Peto. The ship was built on the Clyde by John Brown & Co. and the decorating work was carried out by the entire panoply of leading firms in the field, including Messrs George Trollope & Sons, George Jackson & Sons Ltd, Wylie & Lochhead, Waring & Gillow, Ltd, and W. & E. Thornton-Smith of London, plus the Paris based firms of P.H. Rémon & Sons and Marcel Boulanger, at an overall cost of £36,849. A suggestion from the Holland America Line in December 1910 that Cunard consider employing their decorating firm of Messrs H.P. Mutters & Zoon of the Hague, who had just been commissioned to decorate 24 staterooms on the *Olympic* and *Titanic*, was declined in April 1911 (Cunard D42/S7/3/35).

The first voyage of the *Aquitania* took place in 1914; it was of 45,647 gross tonnage, with a length of 901 feet and accommodation for 3,250 passengers and crew of almost 1,000. The first class accommodation was situated on two decks – A and D. On A deck was the capacious smoking room at 78 feet by 54 feet, the lounge/ball room measuring 74 feet by 54 feet, the drawing room, hall and galleries plus veranda café. On D deck were the dining facilities, including the 138 feet by 93 feet dining room and more intimate grill room, measuring 71 feet by 35 feet. The flavour of the interior decoration in first class was certainly historicist, with the added kudos of fine art. There were several examples of detailed copies of works of art, including a portrait of James II after Kneller, taken from an example in the National Gallery in the smoking room. The room was decorated in Jacobean style, with carved oak panelling, half-timbered ceiling and dark floorboards. In the first class lounge there was an authentic Dutch ceiling painting and a full-scale reproduction of the Mortlake tapestry depicting the Battle of Solebay. The space was decorated in Stuart style, and the walls and supporting ionic columns were predominantly white. The chairs and sofas were upholstered in a range of traditional patterns and the carpeting was also heavily patterned with acanthus leaves. The drawing room was in a more refined Georgian style with Corinthian columns and delicate oriel windows in the ceiling dome. The suites were decorated with prints of famous masterpieces, and named after the relevant artist – whether it be Holbein, Van Dyck, Velazquez, Rembrandt, Reynolds, Gainsborough, Romney or Raeburn. The second class accommodation included a 104 foot dining room, drawing room, Adamesque lounge, oak panelled smoking room and veranda café. The third class accommodation was, as ever, even more basic, again reflecting the extreme social divides of Edwardian Britain.

But floating grandeur was not restricted to ships bound for New York. Liners destined for Canada carrying mainly emigrants, also sported lavish interiors, particularly the ships of the Canadian Pacific Line, founded in 1903, and the Allan Line, which Canadian Pacific bought out in 1917. It was a friend of Davis, George A. Crawley, who designed interiors for both lines. Crawley had just completed the

3.9
**Arthur Davis,
First class lounge,
Aquitania,
Cunard, 1914.**
Source: National
Maritime Museum

interiors of a prestigious commission on Long Island, Westbury House, in 1906, where he worked with the American architect Grosvenor Atterbury. Westbury House is a magnificent Charles II-style mansion furnished with fine English antiques and decorative arts set in 160 acres of landscaped grounds. The *Empress of Asia* and *Empress of Russia* took their first voyages in 1912 and 1913 respectively. At just under 17,000 tons they were far smaller than their American bound counterparts. Nevertheless, they both displayed the importance of representing national idenities. The *Empress of Asia* used period English styles, predominantly Jacobean and Georgian. The dining room was decorated in white painted wood in Georgian style by Waring & Gillow with a wrought iron balustrade around the gallery. The writing room was again Georgian, featuring Chippendale style furniture. The Jacobean smoking room was lined with toned oak panels, by H.H. Martyn & Co. of Cheltenham. The half-timbered ceiling was punctuated by naked light bulbs, demonstrating they were still a novelty in 1912. This was also a feature of the veranda café, which was in 'Olde English' style, complete with leaded windows and half-timbered walls. The *Empress of*

3.10
George A. Crawley, First Class Smoking Room, *Empress of Asia,* **Canadian Pacific Line, 1912.**
Source: National Maritime Museum

Russia was decorated: '. . . in French styles, out of compliment to French Canadians' (Davis 1914: 102). The dining room was a tasteful grey in Louis XVI style, and the smoking room Louis XIV style, and panelled in African beanwood by George Trollope & Sons and Colls & Sons of London. George Crawley was also commissioned to design the first class interiors of the Allan Line ship, *Alsation*. The ship entered service on the Britain to Canada route in 1914, and reinforced elements of British national identity. The public rooms by Crawley were largely inspired by the Stuart period, with an oak panelled, early Jacobean style dining saloon and a hand crafted, plasterwork ceiling by George Jackson & Sons. The smoking room was also oak in the style of James I era, with a chimneypiece copied from an example taken from Old Place, Lindfield in Sussex and period furniture, including Knole sofas. The card room was the only room to veer from the Jacobean theme, and was decorated in neo-classical style with fine plasterwork ceiling and Adamesque panelling. The library was in the style of William and Mary and made extensive use of walnut, modelled on the Pepysian Library at Magdalene College, Cambridge. For Arthur Davis: '. . .

unquestionably the finest apartment on the ship is the lounge. . . . The whole forms a very rich and beautiful apartment' (Davis 1914: 107). The space had a barrel vaulted ceiling with skylights and painted murals by the Australian artist, George Lambert, at either end of the wall space. The walls were panelled with wood featuring pilasters and decorative mirrors. At one end of the room was a richly carved fireplace and surround, complete with an original painting by Philip Connard of flowers and parrots. At the opposite end of the lounge was a large, decorative mirror featuring nautical motifs in its frame. The floor was covered by a richly patterned rug and the furniture was Jacobean in style and the chairs and sofas were upholstered in a variety of strongly patterned textiles.

The overall effect in the first class public rooms was of a rich, British tradition in interior design, dating back to the seventeenth and eighteenth centuries. As the, predominantly, British, passengers sailed to what was then known as the 'Dominion' from the 'Mother Country' they must have had their sense of British national identity reinforced by the interior design of the ship, as numbers emigrating to Canada escalated in the early twentieth century (Fletcher 1913: 263). Sailing between the Mersey and the St Lawrence, first class passengers benefited from the latest technology, with Parsons turbines driving four shafts to reach speeds of 18.5 knots, whilst relaxing in British, period interiors. Passengers travelling to Australia during this era on British ships enjoyed a very similar experience. For example, the Orient Line's Royal Mail steamships, *Orama* and *Orvieto*, which sailed between

3.11
Nelson, first Class Grand Salon, *France,* **French Line, 1912.**
Source: Eco Museum Saint-Nazaire

London and Australia, had period decorated first class rooms by Robert Whyte, who designed more grandiose interiors than his predecessor Norman Shaw for the former and Andrew N. Prentice for the latter. Ships built for the Union Castle line, which mainly served the route from Britain to South Africa, also plundered past styles for the decoration of their first class spaces. The *Saxon*, which entered service in 1900 built by Harland & Wolff is a prime example. It was during this pre-First World War period that France joined the market in the provision for transatlantic travel. French designers also sought to reinforce national identity through the use of period styles in the interiors of the ships.

The Compagnie Générale Transatlantique (C.G.T.), also known as the French Line, had been founded in 1861 as a result of a mail contract with Napoleon II's government. The line provided a service between Le Havre and New York from 1864 onwards; additionally the company served Mexico and the West Indies. There wasn't the level of emigration to other parts of the globe by the French population as there was from the British or Germans. However, by 1912, and the introduction of their largest and most prestigious ship, the *France*, the company was firmly established as a provider of transatlantic passenger transport. The *France* was built at the major French dockyards at Saint-Nazaire, created to build ships for C.G.T., and the interiors drew on the past traditions of eighteenth-century luxury. At only 23,769 tons the *France* was dwarfed by rivals such as *Aquitania* at 45,647 tons, and she was also not the fastest ship to cross the Atlantic. However, her ambience of gallic *grande-luxe*, co-ordinated by French ébéniste-décorateur, Nelson, with the work carried out by Establishment Remon, made her popular with French and Americans alike who could afford to travel first class. The ship could transport a maximum of 535 first class, 442 second, 226 third class and 724 steerage.

The Grand Salon on the *France* drew heavily on Louis XIV period decoration. The room was panelled in white, gilded wood, punctuated by ornate pilasters and oval portraits of figures such as Princesse de la Tour-du-Pin, Madame de Maintenon, Henrietta of England and the Duchess of Burgoyne. There was an imposing portrait of Louis XIV by Hyacinthe Rigaud, copied from the original in the Louvre over the fireplace at one end of the room. At the other end hung another painting of the Sun King, copied from an original by Van der Meulen in the museum at Versailles. The ceiling was also white and gold, with a central dome surrounded by four lunettes. The dining saloon was based on the the Hôtel du Comte de Toulouse, which was designed by Robert de Cotte, a pupil of Mansart, who had worked on the Grand Trinion at Versailles, and the *salon mixte* was in the Régence style with paintings depicting classical ruins by Laroix. Whilst the main first class public rooms reflected France's regal past, the Moorish saloon, or *Salon Mauresque*, reflected France's colonial interests and vogue for the Orient influence, particularly in Algeria and Tunisia. The contemporary publicity boasted: '. . . where decorations reflect the far, desert outposts of the great French Empire . . . and a silent Algerian serves his country's beverage as Americans like it best' (as quoted in Brinnin and Gaulin 1988:

99). The exotic saloon, tucked in a corner beneath a first class staircase, was tiled with oriental ceramics with an Algerian fresco by Poisson at the top of the walls. There were Turkish rugs scattered across the floor on which stood luxurious sofas, pouffes and tiny, occasional tables for coffee. A fountain sprayed cool water continuously. The stewards would dress in Turkish costumes to serve the passengers in the evening.

Chapter 4

Floating art deco showcases

Many of the key ocean liner interiors of the inter-war years were examples of the national showcase, framing what was considered the best design style and the best designers by the line owners. Some designers would be commissioned to design one particular space on the ship, or execute elaborate fittings or objects in their specialist field, for example, decorative painting, glass or metalwork. The French *Normandie* and British *Empress of Britain* were significant examples of this type. Following the First World War, the competition between vying national identities escalated, with America and Italy joining the fray and using indigenous designers to express a more contemporary style in the service of national identity. P&O still used professional decorating firms, but in 1929 the lavish interiors of the *Viceroy of India* were designed by the Hon. Elsie Mackay, one of the first examples of a woman working on ship interiors. Largely unacknowledged at the time, and subsequently derided in the professional press, this was a key example of a British ship designed in period style, with touches of international art deco. Contemporary reviews expressed anxiety about the '. . . distinctive modern note . . .' of some of the décor (*The Shipbuilder* 1929: 263). Although by 'modern' the critic was referring to what would be termed art deco now, it revealed a British resistance to using contemporary, international design styles for the interiors of ocean liners. This seemed to be an inappropriate design style for British vessels.

The sumptuous days of first class travel around the globe were halted with the outbreak of the First World War in August 1914, and the ships built as part of an escalating, competitive international contest were put to the service of war, mainly as troop carriers, with the finest furniture and fittings removed. The war saw the loss of many ships, including Cunard's *Lusitania, Laconia* and *Franconia*, White Star's *Britannic* and P&O's *Persia*. Following the end of war in 1918, Britain and America requisitioned the three giants of the Hamburg-Amerika line – the *Imperator, Vaterland* (renamed the *Leviathan* following American seizure in 1917) and the unfinished *Bismarck*. America retained the *Leviathan*, and Cunard was awarded the

Imperator and White Star the *Bismarck*, which was finally completed in 1922 by Blohm & Voss. The shipping lines also gained property. The British government had requisitioned Hamburg-Amerika's London office in Cockspur Street, which was bought by P&O at the end of the war, and used as a passenger office until the 1970s.

The German ships were extensively refitted to reflect the national identities of their new owners. The *Leviathan* was extensively refitted by the United States Line at Newport News, Virginia, with new interiors by the designer, Eugene Schöen (1880–1957). The cost of refitting, at 8 million dollars, was greater than the cost of its original build by Hamburg-Amerika, and the relaunch of the ship in 1923 brought America into the provision of transatlantic travel in the twentieth century for the first time. Hamburg-Amerika's company livery of black, yellow, red and white was obliterated by red, white and blue. The carved panelling by Mewès and Davis was preserved in the Social Hall, but the Palm Court was transformed into an art deco style nightclub. However, the ship did not match the success of British counterparts. The flagship had no other equivalent ships to form a regular and reliable transatlantic service and, due to Prohibition introduced in 1919, the America Line could only offer an alcohol-free, 'dry' service.

Cunard meanwhile refitted the *Imperator* and renamed the ship the *Berengaria*, after the wife of Richard the Lionheart. It was revamped on Tyneside in 1922. The interiors retained the Mewès and Davis flavour, with the Olde English

4.1
**Eugene Schöen,
Night Club,
Leviathan, 1923.**
Source: Author's
collection

smoking room and French style public rooms. The Pompeian swimming bath remained as it was. The Prince of Wales travelled on the ship in August 1924 in one of the two Imperial suites, which was largely unaltered from its pre-war era. White Star awaited the delivery of the completed *Bismarck* from a dispirited workforce at Blohm & Voss in Hamburg. In 1922 the ship was delivered to White Star and renamed *Majestic*. At 56,551 tons this was the biggest liner afloat, and added to the transatlantic fleet with *Olympic*.

Whilst post-war reclamation and refitting was taking place, C.G.T. introduced its second prestige ship to follow the *France*; this was the *Paris*, completed in 1921. At 34,569 tons it was larger than its predecessor. The ship was designed to carry 560 first class, 530 second class and 840 third class passengers. The décor of the first class displayed a transition from the conventional period styling to art deco, as France sought to reassert its dominance as fashion leader, culminating in the 1925 Paris *Exposition Internationale des Arts Décoratifs et Industriels Modernes*, the planning of which was well underway by this date (Benton *et al.* 1975: 62; Massey 2001: 42–3). France seized the initiative for leadership in modern design from humiliated and war torn Germany, who had begun to introduce more contemporary styling to their liners just before the First World War.

The original interiors were designed by the architect, Richard Bouwens Van der Boijen, son of Second Empire architect of the first Paris office of the Credit Lyonnais (1876), William Bouwens Van der Boijen. The cabins were designed by art deco designers Louis Sue (1875–1968), Andre Mare (1887–1932), Paul Follot (1877–1941) and René Prou (1889–1947). There were traditional cabins to suit accepted tastes, but innovative design was introduced with square windows replacing round, and restrained, geometric ornament inspired by the eighteenth century, but not directly emulating it. The two-storey foyer by Van der Boijen was characterized by the repeated use of a small, scroll shape on the ironwork balconies on the first floor and on the paint work which decorated the supports for the dome. The intricate ironwork in the foyer was designed by Edgar Brandt (1880–1960). This consisted of a wrought iron staircase plus, more unusually, wrought iron was also used for the columns supporting the cupola, the balcony and mezzanine in a style which bridged art nouveau and art deco. The first class lounge, designed by René Lalique (1860–1945), also had a dome, lit at the centre with scaled decorations punctuated by lights to create a grotto effect. There was an art deco iron banister running round the upper floor of the double-storey room. The two-storey smoking room was designed by Raguenet et Maillard, in a style which also linked art nouveau and art deco, with a gilded ceiling. The dining room was decorated by Remon & Fils and featured a large mural by Albert Besnard, which dominated one end of the two-storey room, and featured a classical scene with the French and American flags intertwined.

This was a shrewd move, as America, in a mood of growing isolationism prompted by the experience of the First World War, had introduced a new act in the year of *Paris*'s launch, which limited the number of immigrants to the country. The Emergency Quota Act, also known as the 'Three Percent Act', restricted the admission of immigrants to 3% of that nationality already resident in the US, based on figures yielded by the 1903 census. This had a huge impact on transatlantic travel, by significantly reducing the volume of passengers travelling westward in steerage class. In the five years leading up to the First World War, there had been 700,000 immigrants annually to the United States. With the introduction of the quota system, this dropped to only 230,000 in 1922. This had an impact on the European shipping lines, which needed to adjust their ships to carry fewer lucrative steerage passengers, and more second and first class and provide a higher quality tourist or third class. Hence, the emphasis changed to providing more distinctive, stylish accommodation for the upper echelons, particularly North Americans, who were enjoying an unprecedented level of prosperity and had the leisure time to travel to Europe. And it was a matter of status for the European nations to provide luxurious ships for the prestigious, transatlantic route. Paris was a particularly popular destination, and France capitalized on this allure, promoting the city as the City of Light (Gronberg 1998). Thousands of Americans flocked to Paris for the 1925 *Exposition des Arts Industrielles et Modernes* on the *France* and the *Paris*, including a trade delegation of over one hundered, who brought back examples of the latest French design to America. The ideas were also taken, and inspired the building of art deco skyscrapers and Hollywood film sets (Massey 2000).

Richard Bouwens de Boijen designed a luxury suite for C.G.T. at the 1925 *Exposition*. This was located in a section entitled: 'Means of Transport', which included glassware by Lalique and lacquerwork by Jean Dunand (1877–1942). C.G.T. then launched the 45,153 ton *Ile de France*, which was a floating symphony of art deco. All the foremost French designers who had been involved with the 1925 Exposition contributed to France's new national symbol of modernity. There were 439 first class cabins, each uniquely created in its own style. Moreover, there were four apartments of great luxury and ten luxury. Brinnin characterizes the designers involved with the *Ile de France* as a '. . . dubious litany of forgotten names (which) can be explained – if not excused – by the fact that the great painters of "*le bateau lavoir*" and the age of Picasso and Matisse were still *avant-garde* artists and not figures of wide public concern' (Brinnin 1986: 465). However, the French were using the most prestigious designers of the time to promote the accepted notion of French national identity, which encompassed chic, luxury and glamour. Modern painters would not have fulfilled this purpose. Ship interiors were rarely featured in *The Studio*, a British magazine with a strong international following, established during the time of the development of the Arts and Crafts movement. 'S.S. "ILE DE FRANCE": A FLOATING MUSEUM OF FRENCH DECORATIVE ART' was the title of the review by Gabriel Mourey (Mourey 1927). In it he described the interiors of the *Ile de France* in glowing terms, as an example of : '. . . that bold and progressive spirit which was made manifest at the International Exhibition of 1925' (Mourey 1927: 242).

The main circulation route for the first class passengers was by means of the three-storey Grand Staircase and halls at each level, designed by Bouwens de Boijen of the earlier *France* and the C.G.T. section of the 1925 Paris *Exposition*. The area was clad in grey marble throughout and the bannisters for the staircase were designed by Raymond Subes in geometrically patterned wrought iron. On the first floor was access to the chapel, designed by architect M.R. Danis with sculptures of Christ, Martha and Mary by Henri Navarre.

The tea salon on the promenade deck was designed by Emile-Jacques Ruhlmann (1879–1933) in white ash and silvered bronze panelling, with white ceiling and lighting concealed in six large, white Sèvres vases. Alfred Auguste Janniot (1889–1969), created *Youth and Love*, a large sculpture featuring two women standing in front of a stag, for the space. The red curtains were designed by Ruhlmann to tone with the red and grey carpet and upholstered furniture in grey. Raymond Subes designed an immense, octagonal mirror which was placed at the top of the Grand Staircase, reflecting the whole tea room. The large lounge was also placed on the promenade deck and was designed by the Compagnie des Artistes Francais directed by Louis Süe and André Mare. The coffered ceilings were supported by groups of deep red columns and concealed lighting, hidden behind the gilded mouldings and roses. The art deco, sumptuous chairs were upholstered in Aubusson tapestry and the art deco carpet was also Aubusson. There were four sculptures in gilded cement by Pierre Poisson and Albert Pommier depicting *The Seine, The Aisne, The Marne* and *The Oise* in classical style.

The same wrought iron grille used for the main staircase was used in the deluxe cabins, to separate the sitting room and dining room. These were: '. . . destined for rich travellers from the land of dollars' (Mourey 1927: 246). The ceiling of the sitting room had a circular area of concealed lighting, and alcoves decorated the corners of the room with elegant vases on plinths. The walls were decorated with a painted mural on one side and large, circular mirror on the other. The most striking art deco feature of the space was the upholstery of the six angular chairs – bold and geometric, featuring abstract cog shapes and asymmetrical grids, accentuated by a plain floor covering. The apartment also featured uplighters and circular, occasional tables with four stepped legs, inspired by the ziggurat shape. The luxury bathrooms on board were lushly decorated with murals featuring monkeys in a jungle setting. The writing room was pure art deco, by Leleu from the square ceiling lights, through fretwork screens to the bold, zig-zag carpet. The first class dining room by Pierre Patout was rather more restrained, faced in grey Pyrenees marble and illuminated by 110 Lalique lamps in amber glass, which: '. . . add to a general effect of astonishing novelty and modernity, equal in splendour and and originality' (Mourey 1927: 244). The dining saloon seated 700 on distinctive sycamore chairs, upholstered with Veronese green wool with adventurous, art deco patterns. The floor was highly polished India rubber and at the centre of the room was a *faux* fountain, constructed from illuminated chrome tubes. The smoking room also broke the traditional mould; it was an uncluttered and light space with simple furniture and plain, light walls. The *Ile de France* was a fantastic success for the French, and was regarded as the most glamorous liner of the 1920s, with little competition emanating from Germany or Britain at this time. The aspiration to attract the American traveller was fulfilled,

with passengers including Greta Garbo and Ernest Hemingway choosing to cross the
Atlantic by means of the French liner. Following the launch of the *Ile de France*,
the *Paris* was given an art deco refit in 1929. Edgar Brandt's wrought-iron balustrades
and staircases were left intact, but the public rooms and private accommodation
were reworked by a galaxy of French design stars, including Maurice Dufet, Maurice
Dufrêne, Paul Follot, Léon Jallot, René Lalique, René Prou, Marc Simon and Süe et
Mare. The major alteration was the replacement of the traditional, wooden panelling
with large expanses of mirror glass and other types of reflective surface; the tearoom
floor was also recovered in glass (Bayer 1988). The furniture was smooth with
rounded edges, rather than the geometric lines of the first design (Diard 1930: 20).
This refit reflected a general move to a more modern type of art deco, which was
streamlined rather than angular, but still represented glamour and luxury.

One nation to join the battle for prestige by offering passenger transport
across the Atlantic was Italy, building on the experience gained in providing a service
to South America. Created to provide transport to North America, mainly for Italians,
the Lloyd Sabaudo Line offered a service via the southern route from Genoa and
Naples to New York on the Clydebank built *Conte Rosso* and *Conte Verde*. The ships
entered service in 1922 and 1923 respectively, and their interiors were designed by
the family firm of La Casa Artistica. The company was founded by Mariano Coppedé
in 1885 and involved his sons, Gino (1866–1927), Adolfo (1871–1951) and Carlo
(1868–1952). The firm catered for a wealthy clientele, including J. Pierpoint Morgan,
the Rothschilds, the Marquesa de la Motilla and the Royal House of Savoy. As early as

4.2
**Pierre Patout,
First Class Dining
Room,** *Ile de
France,* **French
Line, 1927.**
Source: Eco Museum,
Saint Nazaire

1908 the firm had designed the interiors of the British built *Principe di Udine*, for the Trieste based line, Lloyd Sabaudo. Therefore, La Casa Artistica was the ideal firm of interior designers to offer prestigious, historically based design which drew on Italy's traditions. Although the *Conte Rosso* and *Conte Verde* were built at Clydeside by William Beardmore & Co., La Casa Artistica sent their own carpenters, ironworkers and upholsterers to Scotland to fit out the ships. The smoking room of the *Conte Rosso*, for example, emulated sections of the Moorish Alcazar in Seville. The first class public rooms drew on the glories of the Italian Renaissance. The ballroom was a feast of decoration, from its huge chandelier, to its Roman inspired frieze to carved caryatids aand marble topped tables. The same firm decorated the next Italian liner to be launched by Lloyd Sabaudo, the *Conte Grande* of 1928. The three-storey ballroom was decorated in a style which fused the Moorish, Liberty (the Italian equivalent of art nouveau) and the Renaissance.

4.3
La Casa Artistica, Ballroom, *Conte Grande,* Lloyd Sabaudo Line, 1928.
Source: Author's collection

Another Italian line, the Cosulich Line, offered a service via the southern route from Trieste. The *Saturnia* and *Vulcania* were introduced in 1928 and at 23,346 and 24,496 tons respectively, had a maximum speed of 19 knots. The interiors were designed by La Casa Artistica again, but with contributions from other design firms from Austria and Britain. La Casa Artistica designed the lavish, Louis XIV ballroom in white and gilt, the grill room in Tuscan Renaissance style and the extravagant Pompeian swimming pool. The Leeds based firm of Marsh, Jones and Cribb designed the first class dining room in a restrained, classical style complete with a mini-reproduction of the Parthenon frieze along the bottom of the domed ceiling. The Vienna based firm of Partois & Fix also designed first class public spaces, including the writing room. A younger Italian designer also contributed to the interior design of the *Saturnia* and *Vulcania*: Gustavo Pulitzer Finali (1887–1967) designed the 'Solemn Room', a blend of chapel and writing room in early Renaissance style, and the smoking room in English Tudor mode, complete with oak panelled walls and galleon above the fireplace.

The floating design showcase was also developed in Sweden by the Swedish American Line, which had been founded in 1918 for travel between Gothenburg and New York in the high season. The *Gripsholm* was introduced in 1925 and at 18,815 tons was a modestly sized liner, but innovative in so far as this was a motor powered ship rather than steam. Built at the Newcastle yards of Amstrong, Whitworth & Co. its interiors reflected the standard, historicist style of British shipbuilding companies, with oak panelled smoking room, complete with leather armchairs and decorative rugs, and white painted dining room. The *Kungsholm* was, at 21,532 gross tons, larger than the *Gripsholm*, and was built for the Swedish American Line by Hamburg based Blohm & Voss in 1928. The *Kungsholm* featured the work of Swedish designers and artists, as the Swedish American line wanted it to be a showcase for the nation's design. For example, the first class smoking room featured two murals by Kurt Jungstedt of the New York and Stockholm skylines facing each other on the forward and aft walls. The African pear wood panelled first class lounge and music room featured original paintings by Jerk Werkmäster and Rolf Engströmer of Gothenburg. The second class accommodation was comparatively expensively fitted out, with Javanese teak and ebony panelling in the smoking room. This was because the line also planned to use the *Kungsholm* for one class cruising, bringing the passenger capacity down from 1,344 to approximately 600 for holiday travel.

Back in Britain, the Cunarder *Mauretania* continued to hold onto the Blue Ribbon throughout the 1920s. It was refitted at the end of 1926 in response to the introduction of the *Ile de France* when the verandah café was converted into an indoor greenhouse; in the lounge new carpets were laid and palms added, and private baths were added to the first class cabins. White Star entered into decline, prompting the government-led merger of Cunard and White Star in 1934. No new ships were launched for the prestigious North Atlantic crossing and so accepted histories make little mention of the later 1920s. This is largely due to the main focus of interest being travel by ocean liner between Europe and North America (Brinnin and Gaulin 1988; Miller 1977). However, P&O's *Viceroy of India* entered service for the journey to Bombay in 1929, as well as providing a cruising service, but rarely features in mainstream publications on ocean liners, even when the subject of the books is broadly passenger shipping (Miller 1987). This is mainly because it did not sail on the transatlantic route. It was a significant ship from the point of view of P&O – at 19,648 gross tons, this was the largest ship that P&O had built to date. In 1926 P&O had reported a net loss of £306,237 and Lord Inchcape: '. . . saw it as imperative that the P&O's standards especially in the luxury liner business, should be as high as possible' (Jones 1989: 142). The *Viceroy of India* was the ship designed to rescue P&O's failing fortunes, with luxury interiors and technical innovations. From the technical perspective, the ship was important, as it was the first European owned turbo-electric ship. As *The Shipbuilder* announced in April 1929: 'The successful completion of the twin-screw turbo-electric mail, passenger and cargo steamship *Viceroy of India* represents an epoch-making event in the annals of British shipbuilding' (*The Shipbuilder* April 1929: 260).

The ship was built by Alexander Stephens & Sons at Glasgow, and the interiors were designed by the Hon. Elsie Mackay. There was an element of friction between Elsie and her parents; at the age of 20, in 1914, she had been the youngest leading lady in London. She secretly married a fellow actor, Dennis Wyndham, in 1917, whom she divorced five years later. She was also one of the first women to hold a pilot's licence, which she achieved in 1922 and exemplified the phenomenon of 'The New Woman' (Horn 1995). Her daring exploits reached new heights in 1928 when, sadly, she was killed attempting to be the first woman to fly the Atlantic.

It was agreed by P&O's Board on 29 April 1925 that she be awarded the sum of £600 per quarter for her work on advising P&O on the interior décor of its ships, and the *Viceroy of India* in particular. By this point, Elsie Mackay and her mother, Lady Inchcape, had already advised on the decoration of the public rooms on the *Razmak*, introduced in February 1925 for the Aden and Bombay route. Lord Inchcape, as Chairman of the company, was sensitive about her appointment. A pencilled note by Inchcape asks that his daughter be awarded the salary, but that it should come out of his own 'emoluments' (P&O 1925). Inchcape had spent time travelling with this wife and daughter, and the lack of modern amenities on board the P&O fleet was unstintingly brought to his attention. As Inchcape admitted:

> I feel some diffidence on assenting to my daughter being given this appointment but I conscientiously believe it will be a good thing for the P&O Company – we are building ships, which unless they come to grief will be on the service for the next twenty years, and we have to look ahead. None of our older vessels have the conveniences which people nowadays require. They have no wardrobe, passengers have to keep their clothes in trunks underneath their bunks, they are deficient in handing hooks, the lights are not arranged so as to be convenient, the looking glasses are badly

placed, the arrangement for the wash hand basins are inefficient and inconvenient, (and) the public rooms are in many cases arranged and furnished without any regard to taste.

(P&O 1925)

And the employment of the Hon. Elsie Mackay guaranteed that an upper class, British taste would prevail. As P&O's house magazine, *The Blue Peter*, noted: 'Inside her deck-houses are rooms which, for furnishings and craftsmanship, rival the best art in English houses of varying periods. . . . These rooms have a peculiar interest in that they were the last upon which Lord Inchcape's daughter, the late Miss Elsie Mackay, exercised her taste for interior decoration' (*The Blue Peter*, May 1929: e). This was the only publication to give Elsie Mackay credit for the design of the interiors, with the credit usually going to P&O and Waring & Gillow (*The Shipbuilder*, April 1929: 263). However, she was young and fashionable and was in touch with the glamorous world of stage and screen, and took her lead from the innovations introduced on the transatlantic route. For example, this was the first P&O ship to have a swimming pool. Located on G deck, it was created in the accepted Pompeian style, as had been used on the *Imperator* onwards, including the *Ile de France*. The main first class public rooms were situated on A deck, the front of the deck was reserved for open air sports facilities, with the two classes segregated. The veranda café followed next, which differed from the usual decoration in that it had Moorish style, pointed arches as wall decorations, and fabric dressing the windows. There was a dark, wooden ceiling with electric lights and the flooring was in decorative squares with white wickerwork chairs. Leading from the veranda café was the smoking room. This is the most reproduced image of the *Viceroy of India*; one of the earliest uses was in a special supplement to mark its launch in *The Blue Peter* as part of the advertisement for Waring & Gillow in 1927. The image is rich with immense depth and detailed interest, unusual in images of ship interiors at this date.

The room was based on decorative features of the State Room of the old Palace, Bromley-by-Bow Court dating from 1606, built for James I and preserved at the Victoria and Albert Museum. To recreate the early seventeenth-century ambience, the space had wire brushed, oak panelling with authentic carving on the pilasters and frieze. The mantelpiece was also in oak, with a caryatid at either side and the royal coat of arms above the bare brick grate. On either side of the fireplace were crossed swords in the style of the James I era. The floor was bare wood with decorative 'Turkey' rugs. The ceiling was white plasterwork like the original, with oak hammer beams supporting a dome and painted glass skylights. The furniture was also an authentic Jacobean type and the windows were leaded, with stained glass escutcheons. Further aft on A deck was the first class reading and writing room, decorated in Adam style, with the mantelpiece based on an original at Kedleston and the remainder of the pastel interior taken from Harewood House. The barrel vaulted ceiling was painted in the style of Angelica Kaufman and Cipriani. A

4.4
Elsie Mackay, First Class Smoking Room, Viceroy of India, P & O, 1929.
Source: P&O

particularly witty feature was the lighting concealed in the four Wedgwood vases. On from the reading and writing room was the much larger music room, measuring 60 by 50 feet with a ceiling height of 11 feet. *The Shipbuilder* commented: '. . . a most unusual scheme of decoration has been adopted, blending classical styles with a distinctive modern note' (1929: 263). The panelled walls were painted in a soft, pastel tone with neo-classical gilding, matching the Corinthian pillars and pilasters; the floor was parquet, with patterned rugs which could be moved if the room was required for dancing; the furniture was generally eighteenth century, but it was the light fittings which created the modern note, and which alarmed contemporary commentators. The style of the wall lights, particularly the two above the fireplace, were definitely art deco. They were attached centrally to a square mirror with jade green border. Art deco could also be detected in the 20 cabines-de-luxe, situated on C deck. The rooms were panelled in polished hardwood, with art deco wood inlays on the walls. The pilasters were similarly carved from decorative hardwoods, finished off at the top, not with a classical entablature, but a scroll and tassel. The cabines-de-luxe also had private bathrooms, with a smaller room attached for a valet or maid, and sliding doors, so that adjoining rooms could be converted to a double cabin with sitting room. There were a further 415 first class cabins, which were all single but with the option of converting to larger suites, if necessary, on B, C and D decks. Each stateroom had a wardrobe, polished oak bedstead, dressing table, washbasin with running water, boot rack and coffee tray. The passengers

4.5
Elsie Mackay, First class Cabin- de-luxe No 178, Viceroy of India, P & O, 1929.
Source: P&O

4.6
**Elsie Mackay
on board the
Rawlpindi at
Belfast with Lord
Inchcape to
her left, 1925.**
Source: Ulster Folk &
Transport Museum

enjoyed the novelty of a reading lamp by the bed and fresh air by means of mechanical ventilation through at least two 'punkah' louvres.

In common with all P&O ships of this era, the accommodation was predominately first class, to cater for civil servants and army officers travelling backwards and forwards to India. There was no provision made for steerage or third class. Second class accommodation was provided for 258 passengers, mainly in twin cabins. There was a Queen Anne dining room for this class, contrasted to the lavish George V dining saloon for first class. A second class music room was provided on C deck in Colonial style, but most adventurous was the second class smoking room on B deck. The style was a technicolour Tyrolean, with soft grey oak walls and brightly painted, art nouveau embellishments on the ceiling. To complete the room, the floor was red rubber, manufactured to emulate tiling. Separate accommodation was provided for the ayahs, and the crew was also segregated according to race.

Whilst the *Viceroy of India* combined British tradition with mild modernism, the design of the *Ile de France* had eschewed styles of the past and used glamorous art deco to express French national identity. In response, Germany's North German Lloyd built two huge liners, the *Bremen* and the *Europa*, which surpassed the *Ile de France* in contemporaneity of design and which took the Blue Riband from the British *Aquitania* in 1929. At 51,656 gross tons and over 1,000 feet in length, the ships matched the size of Germany's pre-war giants. The first class interiors of the *Bremen* were designed by the architect, Fritz August Breuhaus de Groot (1883–1960). De Groot had studied with Peter Behrens and acted as a member of the Deutscher Werkbund. He also wrote a key text eulogizing modernism in ship design, using *Bremen* as a case study, and the interiors reflected contemporary trends in German modernism (Breuhaus de Groot 1930). The late 1920s witnessed the growth of modernism in art and design in Weimar Republic Germany, as exemplified by the Bauhaus School of Design, which had moved into modernist buildings in Dessau, designed by Walter Gropius in 1926 (Willett 1978). De Groot reflected the new, republican sense of German national identity in his designs, which rejected the past and historical styles. He stated:

> The ostentatious luxury of former times which no longer appeals to the man of today, has been avoided in the interior decoration by laying stress on the purity of form, on the beauty of line and on the superior quality of the material. The architecture of the *Bremen* emancipates us from a time which is not our own and leads us into the grandeur of the present age, in which we desire to breathe and not to suffocate.
>
> (as quoted in Brinnin and Gaulin 1988: 139)

Compared to German liners of the past, the *Bremen* and *Europa* were sleek and uncluttered in their interior design. The first class lounge of the *Bremen* was simple in treatment, with concealed lighting on the ceiling, reflective, unadorned pillars running either side with chairs and tables upholstered in abstract textiles. A reminder that this was a German ship was communicated by the addition of two bronze busts of Hindenburg and Bismarck which decorated the end of the room. The first class library shared this modern approach, with concealed lighting on the ceiling and illumination for reading also supplied by modern standard lamps. The room was simply panelled in wood, with the addition of quotes from world literature. The smoking room was also distinctly modern, with plain white ceiling, and a marquetry mural of a tropical scene adorned the walls. There was a heterogeneous mixture of chairs, upholstered and the dining type. The swimming pool also used adventurous lighting, with porthole lamps emitting a warm glow from beneath the water. The interiors of the *Europa* were designed by Ludwig Troost and were in similarly classical, modern style, building on the success of his designs for the *Columbus* of 1914.

By contrast, the Canadian Pacific Line introduced the *Empress of Britain* in 1931. At 42,348 tons this was the largest ship the line had commissioned for travel from Britain to the St Lawrence region. It was also designed with the twin purpose of providing cruises during the winter months, when the weather made travel to Canada virtually impossible. The ship was launched by the glamorous Prince of Wales in 1930 and built by John Brown's at Clydebank. There was a further touch of glamour when the Hollywood stars, Douglas Fairbanks and Mary Pickford, were on board for the initial voyage to Canada in 1931. The exterior styling of the ship was striking, painted all white with three buff colour funnels and elegant cruiser stern. The *Empress of Britain*'s attractiveness was confirmed when the ship appeared in the Hollywood film, *Now, Voyager* (1942) as the symbol of the liberation of Charlotte Vale (Bette Davis). The design of the interiors reflected British attitudes to modernism, which were not as all-embracing as those encountered in Germany. The editor of *The Studio* argued that the ship should: '. . . perhaps be regarded as the first British

4.7
Fritz August Breuhaus de Groot, The Library, *Bremen*, North German Lloyd, 1929.
Source: Author's collection

effort on an important scale towards a departure from the stereotyped "period" fashion in ship decoration' (*The Studio* 1931: 21). Canadian Pacific also reinforced the appeal of its modern attractions: 'In her decorations, her speed, her comforts, her gaiety, she is truly a ship for the moderns, but particularly for those moderns who still think space is preferable to crowds' (Canadian Pacific 1931, as quoted in Harvey 2004: 26).

The design of the *Empress of Britain* was not well received by the developing British modernist design establishment, represented by the polemical magazine, *Architectural Review*. Edited by Hubert de Cronin Hastings from 1928, the magazine espoused modernism and detested the *moderne*, what we would loosely term art deco today (Hillier 2003: 259–66). Hastings appointed John Betjeman as assistant editor in 1930, and he introduced a host of contacts from his Oxford days, including Lord Clonmore. An article by Clonmore on 'The Architecture of the Liner' was published by *Architectural Review* in September 1931. Although it shared the same title as the seminal article by Arthur Davis some 17 years earlier, this is where the similarity ended. In the article, Clonmore took British ship design to task:

> The number and size of British liners are large, but if we study them closely we cannot, if we have any taste, fail to see that architecturally they are

deplorable. By this I do not mean that from the outside they are ugly – of technical points I know nothing, though I have seen many ships, but on the whole it has seemed to me that our ships have as good lines as those of other countries, and that is saying a good deal, for the modern vessel is a lovely thing. But go inside one of our 'luxury ships,' get over the excitement of travelling, of that particular thrill when the train first reaches the docks, and wander carefully through its 'social halls' and 'winter gardens'. You will be very depressed. If not, you have the kind of taste which admires the new London hotels.

(Clonmore 1931: 62).

By the new London hotels Clonmore was probably referring to the art deco Savoy, Dorchester and Claridge's. Clonmore goes on to criticize ships from other nations, including Italy, which he describes as: '. . . an orgy of vulgarity . . .' (Clonmore 1931: 62). In expected *Architectural Review* fashion, Clonmore identifies the Swedish motor-liner, *Kungsholm*'s simple interiors as an example of good taste. He rails against ship interiors which purport to be something else and chooses an unrepresentative image of the *Empress of Britain* to make his point. A view of the sleek exterior of the ship is juxtaposed with a view of the Charles Allom Mayfair Lounge, rather than The Mall or Cathay Lounge. Beneath it is a caption which points out: 'How strange it is that something so simple and dignified without should not be so within. How odd that so traditional an exterior should have such a "traditional" inside' (Clonmore 1931: 63). Clonmore's attitude was partly based on an identity based on social class, gender and regional origin and a crisis in these barriers. He was appalled by the behaviour of some passengers: 'I can remember one lovely day last year, as we steamed across a bright-blue Bay of Biscay, seeing four vast perspiring women from Manchester playing bridge in the middle of a "Moorish Lounge", all with their backs to the windows' (Clonmore 1931: 62).

The *Empress of Britain* was designed to carry three classes of passenger: 465 in first, 260 tourist and 470 third on a total of eight decks. The sun deck and decks A, B and C contained the spacious first class cabins whilst the first class public rooms occupied the entire lounge deck. The public rooms for tourist class were located on A and B decks and cabin accommodation forward on C, D and E decks. Additionally, the dining rooms for all three classes were on D deck. Further down on F deck were the first class Olympian pool, gymnasium and Turkish bath. Canadian Pacific devoted the comparatively large sum of £250,000 to the decoration and furnishing of the public rooms. In an attempt to emulate the success of the *Ile de France*, Canadian Pacific used a galaxy of quintessentially British artists for the decoration of the first class public rooms, whilst retaining the services of their usual decorative architects, P.A. Staynes and A.H. Jones, in the role of design co-ordinators. Staynes and Jones also designed the writing and card rooms, de luxe and special suites plus the entrance foyer, stairways and corridors. Staynes and Jones also designed the swimming pool and Turkish bath when the designs of the original designer, M. Poiret, were double the estimated amount allocated (Johnston 2000: 183).

There was still evidence of period styling in the first class Empress Room, which was inspired by neo-classical architecture. Situated on the lounge deck, the room measured 40 feet by 70 feet and was designed by the society portrait painter, Sir John Lavery (1856–1941). Lavery was chosen possibly because of his links with America and the millionaire clientele there. Through the art dealer Joseph Duveen, he had exhibited his portrait interiors in New York and Boston to great acclaim – during Lavery's visit there in 1925–6 he was reported to have painted the portraits of 15 American millionaires. The paintings depicted the wealthy situated in their ostentatious homes: 'These works function in the same way as photographs of the rich and famous in a glossy magazine. . . . Country house interiors like *A Bedroom at the Wharf, Sutton Courtenay* and *The Dining Room at Lennoxlove* asserted the superiority of European aristocratic culture, just as Walter Gay's views of empty rooms in French *chateaux* fed upon the new world fascination for the *ancient regime*' (McConkey 1993: 169). The room had silvered classical pilasters topped with gold and panelled walls. The main colour scheme was coral pink and mid blue, with added spaciousness provided by a mirrored wall aft plus silvered pedestals which carried rose-coloured ostrich plumes on either side of the stage and at each corner. A domed ceiling was situated over the polished, Austrian oak dance floor. The dome was dark blue with stars painted as they would have been placed on the day that the ship was launched, which were echoed in the art deco ceiling lights. The room could also be used as a cinema, with projection equipment concealed in a room at the forward end and a drop-down screen placed above the stage. Moving forward from the Empress Room, the first-class passengers encountered the Mall, a broad circulation route placed on either side of the funnel casing. Designed by Staynes and Jones, these broad spaces were lined in elegant, modern style oak. This was a place for promenading and for being seen undercover on the ship. There were places to sit and a buffet; this offered the perfect place for people-watching.

Further aft from the Mall was the capacious foyer which gave access to the grand staircase, the shop, decorated with illuminated glass turrets, and lifts. Moving on from the foyer on the left was the writing room and library by Staynes and Jones and decorated by Waring & Gillow Ltd in Georgian style. The room had a marble mantelpiece, wall panelling and furniture in walnut with oak pilasters, contrasted with art deco ceiling lights and carved pine on the pilasters. On the opposite side of the funnel casing was the amusing Knickerbocker Bar. This was a tiny space, which could sit 21 people, with a semi-circular bar with bar stools. The walls and ceiling were decorated by British illustrator, W. Heath Robinson (1872–1944). Famous by this stage for his sardonic portrayals of golfing, modern living and motoring, Heath Robinson painted a mural, the *Legend of the Cocktail*, around the four walls of the room which depicted the history of the cocktail. On the ceiling the cartoon characters were painted, looking down at the room from circular openings in the sycamore panelling, and a cartoon biplane filled the largest of the openings.

More conventional in style was the Mayfair Lounge by Charles Allom, located after the Knickerbocker Bar. The walls were panelled in walnut with silver decorations, the columns and pilasters were green Scagiola marble with bronze decoration. The mantelpiece and the top of the octagonal table in the centre of the room were made from Scagiola Verdite. The style was classical in reference, and the ancient Temple of Minerva was mentioned in the contemporary publicity. The domed ceiling was glazed in amber glass with a sun ray motif, and each of the intersecting panels was decorated with a sign of the zodiac. The floor was oak parquet, covered with rugs in a sixteenth-century Polish design. The furniture was upholstered in traditional, dark patterns, and the curtains were made from silk damask. There were uplighters situated around the room, and a grand piano at one end. Beyond the Mayfair Lounge was the most innovative room on the ship, the first class smoking room or Cathay Lounge, by illustrator Edmund Dulac (1882–1953). Best known in Britain for his illustrations for children's books, including *Arabian Nights*, he was also familiar to an American audience, as from 1924 he began providing cover illustrations for *The American Weekly*, a Sunday supplement for the Hearst newspaper chain. This was an inspired piece of commissioning, and for the first time on a

4.8
John Lavery, First Class Ballroom, *Empress of Britain*, Canadian Pacific Line, 1931.
Source: Science and Society Picture Library

4.9
Staynes and Jones, The Mall, *Empress of Britain*, Canadian Pacific Line, 1931.
Source: Canadian Pacific Archives

PRESS OF BRITAIN"   *Cathay Lounge.*

prestigious British ocean liner, the smoking room was not modelled on historic, British stereotypes. The room was decorated in a rich red and black, the walls were panelled in grey ash, the ceiling was a shimmering silver, and the floor inlaid Macassar ebony and oak, the geometric pattern of which was echoed on the ceiling in vermilion. The bar was surrounded by illuminated, translucent glass with Chinese fretwork motif. The fireplace had a Chinese fretwork grate; above it was a decorative chimney breast, decorated with peach, gold, green and black mirrors. It was square in shape with the addition of a triangle on either of the vertical sides. On either side of the fireplace in two black alcoves, stood two red Chinese vases; the furniture was red and black lacquer, decorated with pale gold and upholstered in pink fabric with an abstract pattern. Chinese fretwork screens and wall decorations added to the exotic ambience. The same pattern was echoed in the ceiling lights. Alcoves and pillars were also in black lacquer and glass, with mirrored panels. Frida Wolfe commented positively: 'This most interesting departure from the usual smoking

4.10
Edmund Dulac, Cathay Lounge, *Empress of Britain*, Canadian Pacific Line, 1931.
Source: Canadian Pacific Archives

room *décor* is marked by the unity, the consistency – down to the last detail – which informs the whole' (*The Studio* 1931: 41).

From the lounge deck it was possible to take the central main staircase down to A deck, on which were situated first class cabins plus the second class smoking room, squash court and first class ladies' hairdressing salon with adjoining beauty parlour. The décor of the hairdressing salon and beauty parlour was by Staynes and Jones and executed by McEwans of Glasgow. The rooms were art deco in style and used modern materials, including walls which were framed with 'Staybrite' chrome bands and rubber flooring. The hairdressing salon equipment was streamlined chrome and supplied by Emile Paidar of Chicago.

The 120 feet long, first class dining room on D deck was designed by Sir Frank William Brangwyn (1867–1956) and executed by H.H. Martyn & Co. Brangwyn had been an apprentice of the founder of the British Arts and Crafts movement, William Morris. By the 1930s he was best known as a mural painter, most notably his mural, the *British Empire Panels*, destined for the House of Lords, was rejected in 1925. For the dining room, Brangwyn decorated either end with scenes from the life of Jacques Cartier, the French explorer most notably linked with the St Lawrence River. Hence, the room was known as the *Salle Jacques Cartier*, possibly in recognition of French Canadian passengers. There was also a link to the mural painting at the top of the main staircase facing the lounge deck. It depicted 'Champlain Presenting his Bride to the Citizens of Quebec' and was painted by Maurice Grieffenhagen in representational style, and showed the first European settlers meeting the inhabitants of Quebec. Brangwyn also designed the floor covering for the dining room, which was a specially patterned rubber-based composite. The walls were lined with oak panelling and the ceiling was divided by oak beams. The furniture was also in light oak in a simple, geometric style which reflected Brangwyn's Arts and Crafts roots. But in keeping with the heterogeneous styling of the ship, the centrepiece of the *Salle Jacques Cartier* was an art deco, gold mirrored buffet. The ziggurat shape was crowned by tiered lighting and supported by alabaster jars at the base.

Further down the ship, on F deck, was the Olympian Pool, which was also a mixture of the traditional and deco. Designed by Staynes and Jones and executed by H.H. Martyn & Co., the pool measured 40 feet by 20, and was lit by an illuminated ceiling. The ceiling was supported by eight classical turquoise glass and mosaic columns. The pool was surrounded by individual, wooden changing cubicles. A whimsical touch was added by a sizeable carved turtle made from Portland stone and inlaid with blue mosaic, which continuously spouted water into the pool through its mouth. At one end was a modest spectators' gallery with café beneath. Further sporting facilities were provided for passengers, particularly those on a long cruise in the form of full-size tennis court and squash court. The tourist class passenger accommodation on board the *Empress of Britain* did not receive the same attention in terms of design and decoration as the first class public accommodation. Therefore it tended to be simple with the added glamour of exotic wood panelling in either Queensland maple, black bean, anelim, locust, Macassar ebony, figured Quebec ash and avodire. Mahogany, sycamore, ash and oak were also used. Three-quarters of the first class sleeping accommodation was en-suite; two of these suites also had their own private sun balcony.

The accommodation for tourist class centred around three public rooms – the smoking room, lounge and dining room. The smoking room, complete with bar, was located on A deck and was more traditional in design than its first class counterpart; it was panelled in limed and wax-polished oak, with the focal point of the room provided by a marble fireplace above which was placed shaped mirrors; the cosy chairs were covered in tapestry fabric. The tourist class lounge was situated one deck down. The space was panelled with sycamore with contrasting pilasters in Zebrano. A dance floor was situated in the centre of the room with Austrian oak floor covering, surrounded by easy chairs and settees upholstered in orange and green. The dining room on D deck could seat 164 passengers at one sitting. Again, wood panelling was used to add warmth and glamour to the space, with French walnut and Zebrano in this case. The chairs were made from walnut with orange upholstery. An art deco touch was added with glass cascades which topped each pilaster, and which supported a fan of green and silver plaster reaching to the ceiling. None of the tourist class passengers could enjoy en-suite facilities, but there was ample provision made in the vicinity of the two- and four-bedded cabins. The third class lounge, with bar and shop, was also on A deck, and was panelled very simply in the slightly less exotic woods of cherry and oak. The dining saloon was on D deck and could accommodate only 234 of the 470 possible third class passengers at one sitting. The sleeping accommodation was at the forward end of the ship, with cabins for two or four panelled in painted plywood. Despite the investment made by Canadian Pacific, the *Empress of Britain* was never a great commercial success. Launched at the time of the Depression and suffering from intense competition in the provision of world cruises, she was tragically sunk during the Second World War. However, the interiors did demonstrate a British willingness to embrace contemporary design and add a touch of whimsy and fantasy to the ship interior.

As Britain struggled to come to terms with modernism and its relationship to ship design, in Italy efforts were made to match the new German liners and gain the Blue Riband. In 1932 the *Rex* was commissioned by the newly formed Italia Line. Mussolini decided a merger of the three existing passenger line providers would prove economical, and possibly allow more official control. This was part of a more general move to centralize and modernize Italian industry, in which design played an important role (Sparke 1988: 42). Hence Navigazione Generale Italiana (NGI), Lloyd Sabaudo and Cosulich Lines became the 'Italia' Società Anonima di Navigazione Line (Italia Line) in 1932 and the *Rex*, originally started by NGI, was the first product of the new, national company. The *Rex* gained the Blue Riband in 1933, averaging a speed of 28.92 knots on the westbound journey. At the same time as the *Rex* entered service, the *Conte di Savoia* joined the Italia Line fleet from Lloyd Sabaudo. The latter was not a record breaking ship, but compensated for this in terms of grandeur of the interiors. The interiors of the *Rex* were designed in the traditional Italian style, mainly by the Studio Ducrot of Palmero. The interiors of the *Conte di Savoia* were designed by Gustavo Pulitzer, who brought German modernism to Italian ship interiors. The Italian designer had trained in Germany, firstly at Munich Polytechnic and then with one of the founders and first President of the Deutscher Werkbund, Theodor Fischer (1862–1938). On his return to Italy, Pulitzer worked with the Casa Artistica on the *Conte Grande* introduced in 1927, designing the Buddhist inspired swimming pool, complete with mural of Mount Fuji. The ship is best known for its first class main lounge in a rendition of Indian Mogul décor. In an attempt to move away from such historicist styling, Nicolo Constanzi, the director of the Cantiere Navale di Monfalcone, Trieste's leading shipyard, commissioned Pulitzer to design the interiors of the *Victoria* and *Conte di Savoia*. Pulitzer had visited the *Bremen* in 1930, and was favourably impressed. He found there a new aesthetic for naval architecture, and wrote an illustrated article celebrating the design of the *Bremen*, 'New Designs in Ships' (*Casabella*, September 1930: 29, 40). Pulitzer combined modernism with luxury in the Italianate main lounge and Genoese club smoking room.

As the stylistic stakes were raised on an international level, the French introduced the biggest luxury ship yet seen on the Atlantic, in 1935. Capitalizing on French *haut décor* and the image of this country, particularly in America, for fast living

4.11
**Gustavo Pulitzer,
Grand Saloon,
Conte di Savoia,
Italian Line, 1932.**
Source: Author's
collection

and fun, earned during American prohibition which had ended in 1933, C.G.T. employed the full range of French designers and decorators who had been officially supported at the 1925 Paris exhibition to reinforce French national identity. The contract between the French government and the French Line stipulated that the new ship: '. . . had to be not less than equal to the best foreign ship in commission or under construction' (as quoted in Battersby 1971: 25). The cost of the subsidy from the French government for the construction of the *Normandie* was in excess of $60 million. Whilst the *Empress of Britain* had the Knickerbocker Bar, the *Normandie* had the Marquise de Pompadour suite and the Grand Saloon, compared in the publicity to the Hall of Mirrors at Versailles. The French art critic, Jacques Baschet, bemoaned the lack of monumental architecture when writing in 1935. But he found solace with the recent: '". . . floating cities". . . . They are the real 'masterpieces' of our period; creations to which, at the Zenith of their technical and artistic powers, engineers, architects, painters, sculptors and decorators contribute. Thus it has come about that the liner *Normandie* is a perfect expression of French genius and taste' (Baschet 1935: 3).

At a gross tonnage of 82,799 this major liner was only surpassed in size by Cunard's *Queen Elizabeth* at 83,673 gross tons in 1940. The *Normandie* also succeeded in winning the Blue Riband from the *Rex*, making the crossing in 4 days, 3 hours and 14 minutes in May 1935. Writing in 1936, John de la Valette, the British modernist who had a background in the shipping industry, commented on the success of the *Normandie*: '. . . to this day, the most resplendent attempt to turn ships into floating displays of a nation's artistic genius is represented by the great French liner, *Normandie* . . . Architecturally and artistically she is a magnificent achievement, one worthy of the highest French traditions. In fact, she stands pre-eminently for the French outlook on much more than merely ships' (de la Valette 1936: 717). This was a party ship, with the emphasis on artificial lighting rather than natural; dinner rather than petit déjeuner; lounging and people-watching as opposed to healthy, outdoor pursuits. Even the garden was glamorous, it was indoor and included caged, exotic birds.

The design work was co-ordinated by two pairs of architects, appointed by C.G.T. in October 1931. The first pair consisted of Pierre Patout (1879–1965) and Henri Pacon (1882–1946) who had both worked on the interiors of the *Ile de France*. They worked on the main entrance hall and dining room, plus they provided the general schemes for the chapel, swimming pool and stairways. The second duo consisted of Roger-Henri Expert (1882–1955) and Richard Bouwens van de Boijen, the latter having had a long association with the line; they oversaw the design of the promenade deck. The ship could carry 750 first class passengers, 670 tourist and 340 in economy class. In a challenge to accepted divisions between the classes, unusually, first class outnumbered the other two in number of passengers accommodated.

Hence, this was a decadent, luxury ship, which projected a particular French national identity. The main embarkation hall on C deck was two and a half decks in height, the walls were clad in smooth, cream coloured Algerian onyx, offset by oxidized copper and textured glass. One British commentator, the architect Oliver P. Bernard, noted:

> The walls are like crystallized sunshine, unembellished or unblemished by ornamental motives, providing a reception that reveals the understanding of marble for which France is famous, however unprepared one may be for such a massive effect on board ship.
>
> (1935: 287).

The shimmering effect of the space was further enhanced by the glossy, geometrically patterned flooring. The hall featured the purser's office, information bureau, florist, hairdressers and a selection of shops run by Parisian boutiques. At the forward end was a huge cloisonné panel depicting a Norman knight by Francois-Louis Schmied, obscuring the entrance to the chapel. When this panel was moved to one side, it revealed the chapel. This was a sombre place, the walls clad in black marble with reproductions of early Christian murals on the top. The Stations of the Cross was carved in rosewood, and placed around the room in niches, which could be screened off for non-Christian services. The paintings in the room were undertaken by Leon Voguet and Lombard. At the aft end of the hall it was possible to enter through the gilded, bronze double doors to the dining room. The doors, by Raymond Subes (1891–1970), showed major towns and cities of Normandy in bronze roundels with art deco surround.

The most striking feature of its interior layout was the huge public spaces created by the decision to divide the uptakes from the engines to the funnels. Hence, the dining room on C deck, the image which has become emblematic of the ship, measured 86 metres long (305 feet), 46 feet wide, 25 feet high and could seat 750 people. Designed by Patout and Pacon, it had no natural lighting, but the artificial lighting was the aspect of the interior design which made the room so remarkable and enhanced the cathedral-like dimensions. There were 12 luminescent standard lights in art deco design by René Lalique (1860–1945), the effect of which was accentuated by the full-length embossed cast glass panels behind. More light was provided by the 38 vertical wall lights, which measured 16 feet in height. Further illumination came from the two ceiling chandeliers, and the ceiling was constructed from plaster of Paris, treated in gold with indirect lighting inside. At one end of the room stood the female figure of *La Paix* (Peace) in gilded plaster by Louis Dejean, which measured 13 feet in height. Oliver P. Bernard, interior designer of the art deco foyer of the Strand Palace Hotel, London of 1930, was impressed by the interiors of the *Normandie*, finding the dining room: '. . . daringly unlike anything that has been attempted in ship decoration; . . .', but he found *Le Paix* to be a '. . . statuesque presence of maternal mediocrity in gilt . . .' (Bernard 12.12.1935: 287). The vista from the entrance stairway to the captain's table beneath the sculpture was accentuated by the coffered ceiling and total symmetry of the room. The staircase was decorated by a gilt plaster of Paris panel on the right by the sculptor Léon Drivier entitled 'Les Sports et Les Jeux'

MAI_35

and on the left, in the same materials, 'Les Arts et Les Monuments Regionaux' by Raymond Delamarre. Eight private dining rooms and an extra banqueting room led from the dining saloon, decorated with various panels by leading decorative artists.

      The other first class public accommodation was on the promenade deck. At the stern end was the first class grill room, open for lunch during the day, and transformed into an exclusive à la carte restaurant and night club in the evening. The room was oval in shape, and afforded views aft of the ocean. The design of the room, by Marc Simon, was the most modern on the ship. In keeping with the hedonistic nature of the ship, the walls were covered in varnished pigskin, the furniture was in a daring tubular, stainless-steel, the pillars were a shimmering black marble and there was a black grand piano on the tiny stage. The lighting was also adventurous, with abstract shapes on the central part of the ceiling and illuminated strips placed vertically around the room. There was a parquet dance floor in the centre of the room and the bar was decorated with a decorative glass panel by Max Ingrand demonstrating the merits of good wine.

      From the grill room it was possible to enter the gallery, from where you could enter a vestibule to the right or left which gave access to the pair of lifts plus a private dining saloon on one side and a private bar on the other. Straight ahead was the ceremonial grand stairway, leading to the smoking room, and designed by

4.12
Patout and Pacon, First Class Dining Saloon, *Normandie,* **French Line, 1935.**
Source: Eco Museum St Nazaire

Borderel and Robert, the firm of metal designers at which Raymond Subes worked (French Lines 1997 004 6950). At the top of the staircase was a larger than life sculpture, *La Normandie*, by Leon Baudry of a peasant girl. The smoking room was another daring use of space, as it was traditionally the place for men to retire after dinner, whilst the women would gather elsewhere, usually the ladies' drawing room or the writing room. This break with tradition was underlined by the fact that first class passengers had to walk through the smoking room to reach the grand saloon beyond. Bouwens van de Boijen had known the leading French lacquerist, Jean Dunand (1877–1942) since 1914 and asked him to design the interior of the smoking room and of parts of the grand saloon. Bouwens van de Boijen and Expert were responsible for the general layout of the grand saloon, and their detailed drawings, included designs for banquettes, are preserved at the French Lines archive (1998 004 6953). Dunand submitted several schemes to the architects, but they were rejected as being too innovative, and so he opted to produce a set of gold-lacquer panels in 'Egyptian' style (Marcilhac 1991: 144). Each panel was 6m (19ft 6in) high and 5.80m (18ft 9in) across.

The theme of the room was 'Jeux et les joies de l'Humanié' (Humanity's Games and Pleasures) and so the first panel on the right as passengers descended the staircase was devoted to 'Fishing' and the panel opposite, 'Sports'. Further into the space was 'Taming the Horse' on the left and 'Grape Harvesting and Dancing' on the right. The partition between the smoking room and the grand saloon was formed out of a panel depicting 'Hunting' with two double glazed doors allowing entrance beyond. The staircase and access corridor were sheathed in panels of gold lacquer with a dappled effect – there were 1,200 square metres (1,400 square yards) of gold lacquer surfaces in total. In addition there were 14 lacquered gold columns and in excess of 235 square metres of coloured and incised lacquer. All the work was executed by hand. Jean Dunand also created panels for the grand saloon, designed by Jean Dupas (1882–1964), a friend of Roger Expert and also M. Olivier, the newly appointed President of C.G.T. Dupas designed the saloon side of the panel created by Dunand; it represented the 'Chariot of Aurora', and is now on permanent display at the Carnegie Museum of Art, Pittsburgh. It depicts the sea and the sun and the wind in gold lacquer. The four panels in the four corners of the grand saloon by Dunand depicted an epic poem from classical mythology with nautical themes – 'The Rape of Europa', 'The Birth of Aphrodite', 'The Chariot of Thetis' and 'The Chariot of Poseidon'. They were made from painted and engraved glass and involved etching and painting the complex designs on the reverse of the glass. The effect looked three dimensional, but was smooth to the touch. Dunand was also responsible for the 14 columns in the saloon, which were covered in gold lacquer. Dunand also supplied the red lacquer games tables, which were complemented by the red Aubusson chairs by Goudissart and art deco lighting by Lalique. The British interior designer was less than enthusiastic about the choice of furniture and floor covering: 'Against such wealth and quality in classical composition, depicting the History of Navigation, the furniture is unforgivable and the carpet richly deserves to be elsewhere' (Bernard 12.12.1935: 288).

Further aft from the grand saloon was a gallery, lined with black and silver uplighters in deco style, and two panel paintings depicting scenes from Norman history by M. Ducos de la Haillie. There were also four bas-reliefs by M. Bouchard carved in thin slabs of Cruchand stone, depicting rural scenes from Normandy. The gallery lounge led to the first purpose-built theatre to be situated on an ocean liner. It could be used for live shows or screening films, reinforcing the fun, glamorous character of the ship. The entrance to the room was decorated with ironwork by Raymond Subes. There was a low, ironwork banister and the elevator covers were decorated in ironwork and a pattern of repeated scallop shells. The theatre itself was decorated in silver, with seats upholstered in red for 380 passengers. Beyond the theatre was the comparatively small writing room with a panel by Jouve, and library, adjacent to the much larger Winter Garden. The library was in a simpler, more modern design with one wall lined with books, and opposite the bookcase was a wall constructed mainly of glass, allowing a view of the Winter Garden. *Design for To-day* commented positively on this interior scheme: 'A restful room in a rather more restrained style' (1935a: 388). The Winter Garden by Madame de Vilmorin and Emile-Jacques Ruhlmann was furnished with wickerwork furniture, but in a modish drum shape for the chairs, which stood on art deco rugs. There were also bronze fountains and Arabescoto marble arches, hung with creepers. The birds were constrained in ornamental crystal cages, designed by Ruhlmann.

The first class private accommodation on the *Normandie* matched the glamorous appeal of the public spaces. The most exclusive accommodation was provided by the Deauville and Trouville 'Grande Luxe' suites – located on the sundeck, above the grill room. The Deauville suite, designed by Louis Süe was decorated with pink and white walls, a grand piano, and elegant furniture in creamy burl ash. There was also a bas-relief of a reclining, female nude by Albert Pommier in gilt bronze, supplied at a price of 5,000 francs. The Trouville suite was designed by Jules Leleu and did not feature any original artworks. It was rather more sombre, with dark, lacquered furniture and carpets by Silva Bruhns, decorated with abstract patterns. The scale of accommodation was generous for these two luxury suites, at 665 square feet divided into three double bedrooms and one single, three bathrooms, a lounge, a dining room, serving pantry and private terrace looking out over the stern of the ship. The remainder of the first class accommodation, 24 veranda staterooms in total, was located aft on the promenade deck. Each had its own private section of enclosed deck and decorated in a range of styles from the sleek moderne to the traditional. The most contemporary was the 'Grande Luxe' Rouen Suite, designed by Maison Dominique, or 'Domin', a firm founded by André Domain and Marcel Geneviève. The walls were covered in pigskin and lacquer, complemented by black doorways and vertical lighting. The moderne ambience was further accentuated by horizontal, silver bands on the walls and pillars supporting the shelves in the dining room, and the furniture was veneered in Macassar ebony. The bathroom of the suite was decorated with tiles, featuring a youth playing with a deer in a rural setting, by the ceramicist Mayodon. The Jumièges Suite decorated by Nelson was one of the

MA

4.13
**Maison
Dominique, Salle
à Manger de
l'appartement
grand luxe
"Rouen",
Normandie,
French Line,
May 1935.**
Source: Eco Museum
St Nazaire

few interiors with overtly historicist references and was based on the chambers of Marquise de Pompadour, the mistress of Louis XV, at the Château de Bellevue. The interior was enhanced by a copy of eighteenth-century Rococo Francois Boucher work by Chauffrey. There was also a swimming pool on the *Normandie,* located on D deck, directly beneath the chapel. Victor Menu designed a tile frieze in Sèvres stoneware depicting animals. The pool was planned in various depths to cater for the novice swimmer. Leaving behind the usual Greek temple theme, the pool had a stepped, moderne ceiling with concealed lighting. The tourist class and third class accommodation was plain moderne by contrast, and did not use the same level of luxurious materials or craftsmanship. For example, the tourist class dining room was decorated by Establissements Leglas-Maurice et Jamin in moderne style, with a circular ceiling feature with concealed lighting. The tourist class lounge was plainly panelled in polished wood, with cloth and gilt plate glass.

The *Normandie* was the apogee of French *haut décor.* The emphasis in the ship's interiors was on glamour and comfort. First class passengers could escape the outdoors, and remained cosseted in the air-conditioned restaurant with no view of the sea. As with the majority of ocean liners to date, the emphasis was on protecting these passengers from the dangers of the sea on the outside and the second and third class passengers on the inside. As John de la Valette argued in 1935, when advocating the case for modern interior design on ships: '. . . the argument which we have all heard shipowners bring forward, and which has been an instruction to many ship decorators: "The ladies want to forget that they are on board a ship – make them forget it!"' (de la Valette 1935: 715). However, by the early 1930s a new trend in ship interior design was beginning to make an impact. This was the tendency to blur the distinctions between outside and inside, partly inspired by the contemporary vogue for the outdoor life, which made swimming and sunbathing fashionable, and also by modern architecture, which advocated bringing the outdoors in and revealing the indoors to the outside. The burgeoning popularity of cruising in the 1930s also prompted the interior design of ships to acknowledge the ocean and the activities on deck as pleasurable. This in turn influenced liner design, as most ships built during this period fulfilled the hybrid function of both liner and cruise ship.

Chapter 5

Modern designer liners

From 1930 onwards, ocean liner interiors gradually developed away from the revivalism of the earlier twentieth century, towards a more modern and self-consciously contemporary style. It is tempting to polarize this period of ship interior design as a battle of styles, between reforming modernism and intransigent periodization. However, the shift was gradual and the themes of national identities and the growing professionalization of design practice are just as significant to an understanding of the history of the interior design of liners of this era. Frequently, ships of this period were a blend of modernism, art deco and streamlining with touches of humour and wit, luxury and glamour. The designer interior was in the ascendancy in this period, whereby the modern architect would have complete control over the décor, most notably with the Orient Line's *Orion*. This type of interior was to rise in prominence, and begin to eclipse the role of the decorating firm and also the influence of the 'Chairman's wife'. This growing hegemony can best be understood as part of the professionalization of interior design, which marginalized women and decoration, and privileged modernism and the male designer. The move also reflected a prejudice against French art deco. As a result of the decline in emigration to North America and the concurrent rise in the popularity of cruising, liner design began to feature permeable divisions between outside and inside. Beginning with the German *Bremen*, moving through the French *Normandie* and British *Queen Mary*, there was a quest to use designers on behalf of the line owners to express national identities to the world and create the most appealing and fashionable surroundings for travel and leisure in an increasingly competitive market. As Adrian Forty has argued: 'No design works unless it embodies ideas that are held in common by the people for whom the object is intended' (Forty 1986: 245).

The first examples of this trend were the *Strathnaver* and *Strathaird*, introduced by P&O in 1931 and 1932 respectively. The ships were the largest to be built for the company at that time at around 22,500 tons each, with accommodation

for 500 first class and 670 tourist class passengers. The two ships were very distinctive externally, as they were painted all white, which also lowered the temperature on board ship by as much as ten degrees. The first class cabin accommodation was forward on decks A to E and the public spaces were all on B deck, with the exception of the dining room, which was on F deck, along with that of tourist class. The remaining public rooms for tourist class were on D and E decks, with cabins on G and H. The interior design of the ships displayed a mixture of art deco and period style, a look which had become the P&O housestyle since the *Viceroy of India*, and were the overall responsibility of the Chairman's wife, Lady Inchcape and her daughter, Lady Margaret Shaw.

The first class writing and reading room of the *Strathaird*, for instance, was gently Queen Anne in styling with decorative plasterwork on the ceiling, English cedar panelled walls, walnut furniture and Turkish rugs. Natural light was filtered by means of leaded windows, decorated with stained glass. Comfortable armchairs were upholstered in chintz. The smoking room was also traditional in style. The interiors of the *Strathnaver* were almost identical to the *Strathaird*, and were also a blend of the old and the new. The smoking room had a Scottish baronial air, with oversized fireplace and wrought iron grate inspired by the original at Holyrood Palace, panels depicting scenes from Scottish history and stained glass. This connection with Scotland may have emanated from the Inchcapes, whose family home, Glenapp Castle in Ayrshire, was built in 1870, and was in traditional Scottish baronial style. The first class lounge was neo-classical in inspiration, but with art deco ceiling and wall lighting. P&O boasted: 'The diffused artifical lighting is of a novel character, amplified by empanelled lights grouped upon sconces of classical design' (1931: 3). The main innovation came with the opening up of the ships to the outside. Divisions between the interior and exterior became more blurred. For example, the first class swimming pool on the *Strathaird* was situated on B deck aft, instead of being much lower down. The glazed screens on two sides of the pool could be folded back to enjoy the sun. Similarly, adjacent to the second class lounge was a dancing space, separated from the promenade space by a hinged glass screen. This reflects the more general fashion for outdoor activities and sports which characterized the 1930s, and also reflects the more conducive climes of P&O's service to Australia, as opposed to harsh conditions of the Atlantic. The *Strathmore* was the next of the set of five to join P&O's service to India and Australia in 1935. At 23,500 tons this ship was marginally larger, and lost the two false funnels of its predecessors. The ship was very similar in structure to the Orient Line's *Orion* and was built at the same shipyard, Vickers-Armstrong Ltd, Barrow-in-Furness, to very similar plans and for a very similar price. The layout of the interior space differed from that of the *Orion*, however, and was designed by A. McInnes Gardner & Partners, a Glasgow based architectural firm with decoration by Waring & Gillow. The dance spaces and veranda on D deck were designed by the shipbuilders.

More space was released for outdoor activities: 'Her one funnel has placed greater deck space at the passengers' disposal and the spacious sports decks will delight both the games enthusiast and those who enjoy basking in the warm sunshine' (P&O 1935: 2). With this ship, the styling of the interiors was more simply moderne than the hedonistically historic. There were hints of period styling, for instance, fluted columns in the first class library and writing room and nods to British tradition, with a portrait of the Duchess of York by Simon Elwes over the moderne fireplace in the library and writing room. However, art deco lighting was used throughout the ship, supplied by General Electric Co. Ltd, and the walls were smoothly panelled in woods from Australia, Canada and India. The first class dining saloon featured a tapestry of the Castle of Glamis, which was located on the Strathmore plain. The room was panelled in Nigerian cherry and walnut banding. Contrasted with this traditional décor were art deco glazed entrance doors, screens and sidelights in aluminium, anodized to give a matt, silver finish. The veranda café was decorated in smooth white sycamore with a trim surrounding the doors and windows in moulded teak. Moderne touches were added with Staybrite steel decorations and blackwood bandings. The veranda café was aft of the lido area. The blurring of the outdoors and indoors was also a feature of the dancing space on B deck, where the glazed screens surrounding the dance floor could be folded back to create an outdoor dancing space. On C deck there was a lido area with swimming pool, veranda café and cocktail bar with deck space for sunbathing. Screens could be erected around the area if the weather was inclement. As P&O boasted: 'While any tendency to elaboration or ornateness has been obviated, the styles of decoration and furnishing are always pleasing and effective' (P&O 1935: 2). The private accommodation on the *Strathmore* differed from that of the *Orion* in two respects. The first were the two, luxury vice-regal suites, created for the use of the Viceroy of India and other wealthy passengers, complete with their own private verandas. Situated on C deck, they included bedroom, two bathrooms, sitting room and dining room. Again, the rooms were panelled in a rich variety of woods, from sycamore, maple, bleached Nigerian cherry and French walnut. The lighting was art deco in style, and the furniture simple and sleek. The spaces were flexible, and could be converted to individual cabins-de-luxe according to demand. The second difference between the accommodation of the *Strathmore* and the *Orion* was in the provision of first class, en suite, single berth cabins on the *Strathmore*. Located on C deck, these were provided possibly to meet the demand of single travellers on British Empire business, as opposed to emigrants bound for Australia on the *Orion*. There was accommodation for 445 first class and 665 tourist class passengers in total on the *Strathmore*. The *Stratheden* and *Strathallan* joined P&O's service in 1937 and were of a similar, simplified art deco design.

The transformation from historicist to modern design was well illustrated in the refit of the Anchor Line's transatlantic liner, the *California*, in 1938. The Anchor Line was essentially a Scottish firm with voyages departing from Glasgow and was founded in 1832 to service the Mediterranean trade and began a service to New York as early as 1856, mainly for the transport of cargo by sail. As the demand for transatlantic passenger transport grew, so the Anchor Line added new ships to its fleet, including the *Columbia* in 1886, which was '. . . most luxuriously fitted for saloon, second and third class passengers' (Burrow 1932: 21–2). The line provided transport from Glasgow to all parts of the globe, including Bombay, Karachi and New York by the 1930s. In 1936 the Board of Directors decided to recondition the fleet, which comprised *Caledonia, California, Transylvania* and *Tuscania*: '. . . to put them in a condition to compete successfully in the trades in which they are engaged' (Anchor Line 20.10.1936: 112–13). A sum of £30,000 for the process was agreed at the meeting, although by the end of 1938 the line had spend £100,000 on reconditioning the fleet. The *California* appears to have been the flagship for the fleet, particularly as it was selected to provide special cruises to London to mark the Coronation of Edward VIII in May 1937. However, following the abdication, this was altered to the King George VI and Queen Elizabeth Coronation Cruise. The original ship had been built by Alexander Stephen & Son and joined the fleet in 1923. With a gross tonnage of 17,250 the ship sailed to New York and also Bombay, providing three classes of accommodation which were decorated in historicist style. The first class public accommodation included a Georgian dining saloon, a William and Mary style first class lounge, an Adam style writing room and Tudor cocktail bar and a smoking room. According to the publicity brochure: 'The Smoking Room is, appropriately enough, in the style of the Tudor period, which witnessed the first introduction of tobacco, and it contains reproductions of fine old Tudor furniture, handsome and comfortable. The floor is covered with the red tiles of the period, the walls are panelled in oak mellowed by time, with stone mullions at the latticed windows. The doors are studded oak' (Anchor Line 1923: 9). The second class public accommodation included a Georgian style dining saloon and Jacobean smoking room.

However, the interior design of the Anchor Line's ships changed radically in the 1930s. Whether it was their decorators, Wylie and Lochhead, suggesting the changes to reflect the current trends in liner design, evidenced with the P&O fleet, or it was the Anchor Line management itself is difficult to ascertain. The line went into liquidation in 1935, but an injection of cash from Runciman Ltd created the new company of Anchor Line Ltd and so it was vital that the company rethink its commercial service in order to survive. The Board were made aware by their New York agent, Mr L. G. Carozzi, in June 1938 that: 'Conditions in the States plus war scares in Europe are definitely the cause of the decline in traffic this year' (Anchor Line Directors' Minute Book: 252). The Anchor Line Ltd used various strategies to attract more custom, including underwriting the Glasgow Empire Exhibition in 1938 for £2,500 in the hope that this would attract more passengers. The line also managed the Atlantic Restaurant at the exhibition. The *California* was refitted by the Glasgow-based decorating firm of Wylie and Lochhead in 1938. The change in styling was striking, and the first class smoking room was no longer Tudor but art deco. The half timbering had disappeared, to be replaced by streamlined horizontal bands on a light, veneered background. The red tiling had been replaced by geometrically patterned lino. The stone fireplace and decorative plates were superseded by an art deco grille and minimal surround, with exotic mirror and clock above. The leather and tapestry easy chairs were replaced by deco dining chairs and the Tudor lanterns by streamlined, flush ceiling lights. There was a similar treatment for the other public rooms, including the first class cocktail bar. The *California* transported 474 Scots and 50 Irish to the New York World's Fair in July1939, led by the Mayor of Glasgow. However, in August 1939 the ship was requisitioned by the government for war service. In 1943 the *California* was destroyed by an air attack and torpedoed off Oporto.

This simpler and less ostentatious form of interior design on the ocean liner, twinned with the fashion for outdoor pursuits also informed the design of the Orient Line's iconic ship, *Orion* launched in response to P&O's *Strathnaver* and *Strathaird* in 1935, but supported by a much more effective public relations exercise, which promoted the interior as a pioneer of modern design, under the control of one architect. The main driver behind the realization of the ship was the young Orient Line director, Sir Colin Anderson, who later ensured its enduring success as an emblem of British modernism through his own activities in terms of lectures and published writing (Anderson 1966). The media launch of the ship in August 1935 sowed the seeds for the accepted image of the *Orion* as the pioneer of modern ship design. British shipping companies who introduced new liners to their service would normally lay on a special, short trip on the new ship for journalists and those who had been involved in its creation, including staff of the shipbuilder and the suppliers,

5.2
Smoking Room,
California, **Blue**
Anchor Line,
before 1923.
Source: Glasgow
University Archives
Service

before the liner would undertake its first, long-distance trip. Before the *Orion* under-took its first voyage to Australia, the Orient Line provided a promotional trip from Tilbury to Southampton on 14 August 1935. This was reported in the national press, including *The Times* (17.8.1935) and *The Manchester Guardian* (15.8.1935), plus local papers such as the *North Western Mail* (15.8.1935). Without exception, the news-papers lauded the modern appearance of the interiors, which had superseded the revivalism of the past, all of which was within the control of the architect responsible for their design, Brian O'Rorke. For example, *The Times* correspondent noted:

> With the treatment by Mr. Brian O'Rorke of the new Orient liner Orion, the paradox that a seafaring nation should prefer to deny the sea in its deco-ration has ceased to be. It now seems stranger than ever that Renaissance fireplaces, Louis Quinze lounges, Tudor dining-rooms should ever have been thought suited to a ship, which, however luxurious, is no more respected by the elements than the veriest tramp.
>
> (17.8.1935)

On board were Frank Pick (1879–1941), the manager who brought modernism to the London Underground and who was also the first Chairman of the

5.3
Wylie & Lochhead, Smoking Room, *California*, Blue Anchor Line, after 1938.
Source: Glasgow University Archives Service

Council for Art and Industry in 1934, plus Charles Holden (1875– 1960), the architect for much of London Underground's expansion in the 1930s. Also in attendance was another modernist architect, Howard Robertson (1888–1963), who was to write up his reflections about the experience in one of many reviews of the ship in the *Shipbuilding and Shipping Record* (22.8.1935: 197–200).

Robertson reinforced the notion that the ship's interior was within the control of the architect, Brian O'Rorke (1901–1974) in fitting modern style. However, he found the style a little too simplistic for his tastes:

> Perhaps the cabins are a little 'mannish', in the sense that there are no symptoms of feminine coquetry; but here again one remembers the length of the voyage and the short-lived attractions of excessive archness in furnishing. The *de-luxe* suite is very sane, and not too *de luxe*. One feels, however, that perhaps the various units of furniture might have been assembled into a more sensitive line, in order better to increase the sense of space.
>
> (Robertson 1935: 200).

The *Orion* did receive a mixed reception from the design and shipbuilding press. The short-lived magazine, *Design For To-Day*, was positive about the ship. There were veiled criticisms of the 'Straths' and the *Normandie* in the article, which applauded the Orient Line for not encumbering the ship with false funnels and ornamental masts, of which P&O and G.C.T. were both guilty. The article complimented the Orient Line on the selection of New Zealand architect, Brian O'Rorke, for the interior design of the ship. This ensured uniformity: 'One is spared the shock of passing from a Tudor dining hall to a Moorish Temple, and from thence into a super-Hollywood Grand Hotel. He has not tried to create a floating palace, but has set out to decorate the interior of a ship to the best of his ability. Throughout, Mr O'Rorke has obtained his effects not by elaborate ornamentation, but by the skilful use of lighting, colour and stressing the lines of the ships by means of flush panels' (*Design For To-Day*, 1935b: 381). It may have been coincidental, but *Design For To-Day* was the official monthly magazine of the Design and Industries Association (D.I.A.) from May 1933 until June 1936. Sir Colin Anderson's father and the chairman of the Orient Line had been chairman of the D.I.A. when it was founded in 1915.

In the shipping press, commentators made little distinction between the *Strathmore* and the *Orion* (*Shipbuilding and Shipping Record* 26.12.1935: 712, 715–22) categorizing them both as modern ships. In the design press, the *Orion* was singled out for detailed but mixed reviews. The architect William Tatton-Brown, writing in *Architectural Review* admired the ship, as it demonstrated: 'The significance of the *Orion* is that for the first time a lay architect has collaborated with the naval architect in the design of the passengers' accommodation. Now that he has been let in, there is no doubt, after the success of the Anderson-O'Rorke experiment, that he has come to stay' (1935: 138). This observation was misleading, given the existing history of Cunard working with Peto and Miller, Mewès and Davis with Hamburg-Amerika and so on. However, there was a close working relationship between Anderson and O'Rorke. Anderson deliberately selected a young, relatively inexperienced architect, who he could work with. He did consider Edward Maufe, Oliver Hill, Wells Coates and Chermayeff for the role, but decided on O'Rorke as he was closest to Anderson's age (26) and was not as established as the other contenders (Anderson 1967/9: 451). O'Rorke was designing a house, Ashcombe Tower near Dawlish, for Anderson's friends, the MP Ralph Rayner and his wife Betty, and Anderson made the contact by these means. Anderson was involved in every detail of the design of the ship from its inception, and acted as a link between O'Rorke, the Naval Architect and the Orient Board of Directors.

The modernist poet and founder of *New Verse*, Geoffrey Grigson (1905–85), was less positive about the *Orion*. He was disappointed in the ship's lack of pure modernism: 'My complaint is that *Orion* belongs to the Liberal Party. *Orion* is an agreeable, and sometimes an irritating, compromise' (Grigson 1935: 192).

Perhaps Grigson's analysis was the most accurate, and the *Orion* represented a moment in the gradual movement in style which characterized this period, rather than marking a seismic shift in taste. In the shipping press, commentators made little distinction between the *Strathmore* and the *Orion* (*Shipbuilding and Shipping Record* 26.12.1935: 712, 715–22; *The Syren and Shipping* 1.1.1936: 44–55) categorizing them both as modern ships. What the design of the *Orion* did characterize was a stylistically unified interior, without the display of different period styles, geographic origins or designers. There was one designer working closely with one patron in one style. Moreover, this simpler style was thought by many to represent British national identity as defined in opposition to highly decorative ships, such as the *Normandie*. *The Textile Manufacturer* argued:

> There is no other creation of man which seems to appeal so widely or so deeply as a ship, which we like to think, is most dear to the Anglo-Saxons. With the revival in shipbuilding, there is a new interest, all the keener because rivals in other seafaring countries have in luxury liners challenged British supremacy in shipbuilding, ship design, and sailing.
>
> (September 1935: 14)

Similarly, the travel writer, Robert Byron, commented in *Country Life*: 'It remains to be seen how passengers respond, and how contemporary styles in furniture, fittings and decoration stand up to the wear of ocean voyages. For the moment we can do no more than express a new pride in English communications, and a hope that this pride may be confirmed by similar examples in the future' (31.8.1935: XXIV). When the *Orion* first arrived in Sydney, the reception again reinforced the link between Britishness and simplicity: 'The true significance of the Orion therefore does not lie in its being a luxury liner and a "floating palace" but in its implications as a symbol of Empire. It stands for achievement in the marine engineering and architecture of Great Britain, for faith in development of Australia, and for the bonds which bind the two countries together in Imperial unity . . . Her fittings and furniture avoid the highly ornate and display only that simplicity and refinement which are typical of truly artistic' (*Sydney Morning Herald* 8.11.1935). And the style was not pure modernism, it was a fashionable, British version of modernism, complete with warm woods, patterned rugs and curtains and decorative wall lights.

Like the P&O 'Straths', the *Orion* followed the trend of blurring distinctions between outside and inside. The deck space for games played a significant part in the publicity, appearing on page three of the first class brochure and also in *Design For To-Day, Country Life, Shipbuilding and Shipping Record* and *Architectural Review*. The outdoor pools were also an important aspect of the ship's publicity. Also, like the 'Straths', there were movable glass screens to open interior spaces up to the exteriors. For example, on B deck level the dancing space, at the centre of the ship, could be opened up to merge with the deck and the galleries. Likewise, the glazed screen which separated the swimming pool from the tavern could be slid back to convert the tavern into a bathing verandah. On B deck the first class café was situated astern of the dancing space, which was panelled partly in white and partly in the same soft, sea-green leather as the bucket seats and banquettes. The room featured horizontal metal bands on the white walls and on the four white pillars. At the centre of the room was a circular dome in the ceiling, accentuated by strip lighting. Directly beneath this, on the patterned lino floor, was a circular, dark green geometrically patterned rug by Marion Dorn (1899-1964) who designed moderne rugs for use throughout the first class, public areas. On the wall was a softly modern seascape by Tristram Hillier (1905–1983). Outside the café was the main stairway, which linked the ship's decks and was clad with warm wood and finished with the addition of a geometrically etched mirror on the main landing with fitted, circular clock and metal, streamlined handrail, the lines of which were echoed with three parallel handrails on the walls. Back through the dancing space, passengers could join the promenade deck or the galleries, which lay either side of the engine casing. The galleries were essentially long corridors, which reached some 160 feet to the first class lounge aft. The long space was lined with plywood, with curtained windows looking out onto the deck and mirrors on the facing wall. More Marion Dorn rugs decorate the wooden flooring. The furniture was in light wood with striped upholstery. The library was situated off the galleries, and again featured a Marion Dorn rug, this time decorated with stars and sycamore furniture. The library could double up as a chapel, and doors set into the bookshelves disguised an altar. The two sides of the library could be thrown open to

5.4
Brian O'Rorke, First Class Café, *Orion*, Orient Line, 1935.
Source: P&O

merge into the galleries beyond. At the end of the galleries was the first class lounge. The walls were panelled with cherry mahogany and the two rows of four pillars were in white, with metal banding at the base and top. The banded curtains were by Allan Walton and the eight navy blue rugs by Dorn. An engraved mirror, designed by the illustrator Lynton Lamb, decorated one end of the space. Each of the eight panels depicted an aspect of travelling on air, earth and water and featured amusing vignettes of swimming prawns, Pegasus and cherubs. The first class nursery and tavern were on the deck beneath. The first class dining saloon was located on F deck. It was lined very simply in beige and brown sycamore, with touches of witty decorations including aquamarine glass seahorse wall lights and a mirror engraved to designs by Edward McKnight Kauffer of the figure of Orion. This room had the luxury of being air conditioned, which meant that the ceiling height needed to be lowered. The shop and barber's saloon were faced in metal and plastic, with a nautical decoration in linoleum by Giraldus Richards at the entrance to the shop.

The tourist accommodation was located mainly on F deck towards the stern, and in the opinion of William Tatton Brown: 'On the whole, the most successful rooms are in the Tourist accommodation. The architect has been less anxious to provide the passengers with their money's worth and the result is something fresh, full of vitality and delight' (1935: 134). Geoffrey Grigson accorded with this view: 'The luckiest of *Orion*'s passengers, really, will be in Tourist Class' (1935: 198). Perhaps O'Rorke's spare, undecorated style did lend itself more to the less lavish tourist class spaces. The tourist class dining room was predominately green with yellow and light green bands and silver stars. The tourist class café on the deck above was also plain, with a mural by Giraldus Richards depicting the voyage to Australia in photomontage. Colin Anderson and Brian O'Rorke had found a winning combination for the Orient Line, and used the same design philosophy to decorate the next ship for the England to Australia run, the *Orcades*, completed in 1948.

The successor to the *Orion* was bolder in the use of colour and pattern. For example, the first class lounge was decorated in red, maroon and blue with cedar woodwork with a 14 foot mural by John Armstrong (1893–1973) of horses in a surreal landscape. The tavern used stainless steel and glass with furniture by modern design company PEL. The first class dining room featured a mural by Ceri Richards, representing Neptune watching over the ship in white wood, ribbed steel and glass. O'Rorke used rugs by Marion Dorn again in his schemes, which were again more adventurous in their bold patterns. The tourist class accommodation was again simpler, and perhaps more successful. However, the ship did not attract the same critical attention as its predecessor as modernism in ship interior design by this date was becoming the norm, rather than the exception.

By the late 1930s, modern interiors by professional architects had become the preferred trend, not only of British shipping lines, but entire Western nations too. For example, the *Nieuw Amsterdam* was deliberately modern in design. The interiors were designed by a plethora of Dutch, modern architects and designers, including J.J.P. Oud of the De Stijl movement, as opposed to the more traditional decorating firm of Mutters & Son, which had been responsible for all the major HAL liner interiors from the *Amsterdam* in 1888 onwards. The liner was not built by Harland & Wolff in Belfast, as the majority of its predecessors had been since 1886, but in the Netherlands. The contemporary shipping press noticed this change:

> In planning the decoration and appointment of the passenger spaces of the *Nieuw Amsterdam*, the owners have directed their efforts to the creation in the ship of an atmosphere of refined comfort rather than of ostentatious luxury. This is not to say that the highest standards of modern interior decoration, furnishing and appointment have been in any degree sacrificed. On the contrary, many well-known artist and architects have collaborated to produce some of the most gracious interiors we have seen on shipboard, and the accommodation throughout the vessel bears the stamp of the best modern craftsmanship even in the smallest detail. We venture to predict that the discriminating traveller will find in his surroundings on board the *Nieuw Amsterdam* a pleasant relief from obtrusively lavish interiors with which he is perhaps in some danger of being surfeited.
>
> (*The Shipbuilder and Marine Engine-Builder*
> June 1938: 409–11)

Likewise, *The Studio* described the interior design of the liner as being: '. . . based on the practical and rational planning on which the modern architect prides himself, but it has more than that. It is definitely not a collection of skittishly exuberant and fancy decoration. It has the outstanding advantage of a controlled scheme which combines architecture and decoration together in beautiful unity' (*The Studio* 1938: 6). And HAL's publicity celebrated: 'Artists and architects of the most advanced Netherlands schools of art have co-operated and rivalled with each other in decorating the ship' (HAL *c.*1938: 3).

The national importance of building a prestigious liner as the new flagship for the Holland America Line was confirmed when the Dutch government provided generous subsidies for the building of the ship. The Dutch national effort was further enhanced by the shipbuilding trade union members, who worked on reduced rates to construct this vital and prestigious symbol of Dutch national identity (Dalkmann & Schoonderbeek 1998). At 36,287 gross tons this was the largest ship to be built in Rotterdam at that date, and it could accommodate 1,232 passengers in cabin, tourist and third class – and the 568 passengers in cabin class all enjoyed en suite facilities, the first time that this was offered on a transatlantic service. There were 12 cabins de luxe on the lower promenade deck amidship. Each was decorated in a unique style by a range of eight architects: Mrs Elisabeth de Boer, with Cornelis J. Engelen; Jaap Gidding, Willem H. Gispen, Harry Kammer, Charles Karsten and Ben Merkelbach, and Hendrik Wouda. The cabins were lined with simple, light woods, with well upholstered furniture and art deco occasional tables. Jac F. Semey designed the cabin class dining saloon on A deck, which could seat 427 and was particularly striking with its arched dome, covered with padded gold fabric. The cream walls beneath had a frieze of pink mirrors, punctuated by carvings in teak by Joseph Cantre and decorated with silhouettes by Joep Nicolas. The floor covering was simple, with alternating squares of dark and light blue contrasting nap. The four central pillars which supported the quilted arch were decorated with varnished gold leaf, and the furniture was in satinwood. A tapestry by Christiaan de Moor depicting a rural scene decorated one end of the space. The art deco ceiling lights and shell shaped wall lights were made in Venice from Murano glass. This simple, but glamorous space was in contrast to the library by Hendrik T. Wijdeveld, which was decorated in a neutral black and silver with modern, circular ceiling lights. The circular Ritz-Carlton room, by the same designer, was decorated in white, gold and brown with an oval dance floor. There were coloured aluminium trellises by Willem Niijs and two murals by Han Hulsbergen. Beyond the Ritz-Carlton room was the secluded cocktail bar, in oyster white leather and coromandel wood. Hendrik T. Wijdeveld also designed the Grand Hall on the promenade deck, which was 73 feet long and 52 feet wide with a double deck height. The room was sleek and modern, in silver and grey with glass and stainless steel doors and ceiling by John Raedecker in aluminium. There were curved glass screens in the room, with sand-blasted designs and the 20 large windows were decorated with engraved designs by Charles Eyck. The four pilasters were decorated by Johan Polet with aluminium figures. The use of modern materials was extended to the glass top and stainless steel base tables.

The De Stijl architect J.J.P. Oud designed the cabin class swimming pool and smoking room and lounge for tourist class. In the tourist class lounge, Oud designed striking, large circular windows, complemented by circular lighting and simple furniture. Overall, the ship's interiors are in the modern style, sleek and simple with a confidence that this is an appropriate reflection of Dutch national identity, which was well received in the shipping and design press.

By contrast, within the discourse of design criticism, the *Queen Mary* was not being positively received. Supposedly lacking the modernist design credentials of the *Orion*, the history of the *Queen Mary* is best known for its rejection of modern paintings by Duncan Grant and refusal of Stanley Spencer's mural depicting riveters from the Clydeside shipbuilding yards (Hughes-Stanton, C. nd: 26–7). Contemporary commentators, including Clive Bell in the *Listener* and *The Architect and Building News*, were critical of the ship's interiors, the latter commenting: 'The general effect is one of mild but expensive vulgarity' (*The Architect and Building News* 1936: 240). Cecil Beaton, writing for *Vogue* concurred: 'The decorations have a monotony without uniformity – there is too much woodwork. The effort at being modern is decidedly forced' (Beaton 1936) The special correspondent for *The Times* commented:

> It is early yet to assess one's impressions of a ship which is still something to be looked at rather than to be lived in. A tour of the ship suggests that, although each of her talented decorators has been more rather than less

successful in their own vein, the inevitable lack of homogeneity precluded unity of atmosphere. All concerned, however, seem agreed that, whatever else the interior of a ship should be made to look like, it must in no circumstances suggest the interior of a ship. In converging from labyrinthine depths of magnificence on to the deck, the temptation to exclaim *Thalassa, Thalassa* is overwhelming.

(The Times: 27.5.1936: 16)

The *Queen Mary*'s blend of luxury, tradition and hint of contemporaneity has been well documented (Walmsley 1991, 2004). In addition, the design of the ship needs to be considered within the broader, historical context of ocean liner design. It was designed as a direct repost to the art deco splendours of the *Normandie* and to regain the Blue Riband for Britain. As such, Cunard attempted to emulate the success of the showcase interior design of the *Normandie*, but lacked the cachet of French art deco. The commissioning and execution of the interior decoration followed the blueprint laid down by Cunard from the time of the inception of the *Mauretania* and *Lusitania*, when the line first employed an architect. Moreover, the ship was constructed as a national symbol which would attract the wealthiest clients and, as such, avant garde modern design was not appropriate to the image of the ship. As Raymond Mortimer argued in 1936 in the *Listener* over the rejection of Duncan Grant's work:

> For my part I think the mistake was not so much to reject the pictures as ever to commission them.
>
> A super-luxury transatlantic liner depends largely on the patronage of international film stars, financiers and opera singers, and their taste is presumably reflected in the international style of decoration which they find in the palatial hotels all over the world from Palm Beach to the Lido. I cannot think that such persons would take much notice of Mr Grant's panels, and it would obviously have been unwise not to give them what they prefer.
>
> (As quoted in Lacey 1973: 56)

Even the ' . . . modified Millionaire Land' of the *Orion* was not deemed appropriate for the design of such an important national symbol as the *Queen Mary* (Grigson 1935: 194).

When Cunard was looking for an appropriate style for the *Queen Mary*'s sister ship, the *Queen Elizabeth* in 1936, Cunard's Chairman, Sir Percy Bates (1879–1946) visited the *Orion* but found:

> The ship is essentially designed and decorated as a hot weather ship and everything had been subordinated to giving an effect of coolness. The decoration has been reduced almost to a minimum and is mostly carried out in veneered plywood . . . The general style is I think, too plain for an Express Atlantic steamer and would be considered mean by many of our

passengers. . . . The furniture in the ship looks cheaper and simpler than ours . . .

(Percy Bates in Memo to Lord Brocklebank,
14 September 1936)

It was Sir Percy Bates who took ultimate responsibility for the design of the interiors of the *Queen Mary*. The design vision for the ship lacked clarity from the outset. The uniformity offered by historic period styling, art deco or the modern was absent. What the Cunard Board, led by Sir Percy, were seeking was an appropriate architect to produce a fitting style to represent the country and attract passengers, knowing what they didn't want but unclear about what they did want. The architect selected for this challenging project was Arthur Davis, who had designed the interiors of the *Aquitania* for Cunard before the First World War. Unfortunately, his erstwhile partner, Charles Mewès had died in 1914, partly as a result of his punishing work schedule. It was agreed that Davis should work with New York based architect, B.W. Morris, of Morris & Connor. Morris was a friend of Bates, and was appointed as advisor to him. He had also designed the New York offices of Cunard. Davis wrote to Cunard on 23 September 1931 outlining the agreement: 'That Mr Morris and myself should act as joint architects, in co-operation with your company's representatives and decoration experts in the production of this scheme' (Cunard 23.9.1931). The Furnishing Department, and Ernest Leach, its Superintendent, however, saw Cunard's role as rather more central. They did not wish to mirror the practice of land based building, where the architect supervised the decorators and proposed: '. . . the specialist interior designer often of high qualifications, measured by the standard of such organisations as the Royal Society of Arts, is usually without Architectural qualifications. It is imagined that the Company is not prepared to take sides in this perennial dispute but will adhere to the policy of forming, as it were, a reserve set of designs' (Cunard 14.9.1931: 4). Friction between Davis and Morris, and Davis's successor, J.C. Whipp, as the joint architects, and between themselves and the Cunard employees characterised the process of the fitting out of the *Queen Mary*. Ultimately, the power lay with the Cunard Board, and Sir Percy Bates in particular, as to what the ship should be like. His intent was to build a ship with: '. . . no thought of boastfulness or thought of megalomania', adding that it was '. . . a ship of peace' (*The Times*: 1.6.1936). This perhaps reflects the growing international, maritime rivalries which would eventually contribute to the outbreak of the Second World War in 1939.

The ship was commissioned in 1930, and John Brown Ltd was selected as the shipbuilder. In keeping with the history of ship interior design at Cunard, the selection of the interior design and suitable architects began after the construction of the ship had been initiated. Davis, appointed in 1931, looked at other ships for inspiration and to gauge the competition. Upon appointment he asked to view the *Empress of Britain* and also crossed the channel on the *Bremen* and the *Europa*. Earlier in 1931 Morris had visited Britain and consulted with leading figures in the art world about suitable artists to commission for work on the new ship. Kenneth Clarke, then director of the National Gallery, suggested McKnight Kauffer; Grey Wornum of the RIBA, James Woodford, Morris Lambert, George Ramon, Bainbridge Copnall, Jan Juta and Norman Forest; Frank Pick suggested Stephen Bone whilst the modern art dealer, Dudley Tooth, was the most adventurous, putting forward the names of British modernists such as Duncan Grant, Rex Whistler, Paul Nash, Edward Wadsworth and Stanley Spencer (Southampton City Art Gallery 1986: 5). Morris and Davis met in London in September 1931 to agree on a working arrangement. They firmly rejected plans already submitted by various decorating firms, who were appropriately compensated for their work. The firms were then invited to tender for the decorating work, which was to be agreed by Morris and Davis. However, the control they attempted to exercise was to be undermined by circumstances, most notably Davis's long-term illness, and by Cunard themselves.

In December 1931 work was halted on the construction of the *Queen Mary*, known as Job Number 534 at this early stage. Thousands of men were laid off at John Brown's, as, due to the Depression, Cunard had problems raising sufficient finances from the banks. Work was not to resume until April 1934, after Cunard had managed to secure a loan from the British government of three million pounds to complete Number 534, a further £1.5 million as capital for the new company and a further £5 million for the construction of a sister ship for the *Queen Mary*. The new company that had been formed under government pressure was a merger between Cunard and the ailing White Star Line. Work on the hull resumed in April 1934 for the new Cunard White Star Line. Despite the interruption in construction, work on the interior design appears to have continued, with Morris supplying the design ideas and Davis translating these into drawings until July 1932, with a hiatus in 1933 and resumption in May 1934. A meeting was held in Mewès & Davis's office at 1, Old Burlington Street on 31 May 1934 to finalize plans, which was attended by Davis and Whipp representing the architects, and Brockelbank, Leach and Barnard for Cunard. Davis reported: '. . . coming back after two and a half years interval, developments had taken place in decoration since that time. Everything tended to more and more simplicity and that Mr. Morris had agreed with him that it would be an advantage to eliminate much of the unnecessary details' (Cunard D42/C3/ 400/P.19: 3). In the same meeting, the employment of Frank Pick was considered, who was then preparing the British Art and Industry exhibition at Burlington House, due to open in the autumn. However, time was running out for the interior design of the ship, and the original plans were moderated and modernized, rather than reworked to reflect contemporary modernism.

The Cunard Board agreed a fee of $10,000 for Morris for the design of the public rooms at a meeting of 26 November 1934. The drawings then had to be approved by the Naval Architect's office, the furnishing department, the shipbuilding committee and then Sir Percy Bates himself, before being sent on to John Brown & Company (Walmsley 2004: 160). In February 1935 Cunard agreed that Morris should play a more central role in the execution of the designs, and return to Britain in April; meanwhile Leach was to supervise the work in hand.

A letter from Arthur Davis in 1932 describes his suggestions for the design of the smoking room. Davis argued that an Early Jacobean style, as seen on the *Viceroy of India*, would not be appropriate:

> Personally, I believe that, in this room it would be wise to break away from the modern spirit, which is so skilfully introduced in all the other spaces, and to decide frankly on a Smoking Room which would be of high standard in style – which although traditional – would be in harmony with the general character of the remainder of the first class accommodation. If this suggestion is accepted, I would select a treatment in a late English style, in which large plain surfaces and panels similar to those in other parts of the ship would carry the same scale throughout.
>
> I think Mr Morris's choice of the well known Bromley-by-Bow model is somewhat unfortunate. These early Elizabethan styles are no longer in favour as they demand a very elaborate and rather overdecorated treatment, which no longer fits in with modern ideas. On the other hand some of the later styles – the Charles II and the William and Mary – are eminently suitable for a Smoking Room and would not show a violent contrast with the modern decoration of the other rooms.
>
> (Cunard 4.3.1932)

The *Queen Mary* was launched in September 1934 and transferred to the fitting out dock, and this was when conflicts over the decoration of the ship really began. Davis had been taken ill late in 1934, and could no longer fulfil the role of, what was essentially, project manager for the decoration of the ship. A colleague of Arthur Davis, J.C. Whipp, was drafted in to oversee the fitting out process in January 1935. The Cunard Board agreed that Morris should play a more central role, and Morris travelled backwards and forwards between New York and London. This activity gave him extra insights into the expectations of the potential passengers for the *Queen Mary*. On 27 April 1935 he wrote from the Carlton Hotel in London to Cunard's Secretary, Flewitt, having just travelled from New York on the *Majestic*: '. . . it would seem to me that sofas should be included in order to keep abreast of competition in conversations with a number of American travellers, of particular tastes and of means, indicated a frame of mind that insists on luxury and every convenience particularly when an extra price is paid' (Cunard 27.4. 1935: 2–3).

However, Morris could not sustain the effort of transatlantic travel by ship, and so Whipp became the dominant power in the process of decorating the *Queen Mary*. Morris became increasingly frustrated as his ideas were not realized and an obvious lack of design co-ordination began to prevail. In a memo from Morris of June 1935, he told Cunard that he was not able to remain in Britain indefinitely, and suggested that the furnishing department work with the various interior decorating firms to hasten completion of the interiors of the ship, which was scheduled for December 1935. Morris suggested that Mr Redding of White Allom & Co. be approached, as his experience of their work for the Waldorf-Astoria in New York was positive (Cunard 14. 6. 1935: 1).

However, the suggestion was not taken up and, as Morris's influence began to wane, that of Whipp was on the ascendance. This was confirmed in August 1935, when S.J. Pigott, the chief liaison from John Brown & Co, wrote to Bates: 'We feel much concerned as to the progress being made with the other decorative features represented by the remaining two-thirds of the total allocated sum, and of the effect which any delay with these items will have on the completion of the Public Rooms. . . . I think it possible that you may consider that some modification of the present arrangements such as decentralisation of similar lines to that now adopted with the electrical fittings would serve to expedite the work generally' (Cunard 24.8.1935: 1). A memo from the naval architect, Paterson, to Flewitt, of 27 August 1935 was the final confirmation: 'In order to ensure that the decorative work in the First Class may be of a harmonious character and be completed in accordance with the Schedule as laid down by the Builders, we consider it to be essential that the handling of the whole of the design work, including the designs of furniture, carpets etc. should forthwith be centred in Messrs. Mewès & Davis' Office under the direction of Mr. Whipp' (Cunard 27.8.1935: 1). As Walmsley has demonstrated, Whipp was far more conservative than Morris, and succeeded in overruling many of his design ideas (Walmsley 2004: 165). For example, he expressed concern about the employment of Vanessa Bell to advise on the first class lounge: 'The suggestion that Mrs Vanessa Bell should design the carpets and curtains and direct the general colour scheme of this room gives me serious concern' (Cunard 9.9.1935). Duncan Grant and Vanessa Bell had been invited to advise on the decoration of the lounge and drawing room in May 1935. They both travelled to Liverpool in September 1935 to make their initial selections upon the invitation of Leach. Grant and Bell's suggestions were then quietly dropped, probably due to Whipp's aversion to their work. When Morris heard that Duncan Grant's paintings for the first class main lounge had been rejected, he wrote immediately to the artist: 'I was greatly distressed to hear from Liverpool just before the receipt of your cable that your panels for the Main Lounge have been rejected . . . owing to the fact that none of the details of the completion of the decorative work on the ship are under my direction, you will realize, I feel sure, that I can not do very much unless my advice is requested by the Committee' (Cunard 24.2.1936).

Duncan Grant had been commissioned to paint two large, overmantel paintings in the first class main lounge for £300 each and one painting at £650 to be placed on the forward wall in the same space (Cunard 27.5.1935). Grant had worked on the canvases throughout the summer of 1935, but they were rejected by Bates in the autumn of 1935.

Leach wrote to Duncan Grant on 21.9.1935:

> My Directors have been reviewing the present situation concerning the company's Commitment with painters for the "QUEEN MARY" and I have been instructed to modify and cancel these agreements, as may be necessary, to bring them into line with a definite policy.

> It is felt that too high a proportion of the murals would appeal only to a limited coteries interested in the development of modern painting, and this condition must be changed to provide these pictures with wider general appeal.
>
> A great deal of apprehension has also been expressed concerning the scale of the figures in your sketches and, indeed, concerning the choice of subject at all – Lambert, you will remember, has provided us with a couple of dozen female figures, and there appears to be a case for some change in the paintings.
>
> (Cunard D42/C3/430)

The problem with the paintings was both their modern, Fauvist style, in bright colours and loose brushwork and their subject matter, which was large, female nudes or semi-naked women. Grant was informed of the decision not to include his panels in February 1936 by Leach, who wrote to Bates: 'I am tremendously relieved at your decision about the pictures in the Lounge. I thought the one I saw was simply appalling', although Grant was devastated by the news (10.2.1936: Cunard D42/C3/ 430). The panels were eventually returned to Grant and exhibited at his dealer's, Agnews, in 1937.

The ship finally joined Cunard White Star Line's service in May 1936 and won the Blue Riband from the *Normandie* on its sixth round trip in August, traversing the Atlantic from New York to the coast of England in 3 days, 23 hours and 57 minutes. Therefore, one of the government and Cunard's main ambitions was realized. The ship represented a country which could achieve impressive technical feats, with the construction of a ship which measured over 1,000 feet with a gross tonnage of 80,733 and world beating engines, which could achieve phenomenal speed of 28.5 knots. The efficiency of the *Queen Mary* helped to realize Cunard White Star's ambition of offering a transatlantic service with two ships, rather than the three that currently offered a service: *Aquitania, Mauretania* and *Berengaria*. The ship's interior decoration represented a blend of art deco, modernism and British traditional whimsy. Cunard White Star's official brochure for the American market was designed with an art deco representation of the hull of the *Queen Mary* in gold, placed on a faux wood background. The brochure opened with a celebration of: '. . . British tradition in its influence of pleasant living, the British tradition is manifold. It is this which tempers London's gayety by a racial flair for correctness . . . which adds to the pleasures of today, by the contrast of age-old custom . . . which makes modern luxury warm and inviting, by the intuitive deftness of the true British servant' (Cunard White Star Line 1937: 3). These were interiors which represented a nation at the start of its decline as an Imperial power. As Sarah Crellin has argued:

> However, by the sterling crisis of 1931 it was clear that the natural as opposed to symbolic centre of the world economy was New York, and American influences on management structures and headquarters' grandeur were crucial to the development of buildings like Imperial

Chemicals house and Unilever House. Business rationalisation and the development of the empire as a free-trade area to rival the United States were taken seriously in the 1920s and 1930s for fear of a serious decline in Britain's status and economy.

(Crellin 200?: 89)

Previously, British liners had plundered the past to roll out a display inspired by tradition and achievement. The *Queen Mary* was the first Cunard ship not to employ past styles, and marked an attempt to represent the nation with woods from the British Empire and a mixture of American art deco with homely or lyrical, British touches; the line christened it: '. . . the ship of beautiful woods' (Cunard White Star Line 1937: 1). Sir Percy Bates was astute commercially, and his involvement of an American architect in the designs reflected the need for the company to attract the 80% of transatlantic passengers who were American, with American friendly design. But the American traveller was no longer the millionaire class of the Edwardian era, but glamorous Hollywood film stars and business tycoons. Whilst the French succeeded in achieving this aim by producing the *Normandie*, which showcased the best of French design, Britain did not have the same unified sense of identity in design by the mid-1930s, and the influence of American art deco combined with a hangover from British traditions in ship design, characterized the appearance of the *Queen Mary* interiors, perhaps reflecting the partnership of Morris and Davis.

The cabin class entrance hall on the main deck was in sleek, art deco style with sombre, wood panelling of the walls and dark, striped Korkoid on the floor. There were two anodized aluminium reliefs by Maurice Lambert (1901–64), a British sculptor who had been recommended by the architect, Grey Wornum, who combined acceptable modernism with fashionable overtones and adventurous materials. The panels were placed on the traditional wood panelling, on the theme of 'Speed and Progress' – a motif which was to feature on the cabin class menu cards, printed on board. One showed an aeroplane outpacing Pegasus and the other an express train speeding ahead of a galloping centaur. Impressively executed, these two pieces of 1930s décor summarize perfectly the tensions on board the *Queen Mary*. The reliefs are figurative but stylized to some degree, to reflect art deco fashion. They portray the traditional juxtaposed with the technologically advanced. The images manage to hold the tension between modernity and tradition successfully, but this balancing act was not so elegantly handled in the interior design of the ship throughout.

The ship was designed to carry three classes of passenger – the first class was replaced by the new cabin class; the equivalent of second class was the tourist class, and then third class. Although the names had changed, all three classes were kept rigidly apart, as had always been the case with the interior arrangements of ocean liners. The cabin class occupied the premium parts of the ship with 421 cabin class suites. On the very top deck, or sun deck, was placed an area for games at the stern with the exclusive verandah grill looking out onto it, the decks below and the ocean beyond. This served as the *Queen Mary*'s à la carte restaurant, cocktail bar

5.5
Maurice Lambert, Speed and Progress, *Queen Mary*, Cunard, 1936.
Source: Author's collection

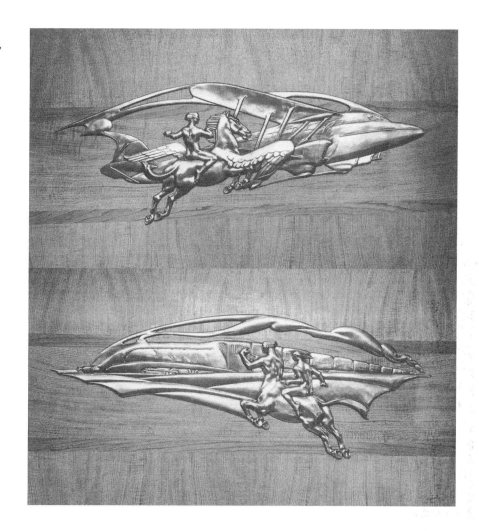

and nightclub which required advance booking for which passengers paid an extra charge of £1. It was a small space, only 29 feet wide and 70 feet long, but the sweep of 22 windows on three sides of the room added a sense of spaciousness. The room's outré atmosphere was enhanced by not only its position, but also its design. This was overseen by the painter and designer, Doris Clare Zinkeisen (1898–1991), a glamorous figure in her own right. She designed costumes for the stage and later for Hollywood, and she and her sister were fashionable figures in London society. Her self-portrait, *Mrs Graham Johnstone* (1929) shows an exotic figure in brightly coloured, Spanish shawl, sleek, jet black hair and vivid red lips. She had been suggested for the job by Morris in a letter to Cunard in June 1935: 'I believe for business reasons it is highly desirable that cultivated feminine thought should have expression, if it can be done in a practical way. For example, it would seem that Miss Doris Zinkeisen (Mrs. Graham Johnstone) or Miss Pinder-Davis have many of the desired qualifications' (Cunard 14.6.1935: 3).

5.6

**Madame Yevonde,
Doris Zinkeisen
painting verandah
grill,** *Queen Mary,*
1936.

Source: Lawrence N.
Hole.

In his 'Partial Inspection of Queen Mary, Cabin Class Accommodations as of June 23, 1936' Morris commented favourably on this room: Very good except for exaggeration of size in electric bowls on the pillars' (Cunard 23.6.1936: 4). This may have been a veiled criticism of Whipp, who had been responsible for the lighting on the ship. The other aspects of the room were overseen by Zinkeisen, and demonstrate a glamour and a unity which perhaps were missing from other spaces on the ship. The walls of the verandah grill were not in panelled wood, as was the case with most of the rest of the *Queen Mary*, but hand painted by the artist with figurative, vaguely erotic scenes of the circus, theatre and the pantomime framed in silver and gold; the largest canvas was situated behind the stage. The floor was covered in black Wilton carpet at the designer's insistence and surrounded a small dance floor in sycamore parquet. The chairs were painted cream with white upholstery, and crisp white linen covered the intimate tables, designed for two. The dance floor was overlooked by the main, raised dining area and separated from it by a streamlined metal balustrade with tinted, etched glass. The balustrade and newels were also illuminated and the colours of the lights could be changed to reflect the rhythm of the music. The windows were dressed with decorative, tasselled curtains in dark red, adorned with gold stars and the ceiling echoed the shape of the dance floor with concealed lighting. The colour scheme for the ceiling and the pilasters was silver etched in gold. White Allom was the decorating firm responsible for the room.

The promenade deck below contained the majority of the cabin class social space, and some tourist class. The designated tourist class area was segregated at the stern end, with the dome over the lounge below and then the tourist class smoking room, flanked by two promenades. The smoking room floor was covered with Korkoid, an amalgam of rubber and cork which was used throughout the ship as a practical and hard wearing flooring, which could be produced in different designs and colours. In this case, it was divided in alternating bands of black, cream and burnt sienna. Geometrically patterned rugs were used throughout, to attempt to create an informal atmosphere in a rather gloomy space, not helped by the low ceiling. The seating was art deco, with bucket style seats and the more traditional armchairs and settees. There was acknowledgement of Cunard's past, with an evocative painting of the *Mauretania* on her last journey to be broken up at Rosyth, by the first president of the Society of Naval Artists, Charles Pears (1873–1958). Placed above the electric fireplace, the painting showed the ship against the silhouette of the Forth Bridge, black smoke emitting from her four funnels and heavy tracts of rust running down from the anchors. The room was panelled in linenfold style oak, with Indian padouk, gold inserts and pilasters lined with walnut.

The remainder of the promenade deck was devoted to cabin class, separated from the tourist class by locked doors. The first space was the cabin class smoking room: '. . . that citadel of male conviviality . . .' (Cunard White Star Line 1937: 12), which encapsulated the heterogeneous styling on board the *Queen Mary*. The room was panelled in dark oaks and walnuts with a highly reflective, smooth surface. The wood panelling which was so prevalent on the ship appears to have been Morris's idea. In a letter to Cunard of 12 July 1934, at the start of the project, he described: 'The large areas of natural woods throughout the room will produce a warm and somewhat restrained colour scheme . . . I think it is safe to predict that architects and artists as well as the general public will find in the "Queen Mary" pleasing qualities of functional design – beauty that is more than decorative and that does not become outmoded, because it is the beauty of logic' (Cunard 12.7.1934: 2). The ceiling's main feature was the domed central section, which gave the room 22 feet in height. The upholstery of the furniture was rather more daring, with arm-chairs and sofas in striped red and cream or dark and light blue hide. The more upright chairs which were placed around the card tables were upholstered in red, green and beige striped fabric, which toned in with the striped curtains. On either side of the fireplace were carved screens in limewood by James Woodford depicting marine life in Eric Gill style. Woodford also designed the bronze uplighters which lined the edge of the dome, and featured playing card 'jokers', almost like gargoyles, looking down at the smokers beneath. It is indicative of how little in control Morris was of the project when he commented in 1936: 'Very successful except for exces-sively heavy electric light buckets beneath the sculptured figures representing playing cards. They are a great detriment to the room and I hope they may be rectified' (Cunard 23.6.1936: 3). Amidst this traditional setting were two works by erstwhile Vorticist, Edward Wadsworth (1889–1949), which hung at either end of the room. 'Dressed Overall At Sea' was the more conventional, and hung over the coal burning fireplace. It featured a sailing ship in harbour with an ocean liner on the horizon and belies the naval inspiration apparent in Wadsworth's work throughout his career. 'The Sea' was more controversial, as it was a surrealist arrangement of pillar, shells, pennants and Georgio De Chirico mask. Indeed, Wadsworth was in correspondence with this Italian metaphysical artist during this time. The still life formed part of a developing series by Wadsworth of mysterious still lifes with a nautical theme. This large canvas attracted the most criticism of any artwork on board.

Adjacent to the smoking room was the ballroom or tea dance room, measuring 35 feet by 50 feet. This again attempted to mix American glamour with British whimsy. The dance floor was in oak parquet with a border of sycamore, pear tree and laurel. On one side was a raised dais for the use of a small orchestra, and on the other a place to set out refreshments. These were separated from the main floor by means of a metalwork banister with a pink hide handrail. The lighting was art deco, with a central light over the dance floor with a base of sandblasted, peach glass. The chairs were upholstered in quilted satin, the curtains were in appliquéd satin and the tables were decoratively veneered. The English whimsy was supplied by back-lit, glass panels designed by Jan Juta around the room. The panels featured ornate vases of flowers, and birds in decorative cages with plumes and tassels. The corners of the room were decorated by Anna Zinkeisen with mythological figures, loosely representing the four seasons. On one side of the ballroom was the long gallery and on the other the starboard gallery with the covered promenade for cabin class beyond. The starboard gallery provided an anteroom for the ballroom. The long, rectangular space was lined with dark, laurel wood which toned in well with the brown patterned Wilton carpet. There was a fireplace at each end of the room, above which hung an inoffensive painting of flowers by Cedric Morris. This provided a sharp contrast to three art deco panels on the inboard wall by animal sculptor John Skeaping (1901–80) which depicted leaping deers in gold and silver relief. The length of the room was accentuated by a central, illuminated panel on the white ceiling which carried circular, art deco lights. Access to the ballroom could also be gained port side with the 118 foot, long gallery. Here there are large, English landscapes by Bertram Nicholls ('A Sussex Landscape') and Algernon Newton ('Evening on the Avon') juxtaposed with Betula wood and metal, art deco standard lights. Traditional armchairs in geometric upholstery sit on art deco rugs, and darkly panelled walls almost jar with floor-length curtains.

Leading on from the long gallery was the cabin class main lounge. This was virtually a square room, measuring 96 feet by 70 feet, subdivided into a higher, central oblong with galleries either side. The space was further articulated with a row of ceiling lights on the higher ceiling, complemented by circular windows at clerestory height. At one end of the central space was a large, raised, fully equipped stage, with a fireplace at the other end. Above the stage was a stylized group of singers and musicians entitled 'Symphony' by Maurice Lambert, who also created bronze panels over the doors.

The colour scheme of the room was the familiar brown, with maple burr panelling and dark green and grey, Wilton carpet runners and rugs in art deco style. The fireplaces were made from onyx and had dark, alabaster floor lights on either side. The tables by Waring & Gillow were made from maple burr to match the walls, and the chairs had curved walnut backs. The room was an uneasy mix of lounge, cinema and theatre decorated in art deco with incongruous maple burr.

The shopping centre further aft of the lounge was more harmonious, using art deco styling and light to achieve a streamlined, glamorous effect, decorated by Waring & Gillow. The mall ran 90 feet from the main staircase between the first and second funnels. The walls and pillars were panelled in oak, chestnut and elm burr. The flooring was in Korkoid in marble effect, light green, dark green and yellow decorative bands. These were echoed in the flow of the elm burr pillars and metal which supported a stepped, white ceiling which had concealed lighting in the soffits and uniform, circular ceiling lights. There were three shops. The main central store panelled in Indian silver greywood banded in Indian laurel was occupied by upmarket, menswear retailers, Austin Reed. A decorative frieze by Maurice Lambert ran the 50 feet around the top of the curved shop frontage, based on the theme of sport and speed, created in plaster and then treated with wax to give the appearance of ivory. W. H. Smith occupied the starboard shop, panelled in makore, and a souvenir and tobacco shop, run by Cunard, was panelled in cedar. Quality, luxury goods such as jewellery were displayed in 24-carat gold and silver framed showcases. There were also dark wooden bucket seats, upholstered in ivory fabric with occasional tables, which again toned in with the overall design of the space. The more conventionally

5.7
Cunard, First Class Sitting Room, *Queen Mary*, 1936.
Source: Author's collection

styled drawing room and library were located port and starboard of the shops. The drawing room could double as a space for religious worship, and housed a large altarpiece, with a painting of the 'Madonna of the Atlantic' by Kenneth Shoesmith (1890–1939) on a gold leaf background. The painting was normally concealed behind another painting by Shoesmith of a harbour scene. Further aft from this area was the children's room and then the observation lounge and cocktail bar. The cocktail bar has become known as: '. . . one of the most architecturally cohesive of the *Queen Mary*'s great public rooms' (Steele 1995: 127). However, Morris was not in agreement:

> Colour a little strong and not in subtle harmony with the beautiful veneer on walls; reds on pillars, electric fixtures and stools not quite in harmony with each other – would be better subdued, and the strong colours omitted altogether from pillars and electric fixtures. Design of table tops and their colours not very pleasing; curved bar very good; vertical pilasters at ends a little dark: figures in Thompson's picture too many and too small, and his colour scheme disappointing.
>
> (Cunard 23.6.1936: 2)

The strong colour Morris referred to so critically was the bright red chosen for the pillars, uplighters, the Formica of the bar top, the hide upholstery of the bar stools and arc framing the bar. The curved bar was the focal point of the room and was panelled in Macassar ebony with metal bands accentuating its form. These deco features were contrasted with the painting by A. R. Thompson above the bar, which showed a circle of figures, hand in hand, celebrating King George V's silver jubilee. The bar looked out across the ocean and the bow of the ship.

Near the observation lounge was the main staircase which led down to the main deck where the special cabin class suites were located. The special cabins each had their own bedroom, sitting room and bathroom and were individually designed. They were panelled in light, Honduras mahogany, deal, bird's eye maple and Canadian birch with ivory satin curtains and bedspread with fitted carpets. These elite passengers had the choice of hot or cold, fresh or sea water, in their baths and showers. The standard cabin class accommodation was situated on decks A and B. A supplementary tourist class lounge was also located on A deck. In simple, art deco style with Canadian birch panelling banded in metal, the most striking feature of the room was a large panel in sprayed nickel by Rebel Stanton. It featured a naked, kneeling female figure in profile with arms outstretched, looking up at the large clock above her. The main tourist class lounge was on the main deck and included a parquet dance floor 33 feet by 28 feet. There was a stage at one end of the room and the lounge, like its cabin class equivalent, could be converted into a cinema. The colour scheme was green, cream and black and there was art work by Margot Gilbert, including a series of painted leather panels inspired by the history of dance. The tourist class passengers, whose 300 cabins were located on decks A to E, could only use sea water in their bathrooms, although 80% did have en suite facilities. There was less wood in evidence in the decoration of these cabins, which contained a range of

single beds to sleep two, three or four passengers. The 214 third class cabins featured bunks in cramped rooms with no en-suite.

5.8
Waring & Gillow, Shopping Arcade, Queen Mary, 1936.
Source: Author's collection

The dining rooms for all three classes were on C deck. The cabin class restaurant was located in the centre of the ship to provide the calmest conditions whilst crossing the Atlantic ocean: it measured 118 by 160 feet with a variable ceiling height, which rose to over 30 feet and three decks in the centre. This huge space could seat 800 at once. The ceiling and lighting treatment were reminiscent of the lounge, with the central atrium lit extravagantly with art deco ceiling lights. The wood panelling was in three shades of peroba, punctuated by reflective, metal bands. The soffits were illuminated to accentuate the stepped ceiling. The floor was covered in brown and gold Korkoid. The focal point of the room was Macdonald Gill's 15 by 24 foot decorative map, which indicated the location of the ship in the Atlantic by means of a crystal model. At the opposite end of the room was a painting entitled 'Merry England' which reached from floor to ceiling, by Philip Connard (1875–1958) showing pheasants in an English, country setting. In the centre of the painting was a bronze door by Walter and Donald Gilbert featuring a range of mythical and nautical episodes. Walter Gilbert had been a leading figure in the Bromsgrove Guild of Applied Arts before the First World War, and had been involved in the design of the *Mauretania*. He then joined the craft firm of H.H. Martyn & Co. in 1919 and moved to their workshops in Cheltenham. From this base H.H. Martyn & Co. became a major fitter and decorator of British liners, including the *Queen Mary* and new *Mauretania* of 1939.

There were more birds featured in panels on the side walls by A. Duncan Carse: 'Birds of the Old World' and 'Birds of the New World' on a background of silver leaf. Fourteen, modestly sized carved panels on the theme of 'Ships through the Ages' by Bainbridge Copnall decorated the walls. Copnall had originally submitted a sample panel of much larger dimensions, which was rejected by Sir Thomas Brocklebank as too overpowering. He: '. . . generally endorsed the opinion that the unlimited freedom which had been given to various Artists to suggest alterations not properly within their sphere should be restrained to more reasonable limits and that the definition of these shall remain with this Office and Mr. Leach' (Cunard D42/C3/400/P19, 25.7.1935: 2). The chairs were in sycamore and upholstered in deep pink fabric. In addition to the main restaurant area, there were four private dining rooms leading from each corner of the main restaurant, one contained the painting 'The Mills Circus' by Dame Laura Knight, another Vanessa Bell's post impressionist painting of a garden scene, viewed through an open window. These two paintings, although tucked away out of sight, are more modern and accord more successfully with the wood panelling and deco lighting of the rooms. The third contained a conventional, floral still life by H. Davis Richter.

The tourist class dining room was of similar width to that of cabin class, but only 78 feet in length with a consistent ceiling height of only 8 feet 6 inches. The room was decorated by Waring & Gillow in a spare, art deco style without the added status of specially commissioned works of art. Wood panelling was still employed, in this case, a light ash burr dado with a lighter, silver-grey blistered maple on the upper parts of the walls. The floor was covered in Korkoid tiling in grey with a black, white and pink linear pattern running though it. The chairs were sycamore and the upholstery rose. The room could seat 400. The majority of the third class accommodation was placed near the bow of the ship, so these passengers suffered the most when the ship hit heavy seas. The public rooms provided were fewer in number and often had to fulfil more than one purpose. For example, there was no library and so books were placed in the lounge on B deck. No swimming pool was provided for third class.

Further down again, on D deck was the cabin class swimming pool in cream tiling, banded with green and red with *faux* mother of pearl ceiling. The tourist class pool was further aft on the F deck, and was plainer and squatter with some decoration afforded by three etched glass panels on marine themes, including that of an aquarium by Charles Cameron Baillie.

The *Queen Mary* remained a popular liner, undertaking stalwart service as a troop ship during the Second World War, and only being withdrawn from Cunard White Star's service in 1967, destined to sail to Long Beach, California where it still functions as a hotel and conference venue. In contrast, the *Normandie* was destroyed by fire in New York in 1940, perhaps adding to her glamorous allure as a fated, tragic beauty. The companion ship to the *Queen Mary*, the *Queen Elizabeth*, was designed once the problems with the heterogeneous design of its predecessor were realized. Frank Pick (1878–1941) had been instrumental in developing a modern corporate identity for London Underground; he was founder member of the D.I.A. and founding Chairman of the Council for Art and Industry (C.A.I.) in 1932. He had attempted to pressure Cunard to take C.A.I. advice on the design of the *Queen Mary*, but failed (Walmsley 2004: 161–2). As early as June 1936 Pick wrote to Sir Thomas

Brocklebank, suggesting Charles Holden as architect for the new Cunard liner. Holden had already designed underground stations for Pick, and was working on the new London University site in Bloomsbury for what would be Senate House:

> I quite agree that the Council is not a body which could, in fact, undertake the work of designing the decoration and completing a ship, and I would like to suggest for your consideration, now, that you should appoint Mr Charles Holden as the Architect for the ship, responsible for the whole of the decoration and treatment of the interior of the ship. I admit he has been Architect as well of the University of London, and therefore is a busy man. He has done one ship already for the Cunard Company. I believe it was the Tuscania. But I am quite sure if you would appoint him and give him authority to deal with the matter, and then if he were asked to consult with our Council, we might have a combination of the experts in various directions he might exercise, and so be enabled to arrive at a more satis-factory result than has happened in connection with the 'Queen Mary'.
>
> (Cunard 17.6.1936:1)

The British government was anxious that Cunard should not employ an American again. The MP Alfred Blossom wrote to Neville Chamberlain in June 1936, pointing out that Morris was an American architect (Cunard 26.6.1936: 1). Therefore, Percy Bates corresponded with Morris, asking if he could recommend an English architect for the *Queen Elizabeth*: 'As to whether such a man should act alone, or be associated with an American architect such as yourself, I have at the moment a completely open mind and would much like to know how you feel about it' (Cunard 4.7.1936: 1). Percy Bates also wrote to Chamberlain's Secretary, V.N. Hopkins:

> In the case of the 'Queen Mary' we realised the desirability of combining American and English ideas in a British ship expected to derive nearly 70% of her revenue from American sources. We were placed very fortunately to give effect to this desire by the fact that Mr Morris, who had designed our New York Office, was a personal friend of Mr Davis, who had designed both our Liverpool and London Offices and who in addition had done a great deal of work on the Company's ships.
>
> (7.7.1936: 1)

Hopkins replied on 13 July 1936 indicating that the Chancellor would like to be kept informed of developments. As the new ship was being built with a government subsidy, then Cunard had no choice but to adhere to the government request that a British architect be employed for the interior design of the new ship.

Morris responded to Bates, indicating that he was willing to work on the new ship, but he did not suggest a British architect whom he could work with. He also regretted not coming over again to supervise last spring and that there had been a lack of co-ordination with the interior design of the *Queen Mary*, and laid the blame firmly at Whipp's door: '. . . but I now think it would have been better . . . (b) if

I had had more to do with the selection of furnishings, and could have visited, with the necessary frequency, the Artists' ateliers during the execution of their work, and (c) if there had been a really sympathetic attempt in London to follow the spirit of the original design, which had been accepted (16.7.1936:1). Later in the year he wrote critically to Bates from the Carlton Hotel, claiming that Whipp ignored his designs: 'I think it would be wise to make use of Mr Whipp's services in the new ship, but in a more limited and subordinate capacity.' (Cunard 4.10.1936:3).

The Chairman of Cunard, Lord Brocklebank, wrote to Bates, asking that British architects be looked at before considering using Morris again. A memo from him set out some clear guidelines: 'In any use we may make of Mr Morris, care must be taken not to antagonise (a) the British Architecture and artistic world; (b) The Treasury (c) Mr Pick and his crowd. . . . I consider all carpets, curtains, etc. should be selected here by professional decorators, working with our own furnishing department, under the general supervision of the architect, as done in Queen Mary' (Cunard 23.7.1936: 1).

S. Lister, head of the Cunard furnishing department, was similarly sensitive about the government funding for the *Queen Elizabeth*. In a letter to Sir Percy Bates he argued: '. . . finally, when we started the "Queen Mary" it was purely a Cunard ship and we were entitled to employ whom we liked. This second one is perhaps more definitely a British ship in which the Chancellor is taking a direct interest. Therefore it behoves us not to bring in at too early a date any American or other non-British influence' (Cunard 24.7.1936: 4).

Various suggestions were made to Cunard over the choice of British architect. Brocklebank wrote to Whipp, suggesting Sir John Burnett, Tait & Lorne, of whom Mr Tait was now the principal partner. The firm had recently completed two prestigious commissions for Sydney Harbour Bridge and Unilever House, London. A letter from Alfred Booth, Cunard London, suggested Grey Wornum (1888–1957), who had just designed the RIBA buildings in Portland Place, London, and was supervising the Coronation decorations, plus Brian O'Rorke, who had designed the *Orion*: '. . . he is a young man and I understand was found to co-operate well with the owners and builders during the construction of the ship' (Cunard 7.8.1936: 1).

Percy Bates replied on 8 August agreeing: 'I have not met Mr Wornum, but I have seen the new premises of the Royal Institute of British Architects, a good deal of which I admired very much'. He also agreed to inspect the *Orion*, but was not favourably impressed. The positive response to the suggestion of Wornum was rein-forced in a letter from Professor Reilly, Head of Architecture at Liverpool University on 4 September 1936. Morris travelled to England to act as a consultant for Cunard in the selection of an architect for the *Queen Elizabeth* in October 1936, when the choice was finally made. Morris, Leach and Brocklebank interviewed the shortlist of architects drawn up by Cunard on 15 October 1936. Adie, Button and Partners were rejected, largely because Adie presented a redesign of the *Queen Mary*'s Lounge which Morris took exception to. Burnett, Tait and Lorne were also rejected, on the grounds that, according to Brocklebank: '. . . I do not consider that we should get the personal touch we want from them. Nor should I expect either originality or artistic ideas in their designs' (Cunard 16.10.1936: 4). Oswald Milne was regarded as insufficiently practical and his office lacked the necessary organizational skills to support such a complex project. Therefore, Wornum was selected by the Shipbuilding Committee in October 1936, as, according to Brocklebank: 'He is definitely "somebody" in the architectural and artistic world, and his selection by us would not be criticised by them, or I do not think so' (Cunard 16.10.1936: 3). Bates informed Wornum of the decision later that month; in his letter he suggested wood veneers as the best decorative surface and included his criticisms of the *Normandie*: 'As regards the next ship (your ship), I don't propose there is any real risk of your trying to make extensive use of stone or marble or heavy glass as was done on the "Normandie", but I think I ought to say that I thoroughly dislike all three' (Cunard 27.10.1936).

The design process of the *Queen Elizabeth* was much more tightly controlled than that of the *Queen Mary*. There was an overall schedule, and phasing of the fitting out with realistic deadlines reviewed each month. Wornum was in control of the selection of decorating firms to be contracted; a range of decorating firms were given 50 guineas for preparing designs for the first class state rooms – this included Betty Joel and White Allom. Anna Zinkeisen was given a similar sum for acting as consultant for the tea and dance rooms. Morris continued to act as consultant for the project, and was paid a fee of £13,518 in total. However, friction emerged between him and Wornum soon after his appointment, when Morris asked that Wornum change his letter heading to include his name. Wornum refused and Morris was released from the project in December 1936.

There was still pressure from the government. Following the appointment of a British architect, the Treasury were then insistent that Cunard use only British materials. The *Queen Mary* was referred to as a bad example, and spending abroad on the new ship limited to £100,000. For example, the cost of Formica for lining the walls of the bathrooms of the *Queen Mary* was £15,000 and special permission was sought, and gained, from the Treasury to use Formica in the same fashion on the *Queen Elizabeth*. Work was inevitably delayed on the ship's fitting out, as the ship was called into service at the outbreak of the Second World War. Cunard may have sensed an interruption to their plans as early as February 1939, when the Ship Building Committee agreed that the cabin class children's room should be plain, as the room may be used for other purposes (Cunard 6.2.1939: 1). Cunard's aim had been that the *Queen Elizabeth* should join the transatlantic service in 1940. However, following the outbreak of war it sailed to New York and was employed as a troop ship. The fittings and furniture which had been installed were removed and put into storage at various depots around the world, including Australia, North America and different areas of the United Kingdom. The furniture and fittings were located and transported back to Southampton for reassemblage, a process which took two months in 1946.

The ship eventually entered service as a transatlantic passenger liner in October 1946 and its interior design used the blueprint laid down by the *Queen*

Mary, with a range of over one hundred woods used and Korkoid for the flooring. Many of the same artists and decorators were commissioned to produce very similar objects. The Verandah Grill was still a feature, but was decorated with ivory coloured, sycamore panelled walls with pale blue upholstery. The same illuminated balustrade was used and variated coloured lighting when the room was converted into a night-club after dark. The room was decorated by White Allom Ltd, largely because they submitted the lowest tender of £8,400. The main lounge on the promenade deck was panelled predominantly in Canadian maple burr; this was contrasted with leather covered panels in light grey. The fine art focus of the room was provided by two flower paintings by Cedric Morris and a marquetry panel on the theme of Canterbury Pilgrims, designed by George Ramon and crafted by J. Dunn. Ramon also designed panels for the observation lounge and cocktail bar on the subject of 'Scenes of the Circus'. The ballroom featured decorative glass work, just like the *Queen Mary*, with a screen depicting a jungle scene. There was a raised platform for a band with recessed, coloured lighting and a central dance floor. The walls were lined with quilted satin and ivory sycamore and decorated with tiny, silver stars. The smoking room was still designed as a masculine space, with wood carvings of 'Hunting', 'Shooting' and 'Fishing' by Dennis Dunlop. Macdonald Gill designed a similar map to that in the cabin class restaurant on the *Queen Mary*, only this time it was placed in the smoking room and showed the dual progress of both 'Queens'. Two paintings, 'Elsinore' and 'Dover Harbour' by the leading marine artist, Norman Wilkinson (1878–1931), inventor of dazzle painting for ships, were also placed in the smoking room. Maurice Lambert created sculptures for the main hall, flanking the entrance to the lounge and figures over the deck entrance to the main hall. Jan Juta was again commissioned by Cunard to supply decorative glass and metal panels and screens, this time for the restaurant, salon, dining room, cocktail bar and verandah grill. Bainbridge Copnall (1903–73), who had worked on the *Queen Mary* and also on the RIBA headquarters with Wornum, was commissioned to provide wood carvings for the foyer of the first class restaurant, as well as two large clock compositions and two panels depicting 'The Fisherman' and 'The Huntress' in the restaurant itself.

The ship's design was essentially pre-war, down to its division into three classes, although these were rebranded as first class, cabin class and tourist class. The post-war era was to witness the demise of the ocean liner, as travel by air became more easily available, prompted by a more truncated view of time and the need for more efficient use of hours in the day (Harvey 1989). The swansong of the ocean liner was expressed in an international modernism, which transcended national boundaries on the one hand, but acted as a backdrop for the projection of national identities, based on media forms, on the other.

Chapter 6

Transatlantic modernism and the interior designer

The trajectory that this book has mapped began with the anonymous decorating firm, moved through the fashionable architect and the art deco showcase to the modern designer ship. This concluding chapter maps the entrance of the professional interior designer to the field of ocean liner design after the Second World War. The history of the interior design of ocean liners in the post-war era was determined by the economics and politics of the Cold War era. As America rose to dominance on the world stage, modernism was appropriated as the style of democracy and freedom. A period of reconstruction followed the devastation of the Second World War, financed by the Marshall Plan. The ease with which liners could reflect distinct national identities was eroded, as international modernism became the prevalent style used by all Western nations, who followed America's lead. Moreover, it was in America that the profession of interior design had first emerged, and so western Europe was emulating the US's lead in this respect also (Massey 2001; Sparke 2005). Hence, new ships built by France, Britain and Holland were closely related in style and distinguished only by surface detail and references to different histories, overseen by teams of interior designers. There was an optimistic faith in the future as reconstruction got underway, fuelled by a trust in new technologies and the power of consumer freedom. The actual process of designing liners changed little, but the responsibility for the overall design became more within the realm of the professional interior designer, rather than the system of an architect or interior decorator overseeing the design process or the showcase model. By the end of the 1960s, the status of the ocean liner began to wane as air transport offered faster and more prestigious travel, with France and Britain investing in the supersonic Concorde and America in space travel, and the massive, ocean-going ships destined to be built only for the burgeoning cruise market. The *Queen Mary 2*, Cunard's latest vessel, contains references to the past, and to representations of luxury and glamour. However, cruise ships such as this offer a safe, holiday retreat from a world where, since 9/11, the threat of terrorism is ever present and the ship represents safety from a turbulent reality, rather than the a perilous journey or one way journey to a new beginning. But the ship remains a supreme example of Foucault's concept of heterotopia; whether it be ocean liner or cruise ship, the spaces within are regulated spaces of illusion and exclusion.

Recovery for the Western world from the Second World War was slow. Cunard's refitted *Queen Elizabeth* began to offer a transatlantic passenger service from 1946. However, the style of the ship was essentially pre-war, with woods used extensively for decorative purposes, and it was firstly America, then Italy, Sweden and France which launched ships that represented nationhood within the context of modernism and the new Cold War culture. The first significant, new passenger liner to be built after the Second World War was the *United States*. It was commissioned by the United States Navy as a troopship at a cost of $77 million, and sold to the United States Line upon completion for a total of $33 million. The ship took the Blue Riband from the *Queen Mary* on its first voyage in July 1952, with engines to match the *Queen Elizabeth*, but a much smaller and elongated hull, narrow enough to pass through the Suez Canal. The 53,329 gross tons provided accommodation for 882 first class, 525 second and 551 tourist class. The interiors were designed by the architectural partnership of Eggers & Higgins in close collaboration with the interior design firm, Smyth, Urquhart & Markwald. It was Anne Urquhart and Dorothy Markwald who were responsible for the cabin designs, as they had the experience of working on the *America* (Kirkham 2000: 315). The designers were not allowed to use wood in the outfitting of the *United States*, as the ship needed to be completely fireproof. The main structure of the ship was aluminium, a material which was lightweight and flexible and much in vogue during the 1950s. The ship was designed to convert easily into a troop ship, although never used for that purpose apart from being on standby during the Cuban Missile Crisis. The interiors were therefore simple and modern in design, with minimal decorative detail but used modern materials, including all-metal furniture, glass fibre for curtains and bedspreads plus plastic upholstery. Aluminium was selected for 22,000 pieces of shipboard furniture. As the editor of *Architectural Review* observed in 1956, the ship's interiors were successful as they acted as a contemporary setting for the knowing consumer:

> It would seem self-evident that where a number of people move and congregate, the background should be what its name suggests. This does not rule out pattern, texture, colour and ornament whether in the form of sculpture murals, tapestry or, as in the liner *United States*, 1951, etched glass. But where they are exploited, as they so ably are in the *United States*, they must take their place as part of a controlled environment.
>
> (McCallum 1956: 135)

The only German transatlantic liners to remain intact after the Second World War were the *Milwaukee* and the *Europa*. The former was destroyed by fire in 1945 whilst undergoing conversion to a troop ship by Britain, to whom she had been awarded, and the latter was awarded to France. After undergoing extensive refurbishment and conversion at St Nazaire, the *Europa* was relaunched as the *Liberté* by C.G.T. in 1950, providing accommodation for 569 first, 562 second and 382 tourist class. This was a case of changing national identities: 'La metamorphose d'un style Germanique en un subtil parfum Francais' (Vian 1992: 278). André Domin of La Maison Dominique was the overall designer for the ship. The renamed Café de l'Atlantique enjoyed the addition of a dancefloor and the Grand Salon had lacquer-work by Dunand added. The salle à manger was overhauled by Marc Simon, who was also responsible for the cabins de luxe and the first class cabins. The last great liner to be built by C.G.T. with French government subsidies was the *France*, launched in 1962. At 66,348 gross tons, this was the largest ship ever to be built at the Chantiers de l'Atlantique shipyard in St Nazaire. President de Gaulle hoped the ship would provide a morale booster for the French, and build on the global success of the *Normandie*.

6.1
Eggers & Higgins, Dining Saloon, United States, 1952.
Source: Mariners' Museum

The interiors were designed by G. Peynet and were brightly patterned and multi-coloured, making a statement about the currency of modern French design. The ship was designed to operate as both a transatlantic ocean liner and a cruise ship, and segregation of the classes was less marked, with vertical circulation of the two classes enhanced by lifts and staircases which could bypass the other class. The first class accommodation on the promenade deck consisted of a modern smoking room aft, decorated with star shaped ceiling lights, white ceiling, pillars and banister with wall panels by Jean Picart le Doux. The large central panel measured 4 × 17.5 metres and depicted 'Les Phases du Temps' in black, dark blue, light blue and gold. They consisted of a large, central section with a sun radiating angular rays, surrounded by stars and planets. One panel either side was a bold representation of a lyre shape with patterned fish swimming by. The furniture echoed the angularity of the lighting and the wall panel. Further along the promenade deck was the grand salon amidship, decorated mainly in white, with concealed lighting in the ceiling, white leather uphol-stered chairs and glass and metal coffee tables. The addition of luxury was attempted with the addition of a multitude of contemporary French art, including decorative ceramic plaques by Picasso in the tourist class dining room, and watercolours by Raoul Dufy in the first class private bar and Cabaret Atlantique. Both classes had libraries and writing rooms, shops and cabaret bar. The second class was called Rive Gauche, and was perhaps more successful than the first class, as the style of mod-ernism was more in tune with bare simplicity than luxurious surface decoration. For example, the smoking room had walls and ceilings faced with a plain, plastic surface, with some multi-coloured rectangles for decoration behind the bar. The furniture was simple, with metal frames and fabric upholstery. The floors throughout the ship were carpeted, predominantly in plain colours. The Rive Gauche class also had a glass-domed indoor swimming pool and lido bar aft on the upper deck, comple-mented by a glass-roofed sports centre on the sun deck. The *France* was initially a success, but the challenge of travel by air soon led to the demise of the ocean liner globally. The *France* was also hit by a withdrawal of government support and C.G.T. desperately tried to market the ship and various cruises during the early 1970s. However, this was unsuccessful and the ship's future remains uncertain, as it lies in dock in Germany.

The Dutch government also subsidized prestigious liners in the post-war years, and contributed one-third of the cost for the building of the *Rotterdam* by the Holland-Amerika Line. The liner entered service in 1959, with a gross tonnage of 38,650 and accommodation for 580 first class and 789 tourist, which could be altered to 301 first class and 1,060 tourist. Designed primarily as a cruise ship, running holidays from New York to the Caribbean, the ship made occasional transatlantic trips too. The interior design of the ship was executed by a panoply of Dutch designers – nine in all, with the most prestigious dining rooms, library, ambassador room and main staircase and vestibule designed by J.A. van Tienhoven. The two dining rooms were adjacent on B deck and could seat 894 passengers. They could be combined when there was one class cruising, or separated when the ship was sailing on liner

duty. The aft dining room was two storeys high and resplendent in gold coloured facings and geometric patterns. The ambassador room was situated on the boat deck and was circular in shape, with a star-shaped dance floor and space for a dance orchestra, small bar and seating for 142 passengers. The décor was a brightly coloured turquoise, beige and orange.

6.2
G. Peynet, First Class Dining Saloon, *France*, **French Line, 1962.**
Source: Author's collection

The lounge and adjoining Ocean Bar were designed by Mutters, the firm which had decorated the very early Holland America Line ships. The lounge extended the full width of the ship and featured a kidney shaped dance floor, sunken in the centre of the room and reached by means of two steps. The other public rooms in the ship, for instance the Café de la Paix by Jan van Bommel, cardroom, smoking room, Tropic Bar by Carel L.W. Wirtz and N.V. Muttero and Ritz-Carlton Room by Muttero were united by a style which was modern and brightly coloured with a light-hearted, holiday ambience. There was also an emphasis on deck activities, with a sun room and sun deck for patio based leisure. In total, the *Rotterdam* had 55,000 square feet of deck space for passenger amusement: 'A unique feature is the Atlantic Promenade, which will appeal particularly to the "teen set". A genuine American soda fountain has been installed, and authentic hot dogs, hamburgers and milk shakes are dispensed to the young and . . . recorded pop music provides a properly exuberant note' (Holland America Line 1959b: 11).

Italy too continued to build new ocean liners to reflect national identity and boost esteem. Post-war recovery was funded by Marshall Aid totalling $1.5 million,

6.3
J. A. van Tienhoven, Aft Dining Room, *Rotterdam***, Holland-America Line, 1959.**
Source: Rotterdam Maritime Museum

with which Italian industry was revitalized. There was an optimism and trust in the new democratic government to build a new future for the country. Shipbuilding was aided by the availability and cheapness of steel, and design styling was reinvented in emulation of the American blueprint, with the consultant designer model and mass production and consumption based on Fordism (Sparke 1988: 75–83). The leading figure in developing a distinct identity for Italian post-war design was Gio Ponti (1891–1979), editor of the leading design journal, *Domus*, and designer of several ship interiors. The new Italian approach eschewed Rationalism and pure modernism in favour of a more organic style, which affirmed the active role of the consumer. He was responsible for revamping the first class areas of the *Conte Grande* in modern style in 1949. He designed the first class spaces of the *Giulio Cesare* in 1950 and the *Andrea Doria* in 1953. At 29,082 tons the *Andrea Doria* was smaller than the Italian Line's pre-war vessels, the *Rex* and the *Conte di Savoia*. The *Cristoforo Colombo* joined the service in the following year and was 29,429 tons with interiors by Matteo Longoni (1913–84) who had designed the second class accommodation on the *Andrea Doria*. Ian McCallum admired the styling of the *Cristoforo Colombo*, remarking: '. . . perhaps a little mannered, but where, in the morass of ship interiors, there is lightness of touch, elegance, assurance – in one word, style (in the non-historical sense) – complaint on such small scores becomes carping' (McCallum 1956: 136).

The post-war British recovery was markedly slow and, following the introduction of the *Queen Elizabeth*, the Union-Castle Line were amongst the first to build new passenger ships. The *Pendennis Castle* was the first ship to be built under the new ownership of Union-Castle, having been taken over by Cayzer, Irvine & Company, owners of the Clan Line and other shipping companies in 1955. Lord Rotherwick became the new Chairman with his nephew, Nicholas Cayzer, Deputy Chairman. When Lord Rotherwick died in 1958 he was succeeded by his nephew as Chairman and Nicholas's younger brother, Bernard Cayzer, became Deputy Chairman.

Harland & Wolff had built and fitted out the Union-Castle ships since the creation of Union-Castle in 1900; the company had been bought by Sir Owen Philipps and Pirrie of Harland & Wolff in 1912 (Moss and Hume 1986: 155). The ship had been ordered from Harland & Wolff before the takeover of Union-Castle: '. . . the last vessel ordered from Harland & Wolff by that old-established customer. For well over half a century Union-Castle had ordered all its ships, with one exception, from the company, and this link was reflected in the close friendship between Sir Frederick (Rebbeck) and Sir Vernon Thomson, chairman of Union-Castle' (Moss and Hume 1986: 373).When Harland & Wolff won the 40th contract from Union-Castle in 1955 for the building of the *Pendennis Castle* the Company Secretary wrote to Union-Castle:

> Sir Frederick Rebbeck desires that you should convey his personal thanks to Sir George Christopher for the message communicated in the last paragraph of your letter and to express his pleasure that the pleasant association which has existed between our two companies for so long is thus being continued'.
>
> (Harland & Wolff 16.3.1955 D/2805/PRO/A/113: 1)

Planning for this new passenger and cargo ship for the South African service had begun in the previous year, and the designs were based on the interiors of the *Edinburgh Castle*. There was a visit by Sir George Christopher, Chairman of Union-Castle, the Naval Architect Lees and representative of Harland & Wolff to see experimental cabins on *Edinburgh Castle* in January 1955. Heaton & Tabb mocked-up a sample first class and tourist class cabin for inspection. In July 1955 Union Steamship's naval architect, J.A.H. Lees, wrote to Harland & Wolff to ensure that Heaton & Tabb were to be involved:

> We are not certain of the extent to which you propose to sub-contract this work to Messrs Heaton & Tabb, but where they are likely to be concerned we suggest that you may care to let them have a copy of the appropriate note and arrange with them to discuss their proposal with us direct. Because of the structural work etc. which is involved, we think it is important that very early consideration be given to this matter and for details to be worked out as between yourselves and Messrs Heaton & Tabb prior to submission to us.
>
> (Harland & Wolff D/2805/PRO/A/114 13 July 1955)

However, the association between Union-Castle and Harland & Wolff was not to continue for much longer, and the Union-Castle Steamship Company was bought out by Cayzner, Irvine & Company later in 1955. It had been the established practice at Harland & Wolff to use their subsidiary, Aldam Heaton & Co. for the interior design of their ships and the *Pendennis Castle* was no exception.

This was to be challenged when Bernard Cayzer introduced a new interior decorator to Union-Castle for the fitting out of the 28,582 ton *Pendennis Castle*. Jean Monro (b.1916) was a society decorator and had joined her mother's business, Mrs Monro Ltd, after the war. On holiday in Jamaica, Jean Monro had met Bernard Cayzer, and he invited her to decorate the interior of his new house in Eaton Terrace, which had been designed by Brian O'Rorke. Following the success of this commission, Bernard Cayzer invited Jean Monro to design the interiors of the *Pendennis Castle*, which was in the process of being built at Harland & Wolff, Belfast. From the Harland & Wolff records, it would appear that work was already well advanced along traditional lines. Monro found that she was challenging the traditions of the shipbuilding industry there. On her first visit to Belfast:

> We had a very unpropitious start: Sir Henry Rebbeck, the chairman, was not keen on women in shipyards except to clean up the ships before they sailed, which by tradition was 'women's work'! I was therefore taken out to lunch by his secretary at a hotel in Belfast instead of lunching with him in the directors' dining room. This was a great waste of time both for his secretary and for me.
>
> Monro 1988: 58)

Monro challenged the status quo by being the first woman designer to work with Harland & Wolff, but she also represented the new owners of the Union-Castle Line. She used new suppliers for the ship, not only Harland & Wolff's usual choice of firms, possibly controlled by Heaton & Tabb. Monro also encountered the traditional method of designing interiors for liners, which had been in place since the beginning of the twentieth century, whereby sample cabins would be constructed in a warehouse, and owners could select their choice of style and layout from the limited range displayed (Moss and Hume 1986: 81):

> One of the traditional methods of designing and building passenger accommodation was to make a mock-up of a cabin of each class and type, plus a sample of a de-luxe cabin or suite. These were built in the vast joiners' sheds, which looked rather like aircraft hangars. Of course, they wanted to do it as they had always done it and to use the same suppliers – much easier for them. I was soon to learn that the 'old boy' network was hard at work between the shipyards and the suppliers of carpets and furniture.
>
> (Monro 1988: 58).

A review of Union-Castle post-war interiors up to the *Pendennis Castle* bear out that Monro did introduce a different and more contemporary styling. For example, an earlier ship, the *Pretoria Castle* of 1948 was not that different to pre-war interiors, with freestanding furniture and art deco mirrors. The dining room was criticized by McCallum: '. . . a system of beams is created in the ceiling for "decorative" reasons, which combine with the lighting troughs to confuse the eye and oppress the spirit' (McCallum 1956: 138). The sample rooms for the *Pendennis Castle* were laid out in the joiners' shop in September 1956. The fabrics and furniture on display were much in the contemporary style (Jackson 1998). At the back were samples of different wood veneers, ranging from oak to sycamore and willow. Against each was a range of suggested textiles, floor coverings and furniture. The finished interiors had fitted furniture and bed with drawers beneath. There was a first class swimming pool on deck and a second class dining room with mural.

Jean Monro then designed the interiors of the *Windsor Castle* for Union-Castle from the time of its original commission, Heaton Tabb being relegated to the decoration of the tourist class public rooms. The ship was built by Cammell Laird at Birkenhead, and was larger than the *Pendennis Castle* at 37,640 tons, and joined the service in 1960. The style again was contemporary, with touches of historical grandeur. In a joint interview for *The Times*, Jean Monro and Bernard Cayzer outlined the design philosophy of the *Windsor Castle* as: 'Yesterday's Elegance, Today's Comfort' (*The Times*: 18.8.1960: 4). For example, the half-landing leading to the

6.4
Sample rooms for
***Pendennis Castle*,**
laid out in
joiners' shop at
Harland & Wolff,
September 1956.
Source: Ulster Folk &
Transport Museum

first class dining room on D deck featured a classic historic French wallpaper, 'La Fête chez Therese' in purple and white plastic. A large glass door then led into the dining room, the theme of which was 'Night and Day'. By night the room was lit by gilt and black chandeliers, wall brackets and table lamps, and by day the curtains were drawn back to reveal white shutters with chintz curtains. The colour scheme was cherry, mauve and regency green with purple curtains shot with silver. The end wall was decorated with three murals by Felix Kelly (1914–94), which spanned the width of the room. Wedgwood produced 6,000 custom made pieces of dinnerware for the ship, each featuring the same view of 'The Long Walk', the three mile avenue leading to Windsor Castle in sepia green, designed by Peter Wall. During the day only the central mural of Windsor Castle was visible, flanked by purple curtains. By the night, the curtains were drawn across the central mural and two further murals were revealed on either side, one of St George's Chapel and the other of the River Thames near Windsor, both painted by moonlight. The space was constructed on two levels, with diners sitting on a raised area around the sides of the room, separated from the lower central area by a balustrade made from ormolu and crystal Perspex, in a typical mix of the new and the more traditional. The floor was covered in black and silver grey squares. Also, a special private dining room led off from this space, which was decorated in a subdued Adam style.

The remainder of the first class public rooms were on the promenade deck. The first class drawing room, according to the press release: '. . . has been designed to represent a comfortable sitting room in a typical English way with sofas and chairs, pale pink walls, green and white marble fireplace, card tables for use when the card room is full, and a large bay window with a window seat. Over the fireplace is a copy of a portrait, by Denis Fioles, of the Queen Mother, who launched the ship' (Union-Castle Line 1960: 2). To add to the typically English ambience there were chintz curtains and upholstery and Adamesque door surrounds. The first class lounge also featured chintz and fluted pillars and the library chintz covered easy chairs near the open fire, in a room panelled in pine. At the stern end of the promenade deck was a verandah café and swimming pool, with a movable glass screen, which could be drawn back in sunny weather to create one space. The cinema had walls covered in plastic, patterned to look like white-washed canvas. The cushions were covered in dark tweed and polystyrene tiles covered the ceiling.

The design of the tourist class areas was less traditional than first class and had a younger ambience. Bernard Cayzer had stipulated to Monro that: '. . . for Tourist Class passengers I wanted great comfort but with a less formal atmosphere and plenty of gaiety in all the rooms' (The Times 18.8.1960: 4). The tourist class dining saloon on D deck could accommodate 296 diners. One wall was decorated with a mural in light blue, terra cotta and white and featured a whimsical treatment of classical architecture with urns and swags by Sidney Smith. Frosted glass windows were lit from behind to give the effect of sun on the sea with 'Grecian Urn' designs for the curtain fabric. A mirror covered the opposite end of the room to the mural, and the walls were covered in plastic to imitate woven glass. The diners sat at long,

6.5
**Hugh Casson
and John Wright,
stairs to the
Crow's Nest,
Canberra,
P & O, 1961.**
Source: P&O

narrow tables on white sycamore chairs covered in sea-blue, tan and pale blue hide. Variety was added with some chairs having black frames with yellow hide upholstery. The remaining tourist class public accommodation was situated on the deck beneath the first class promenade deck. The lounge had: '. . . full length curtains in a charming floral print' (Union-Castle 1960: 2). There was a sunken dance floor with wrought iron balustrade surrounding and wrought iron lanterns which resembled street lamps.

The tourist class smoke room was the most innovative on the ship. It was designed by Michael Inchbald and featured the same iron street lamps. It was divided into three sections: the first was the Cockpit Bar, which reinforced the traditional masculine identity of the smoking room with seats covered in tweed and mahogany chairs covered in hide, the colour of saddle leather and based on the design of chairs used by spectators at cock fights in the eighteenth century. The walls were lined with weathered timber and decorated with firearms and fish in cases. Beside the Cockpit Bar was the Rotunda, a circular room with a fun 'Stovescope' at its centre, which looked like a brick and brass stove surmounted by an armillary sphere. The points of the compass emanate from the 'Stovescope' on the blue, black and white floor, whilst a black cushion topped rail runs around the stove. The domed ceiling is painted to represent a chart of the night sky. Around the perimeter of the room are 12 white tables, each with a compass motif in black. Four model ships in glass cases decorate the walls. The third section is the sitting out area with armchairs, writing tables, etc. At the end of this room is an abstract expressionist mural by the British painter and author, Trewin Copplestone. The overall colour scheme for this room was black and white, pomegranate and brown.

Each de luxe first class cabin had its own name, including Almond Blossom, Dragon Fly, Moonstone, Lavender Blue, Sea Holly, Lilac, Peony, Tamarisk, Red Rose, High Summer and Maple Leaf, and all featured chintz. This was a rather incongruous combination with the contemporary style furniture. The cabin class accommodation was rather more basic, with bunks rather than beds, but they still had chintz covers. The ship is a good example of Corin Hughes-Stanton's assertion: 'The Union-Castle Line has always been chided for its neo-Regency rooms, its fake fire-places and its chintzy furniture. Yet its ships often have a vigour and sense of pleasure missing in the more orthodox and unimaginative contemporary ship interiors' (*c*.1962: 19).

Jean Monro and Michael Inchbald were also to work for the Cunard Line in this period. Cunard had launched two new ships for the voyage to Canada in 1954 – the *Saxonia* and the *Ivernia*. The architect was E.C. Leach and the style was an incongruous mix of the modern and the traditional. The *Saxonia*'s first class chintz lounge, for example, was lined with pink plastic studded with small mirrors, painted with various flowers. The curtains were maroon satin and the floor covered with a patterned, brown carpet. The *Shipbuilding and Shipping Record* commented: 'To my mind this space would have gained dignity had all this wall decoration been omitted, or had it been replaced by one focal piece of decoration' (9.9.1954). Cunard renamed and refitted the ships in 1963, bringing Monro and Inchbald in to remodel the interiors, following the positive reception of the *Windsor Castle*. The *Saxonia* was renamed *Carmania* and *Ivernia*'s new name was the *Franconia*. The main intention behind the changes to the ships was an economic one, and the gross tonnage was increased as the superstructure was enlarged to accommodate a lido area and swimming pool aft. This was in order to use the ships as cruise ships as well as Canadian-bound liners. The ships' facelift was heralded as 'The New Look', resonant of Dior's fashion revolution a decade previously (Cunard, February 1963: 1). Cunard used the name of Jean Monro extensively in their publicity to promote the ships, labelling her: '. . . one of the foremost Interior Design consultants in the United Kingdom' (Cunard, February 1963: 2). The main changes to the interiors were brought about by new forms of lighting, both fluorescent and tungsten, with dimmer switches. There was the addition of a dedicated teenagers' room and new cocktail bar. The cabins were overhauled by Michael Inchbald, Paul Gell and Evelyn Pinching to be contemporary and new without any historical references, a major new point of departure for Cunard.

Meanwhile, the Orient Line and P&O had commissioned two substantial liners independently of one another. So, when the companies merged in 1960, the Orient Line had already commissioned the building of the 41,923 ton *Oriana* and P&O's 45,733 ton *Canberra* was also nearing completion. Both ships were built primarily for the voyage to Australia which, unlike the transatlantic route, was still experiencing high demand. The main stimulus was the post-war assisted passage scheme for emigration to Australia to boost the population, hence the choice of name for P&O's new flagship.

Both ships had modern interiors and were a result of official British support for contemporary design, and would not fall within the interior decorator's remit, as with the Union-Castle ship interiors. The *Oriana*'s interiors were designed by the Design Research Unit (DRU) in collaboration with Brian O'Rorke. The DRU had been founded in 1943 by the Ministry of Information, with the aim of providing a network for designers and engineers to provide advice to industry to make British design attractive and competitive after the war. The British modernist critic, Herbert Read, was the Chairman and members included exhibition designer, Misha Black and graphic designer Milner Gray. The experience gained by British designers during the war, contributing to the design of propaganda, laid the foundations for post-war official 'good design' (Sparke 1986). This was promoted by the newly formed Council of Industrial Design (COID) and through the exhibitions, *Britain Can Make It* in 1946 and the *Festival of Britain* in 1951. The *Canberra*'s styling was co-ordinated by Sir Hugh Casson (1910–99) who had been the director of architecture at the Festival of Britain. Both ships reflected a new sense of British national identity, which was a result of wartime experiences and a faith in the future and in new technology and materials. The styling of the ships was modern and made no references to the past in stylistic terms, but did reflect the past in terms of British popular culture and traditions. There were no Tudor style smoking rooms or Adam style libraries, but there were references to traditional British pubs and to cricket. Both ships were positively received by the design and the popular press, although their place in the history of British ship design has been largely unacknowledged, given the prominence of the more prestigious *QE2*. However, the evidence would suggest that the design of the *Oriana* and *Canberra* influenced that of the *QE2* (Agnew in *Architectural Review* 1969: 411).

The *Oriana* was commissioned by the Chairman of the Orient Line, Sir Colin Anderson, in 1956. The partners in charge of the co-ordination of the design of the interiors from DRU were Misha Black, Milner Gray and Kenneth Bayes. Brian O'Rorke played the role of consulting architect. The ship measured 804 feet in length and was 41,923 gross tonnage. It could accommodate 646 passengers in first class and 1,496 tourist class. This was the first British ship to follow the lead of the *United States*, and have an aluminium superstructure and to have a bulb bow. The work of the DRU succeeded in creating a unified whole for the interiors of the ship in the Contemporary style. This included details down to modern signage and works of art. For example, the first class main stairway featured an abstract relief by the British Constructivist artist, Mary Martin, which toned in eloquently with the paladao panelling and white PVC ceiling covering. The floor and treads were covered in dark and light grey lino. Further unity was provided by modern typography and signage by Christopher Timings of DRU and details such as a uniform design for cylindrical ash bins in spun aluminium, which were anodized and stove-enamelled in sea-green with the white lettering of Orient Line around the top. The first class observation room, 'The Look-out' at the front of the ship, was a light and airy space, with the bulkheads covered in cherry veneer and the white painted acoustic tiles and boarding of the ceiling. The chairs were also lightweight, made from cane in a cylindrical shape resting on dark, metal frames. The flooring again was in dark grey lino. The space featured an exhibition on the history of the *Oriana*; another focal point was the compass, mounted in a matt black, stove-enamelled pedestal with teak surround, designed by DRU.

The first class main lounge or 'Princess Room' measured 80 by 70 feet and combined a sitting area with screened-off library space. The screen was decorated with a mural by British neo-Romantic artist John Piper. The Contemporary furniture was designed by Robin Day and included a librarian's desk in macassar ebony to match the wall covering, with silver bronze metalwork details and stove-enamelled frame. The librarian's chair was covered in black hide. The ceiling was faced with olive ash and acoustic board with concealed lighting. The first class restaurant was the responsibility of R.D. Russell and Partners, another mainstay of the British 'good design' movement. The room was plain and modern, with small tables arranged in rows with chairs designed by Ian Hodgson in rosewood with scarlet upholstery. The passengers ate with stainless steel cutlery designed by Robert Welch, and Wedgwood china designed by Professor Goodden. The walls were panelled in figured Brazilian rosewood and dark green leather cloth, forming a contrast with the Siamese silk curtains in pink, scarlet and orange. There were echoes of British popular culture in the design of the first class 'Plough Tavern'. The Victorian etched glass used to divide the bar from the rest of the ship was salvaged from the demolished *Plough* at Notting Hill Gate. The tourist class accommodation received a less expensive finish, with the dining room, designed by Ward and Austin, with flooring in vinyl tiles, walls panelled in Indian silver grey wood and beige leather cloth and ceiling in white and beige leather cloth. The tourist class ballroom, also by Ward and Austin, had a teak dance floor illuminated by five orange saucer domes. The walls were covered in green hide with settees in orange hide.

The *Oriana* was slightly smaller and less costly to build than the *Canberra*, at £14 million compared to £16 million. The *Canberra* was larger, with a length of 818 feet and gross tonnage of 45,733, in which 548 first class and 1,690 tourist class could be accommodated. Like the *Oriana*, the *Canberra* had an aluminium superstructure but the main technical innovation was the placement of the engines aft, rather than amidship, which released space for passenger accommodation. The *Canberra* was billed by P&O as 'Tomorrow's Ship Today' and the design traded on being futuristic and modern in style and in its use of materials, whilst not jettisoning qualities of Britishness (P&O-Orient Lines 1961: 1). The ship's naval architect, John West, laid out the four objectives which dominated the design upon the ship's launch. He stipulated that the ship should be economical to run and not be a drain on resources by needing constant repairs. He also claimed that the passengers should have priority and lastly that: 'As the ship would be sailing on her maiden voyage early in 1961, there should be abundant evidence throughout the ship of progressive thought and good design' (P&O-Orient Lines 1961: 2). P&O had been careful to maintain control of the interior design of the ship from the outset. William C. Currie of P&O wrote to Rebbeck on 4 November 1955 stipulating: 'The contract for public rooms, including the floor covering, will be placed by the Company and is not to be included in the estimate' (Harland & Wolff D/2805/PRO/A/190 4.11.1955). The ship was well received at the time; for example, the shipping correspondent of *The Times* enthused:

> So much has been written about, and claimed for, the Canberra during her four years' construction at Belfast that it only remains to ask if the execution fulfils the expectations aroused by her imaginative conception and design. The consensus of opinion on board is that she does – with honours. Inside as well as out she is a visually exciting ship, full of radically new ideas. . . . The décor of the Canberra is essentially in the idiom of the sixties – there is no mock Tudor, neo-Georgian, or bogus country club. The accent is on simplicity, cleanliness of line with here and there splashes of colour and excitement, even shock.
>
> (*The Times* 22.5.1961: 4).

And the *Architectural Review* argued that both the *Oriana* and *Canberra* were: '. . . object lessons in the contribution that sensible ship-owners, and the good designers they employ, can make' (*Architectural Review* September 1961: 155).

The interiors were co-ordinated by Sir Hugh Casson, who was a leading figure in the development of the profession of interior design in post-war Britain and had designed the royal yacht, *Britannia* which was commissioned in 1954 (Casson 1968). He was also a Directing Editor of *Architectural Review* and had been director of architecture at the Festival of Britain, and was Professor of Interior Design at the Royal College of Art from 1955 to 1975. He was an enthusiastic supporter of modern architecture combined with touches of British whimsy. Casson established a special office to deal with the *Canberra* project, under the management of Timothy Rendle, which dealt with the main and first class public areas. John Wright (1919–97) designed the tourist class areas. He had worked for the Orient Line on the *Orsova* with Brian O'Rorke in 1960 and with Casson on the *Britannia*. Barbara Oakley designed the cabins, alleyways, officers' quarters and crew mess rooms. She had helped to start Constance Fry's school in London after the war, before forming a decorating partnership with Elly de Broen in 1947. The firm contributed designs to the Coronation decorations and parts of the British Embassy in Paris. From 1954 the company advised P&O on the interior design of its ships, including the *Arcadia* and *Iberia*, and its designs for the *Canberra*, submitted in 1958, were accepted. However, P&O-Orient Line awarded the prestigious parts of the design contract to more eminent, male architects, rather than relying on the experienced, female decorator.

The first class observation lounge or 'Crow's Nest', was right at the front of the ship and was designed by John Wright and decorated by Heal's Contracts Ltd. The lounge made full use of the view out to sea and also the games deck behind, with 41 full-height windows. The spaciousness was further enhanced by flush wall surfaces which were painted eggshell white with close-boarded ceiling cladding, also painted white. The main lighting was provided by modern spotlights and concealed cold-cathode lighting around the edges of the space. The furniture was also light-weight, with chrome plated wire, Bertoia fully upholstered, chairs upholstered in yellow and white tweed, with white plastic and chrome occasional tables to match. This was part of a set of designs the American sculptor undertook for Knoll in 1952. Part of the floor was covered with a patterned carpet, designed by Audrey Tanner, which had a black background with white, lemon, gold and brown compass point shapes, whilst the remainder was covered in teak. Doors port and starboard from the Crow's Nest led out to the games area, whilst a spiral staircase in the centre of the space led down to the first class lounge or Meridian Room, two decks down.

At the far side of the games area was the Bonito Club café and ballroom and first class swimming pool, designed by Hugh Casson. The pool was faced in white mosaic tiling with sunbathing terraces to create a lido ambience with sun loungers designed by Ernst Race, who had designed furniture for the South Bank site at the Festival of Britain. The spaces were integrated as far as possible, with the teak boarding of the pool terrace continuing into the café area to form a dance floor, to convert the café into a ballroom by evening. A movable glass partition was all that divided the two areas. During the evening's dancing, the activity was illuminated by means of a cellular glass, reinforced plastic ceiling which gave a diffused light through the honeycomb shaped cells. Further jolly ambience was created through the tables which were fixed either side of the bandstand, which were illuminated internally. The decoration of the table tops was carried out in foil and painted designs on glass fibre sheet by J.H. Spender.

Down two decks by means of a spiral staircase, first class passengers could reach the Meridian Room from the Crow's Nest lounge. The Meridian Room was the main, public space for first class and was organized by Hugh Casson and Partners as an open plan area with screening used to delineate different activities, which previously would have occupied separate rooms. The staircase itself was a striking architectural feature, curving up to the Crow's Nest; it was lined with dark wood panelling which provided a strong contrast with the white and chrome open staircase, which was dramatically lit from above. The Century Bar lay beyond the staircase at one end of the Meridian Room, and was panelled in exotic, dark woods with bar stools lining the curved, wooden bar top, as this was a 'sit-up bar'. An exhibition of images representing life in the previous century was a feature of the bar area. At the other end of the Meridian Room were the screened-off writing room and library, or Menzies Room, furnished with contemporary style desks and chairs. The central part of the Meridian Room was furnished with comfortable, contemporary style chairs in

6.6
John Wright, Crow's Nest, Canberra, P&O, 1961.
Source: P&O

glass reinforced plastic with foam lining over which brightly coloured, removable covers were placed. A major feature of the central sitting area was an angular ceiling light which measured 30 feet in length.

Dining on the *Canberra* for the first class passengers took place in the restaurant on the deck below. The room spanned the full 100 feet of the ship's width but with a low ceiling and no natural daylight, as it was placed too far down in the ship to accommodate portholes. The restaurant could seat 320 passengers at once and the slightly oppressive nature of the room was addressed by the use of strip and spot lighting in the ceiling, and creating a sunken, central section accessible by stairs. For evening use, small lanterns were placed on each table to create a more subtle mood. The space was also broken up by screen walls formed from the pillar casings. The room was finished in natural wood and leather and the floor carpeted. Decorative features in the room included a half sectional, full-size model of a Manhiki war canoe on one wall and the balustrades were decorated by William Mitchell with bone and metal inlaid into Indian laurel. There was also a much more intimate space, the Crystal Room, which could be used for private dining, cards or cocktail parties. The room earned its title as it had a large mural on one end wall, constructed from resin and glass fragments using a technique taken from the field of botany for setting small specimens in clear, resin blocks. The remainder of the walls were decorated with white, louvred doors and window shutters and light grey wood veneer, laid on in parquet strips. The ceiling was completely covered in a white plastic, louvred grid with concealed lighting. The carpet was a dark, mottled green and black. The table was in satin chrome with a reversible top, one side being black leather and the other baize. The glass reinforced plastic chairs were supported on satin chrome legs with bright orange covers. The first class children's' nursery was also important, as it contained a mural in three sections by Edward Ardizzione. The mural depicted scenes from nursery rhymes, a depiction of *Treasure Island* and scenes of children swimming, fishing and boating. Ardizzione painted the scenes onto melamine impregnated paper, which was then processed into a melamine-faced Perstorp laminate. The room was predominantly pale blue in colour, with blue rubber floor. The room could be opened up in good weather to enable play on deck. Special toys were designed by Margaret Redfern, including: '. . . a miniature cabin, mainly for small girls, and, for the boys, a rocket into which they can climb and view the deck above through a periscope . . .' (P&O-Orient Line 1961: 5).

The overall styling of the first class areas was a subtle and sophisticated modernism, combining an adventurous use of new materials and colour schemes. The tourist class areas were more daring and more fun in their treatment, the most notable feature being the use made of abstract art. The first and tourist class shared the cinema on A deck, but the remaining public areas were completely separate for the two classes. The tourist class restaurant faced the same problems as its first class counterpart; this vast space could seat 704 passengers at any one time, and so the designers introduced white 'fins' in Everflex, which created more intimate eating bays. The sloping ceiling, which was said to resemble the '. . . upper surface of an aerofoil' was covered in white, with the central part being a brightly lit, white fibre glass, although the lights could be dimmed in the evening for dinner (P&O 1961: 11). The walls were clad in green/gold glass fibre and the floor was dark blue, which matched the leather upholstery on the bent plywood seating. The sculptor Geoffrey Clarke (b.1924) had created a set of open cast reliefs for the *Oriana*, and he did the same for the tourist class dining room on the *Canberra*. There were abstract wall panels port and starboard on the outboard side, and flying screens port and starboard on the inboard side. He also created a decorative screen for the central part of the room. All the sculptures were in aluminium and in the style of the 'Geometry of Fear' generation of British, abstract sculptors of the time, who had made such an impact at the 1952 Venice Biennale (Black 1994).

There was more contemporary, abstract art in the tourist class main lounge or William Fawcett room. The large space was decorated with tinted glass murals by Robert Y. Goodden around the translucent, silver-white fibre-glass walls. Goodden was another Festival of Britain veteran, having designed the Lion and Unicorn Pavilion. At the centre of the room, two larger murals were set in black bean wood. John Wright, the architect for the tourist class areas as a whole, designed two fountains for the restaurant which featured bubbling fluorescent water spiralling up through pipes, carrying table tennis balls with it. The furniture was in moulded plywood and veneered in black bean and covered in bronzed green leather and purple tweed. The carpet was dark gold, which contrasted with the mauve and pink curtains. Like the first class Meridian Room, the William Fawcett room was open plan, leading to a writing room and library which was separated from the main area by mirrored walls, with bent plywood furniture with high backs and plain white walls. The Peacock Room was a quiet room for reading, smoking and dancing and also featured abstract, contemporary art by Robert Adams (1917–84). He designed the unusual white canopy, which hung over the central part of the room. Constructed from painted white timber, it belied Adams's constructivist affiliations, with an abstract, linear arrangement. This was reflected on the wall beneath in a 'Sunburst' mural, also by Adams in white timber mounted on board in an abstract grouping. The curved walls of the room were covered in stained blue wood veneer with matching floor-length curtains in blue stripes with orange and gold. The furniture was of a similar style and construction to the dining room. The floor was cream with a diagonal black stripe indicating the dance floor area.

A more traditional form of British art was commissioned for the Island Room from Robert Buhler (1916–95). He created a series of mural panels depicting scenes from the various places which *Canberra* would visit. Like the first class children's room, they were painted on melamine impregnated paper and then processed into a melamine-faced Perstorp laminate. This was a flexible space, used for dances and concerts with a games deck, part of which was used as a children's playground during the day. Both sides of the room could be opened out onto the deck during hot weather. The seating was made from a drum of laminated plywood, from which four different chairs were cut. The main bar for the tourist class was the Cricketers'

Tavern, situated on the port side of B deck, designed with the advice of famous Test British cricketer, Colin Cowdrey, and an early example of a themed bar. This celebration of cricket reinforced the British national identity as a sporting nation with a Commonwealth rather than an Empire, an image which was used at the Festival of Britain and in advertising for British products. Four full-length portraits in oil of the famous English, Australian, West Indian and Indian cricketers, W.G. Grace, Sir Donald Bradman, Learie N. Constantine and K.S. Ranjitsinhji by British portrait painter, Ruskin Spear (1911–90) dominated the room. Cricketing paraphernalia decorated the willow wood, striped covered walls in a display designed by Margaret Redfern. The bar was made from willow and white marble and behind it were over 150 club ties from around the world. For younger tourist class passengers, there was the 'Pop Inn', which was decorated by Royal College of Art students. The teenagers could play music by means of a juke box, dance, play table tennis and buy drinks from machines. The walls were clad in deal and decorated with poker work by students, including David Hockney. Paintings by the students also featured on the walls. The bar tops were made of multicoloured strips of Perspex, with fluorescent strips at random intervals. The upholstery was nylon, fun fur, and a multicoloured strip in the shape of a scribble decorated the ceiling. According to P&O: 'Noise is not obligatory, but there is a juke-box stacked with "pop" records to give full scope for exuberance. There are soft-drink dispensers too – even in shape the room is far from square!' (P&O 1961: 16).

Tourist class was provided with two pools, one of which was called Alice Springs, with underwater views into the pool, decorated with glass mosaics in a peacock feather design by the artist Arnold Machin (1911–99). The remainder of the room was plain white with cane furniture and cane frontage to the bar. The other pool was the lido on the upper deck, which incorporated a paddling pool for children. This space was decorated with multicoloured mosaics by Edward Bawden (1903–89), who had created a large mural in the Lion and Unicorn pavilion at the Festival of Britain. The tourist class playroom was decorated in white and yellow with a mural, laminated into the wall, of fantasy birds and animals by Mary Feddon (b. 1915).

The *Canberra*'s public rooms as a whole combined contemporary furniture and furnishings, with modern art. Further unity of appearance was ensured by the use of a specially designed *Canberra* typeface by Edward Burrett, which was used for all on-board signage, printed material and even the ship's newspaper. It was a medium weight, sans serif which was simple, legible and modern. Use was also made on the ship of new technology and materials, such as aluminium and plastics. The use of plastics for the private accommodation was even more striking. A million and a quarter square feet of Swedish Perstorp plastic laminate was used on the *Canberra*, for the children's rooms, doors, skirting boards, galleys and corridors. The most prevalent use of plastic was for the cabins, bathrooms and toilets. P&O made a feature of their use of the material in a separate section of the press release which accompanied the introduction of the ship. The decorating firm of Heaton Tabb and Company, who had been involved with ship decoration since the time of the *Titanic*, were responsible for bonding the plastic to the plywood cores. The use of the material cut down on the need to constantly redecorate frequently used spaces, like corridors, or places which usually experienced a lot of wear. A feature was even made of the material in the first class cabins, where fabric was laminated into Perstorp panels for the decoration of dressing table tops.

The first class cabins were designed by Barbara Oakley, who worked with Heals Contracts Ltd, on the eight de-luxe suites on C deck. Each of the suites had a dayroom which could be converted to a bedroom, entrance lobby, bathroom, toilet and luggage storage space. The height of luxury was the four veranda suites on B deck, with a double bedroom separated from a veranda sitting room with curtains. The large windows in the sitting area afforded views of the sea; there was also a private bathroom and toilet. The main sitting room was furnished in contemporary style with a low settee and a unit which contained clock, radio, cocktail cabinet and television. Two of the four suites had communicating doors to accommodate a large group travelling together, as did four of the de-luxe suites. The walls of the first class cabins were covered with white Vynide, which was a soft plastic with a texture resembling linen, and fitted carpets. All the 305 first class cabins had either a private bath or shower. The tourist class cabins, however, were faced in ordinary plastic and had a square of carpet on the floor. Heaton Tabb manufactured pre-fabricated glass fibre shower and toilet units for tourist class, and John West designed a compact shower with a cylindrical Perspex screen, meaning that nearly 100 of the 509 tourist class cabins could enjoy en-suite facilities.

Plastic laminate was also to provide a fitting interior finish for much of Cunard's next ocean liner, the *QE2*. The ship was originally destined to be rather more traditional in appearance, due to the influence of the Chairman's wife, Lady Brocklebank. However, after objections from the British government and the Council of Industrial Design, the ship eventually entered service on the Southampton to New York line in 1969 as a modern symbol of British national identity. This transformation could be characterized as a shift from chintz to Formica, a shift in the way that British national identity was represented by an ocean liner. At the time of its launch, the British design press were dismissive of preceding liner design, and looked to the *QE2* for a long awaited confirmation of modern movement design principles. As Sherban Cantacuzino commented in *Architectural Review*, in an introduction to its special issue on the *QE2*:

> In 1914 a serious critic would have dismissed derisively the mock interiors of the 'Aquitania'. A generation later he would have found a change of attitude towards style, but little to recommend, in the design of the 'Queen Mary'. Yet both these ships became in many ways the embodiment of their respective age – an embodiment glamorised by the ephemeral nature of ships. Whether the QE2 will be to the 1970s what the 'Aquitania' was to the 1920s will largely depend on factors outside the control of those responsible for her design. The design quality of the QE2 will continue to

bear fruit long after the tribulations that accompanied her first sea trials have been forgotten'.

(Architectural Review 1969: 397–8)

The *QE2* was a 'Swinging Ship', which used modern design to represent a new Britain. As *Design* magazine commented in 1969: '. . . the QE2 is a floating Swinging London, a Hilton à la Kings Road offering five extra days in London before you even get there' (April 1969: 37). A design advisory board was created to consider the interiors of the new luxury liner-cum-cruise ship. This consisted of the wife of the Chairman of Cunard, Lady Brocklebank; the Vice-Chairman, and Dan Wallace, the Naval Architect, with advice from interior designer, Jean Monro, who had finished her commissions for Union-Castle and the refits of the *Carmania* and *Franconia* for Cunard by this stage. Hence, she was available to advise Cunard on the latest ship.

For two years the group toured hotels in Europe and America, travelling by liners already in service and studying those under construction. During the early 1960s the leading examples the group studied, apart from *Carmania* and *Franconia*, were P&O's *Canberra*, in service from 1961 and the Orient Line's *Oriana* of 1960. Other examples, which may have presented more competition, included the French *France* of 1962 and the American *United States* and Dutch *Rotterdam*. In Britain there were concerns about the self-appointed design committee not making the most of British design. As early as September 1961, the *Architectural Review* was lobbying Lord Brocklebank to reconsider the design philosophy of Cunard:

> The statement by Lord Brocklebank, chairman of Cunard, that he would prefer the proposed new Queen liner to have 'a Georgian type interior', will have deepened the general apprehension felt when the Government announced their intended multi-million pound loan for her construction. But against Cunard's bad reputation in the field of interior design can now be set two new British ships that show how well we can do. The *Oriana* and the *Canberra*, . . . are object lessons in the contribution that sensible ship-owners, and the good designers they employ, can make.
>
> (Garrett 1961: 155)

After questions were asked in the House, Cunard were forced to defend their position by the new Labour government, voted in a year before and perhaps anxious to change the national identity of Britain after Harold Wilson's 'White Hot Heat of Technological Revolution' speech. In February 1965 Cunard met reluctantly with the Council of Industrial Design to view the portfolios of eight selected and approved designers. Lady Brocklebank released a grudging statement after the meeting:

> There was no intention that they should not be consulted. We are in full agreement with the Council that this ship should reflect what is best in British design, but it will be some months before we reach finality and appoint the design team, including those responsible for co-ordination'.
>
> <div align="right">(<i>Sunday Times</i>, 28 February 1965)</div>

However, Cunard needed to bow rather more to government pressure, as the completion of the *QE2* was reliant on a loan of £17,600,000 from the government. When questions were asked in the House of Commons about the design of the ship, Roy Mason, Minister of State at the Board of Trade, replied: 'Cunard know the importance I attach to standards of industrial design in a ship of this kind and are taking full advantage of the wide range of new fittings and equipment now available in Britain. But under the terms of the loan we have no power to insist on any particular interior design or the appointment of any particular designer' (Potter and Frost 1969: 126).

In October 1965 the full list of designers appointed was announced by Cunard. This included Jean Monro and her friend, the interior decorator Evelyn Pinching; the society interior designers David Hicks and Michael Inchbald; veterans of the Festival of Britain and probably recommendations of the Council of Industrial Design, Dennis Lennon and James Gardner, plus exhibition and yacht designer Jon Bannenberg and industrial designer Gaby Schreiber, who had designed the interiors of BOAC aircraft. The team were criticized by the British press for being a heterogeneous group which would lack a unified vision. However, Lady Brocklebank defended the choice, stating: 'It is an exciting project and we have got the best people for the job' (Potter and Frost 1969: 126). Lady Brocklebank attempted to provide design leadership for the *QE2*, despite media criticism.

However, by November 1965 Lord Brockelbank was forced to retire due to ill health and so his wife could no longer be involved with the *QE2*. As his successor, Sir Basil Smallpeice commented: 'Not surprisingly, in view of Liverpool's dearth of management experience in the field, Lady Brocklebank had taken upon herself the responsibility for these matters. Although the chairman's wife, she had no official position in the company, and it was an untenable arrangement' (Smallpeice 1981: 197). Smallpeice came from the London office of Cunard and had worked at BOAC before that. He was from an accountancy background, and was more commercially minded and led a significant change of direction for Cunard. At a meeting at the shipbuilders, John Brown's, in December 1965, Smallpeice: '. . . reviewed the recent happenings in the Cunard Company and outlined their new selling policy whereby emphasis would be on the hotel rather than on the transport function. He stated that it was vital to Cunard that the delivery date for No. 736 be achieved if Cunard's recovery programme were to be successful. Sir Basil stated that as a result of a current survey it might prove advantageous to alter the number of classes of accommodation or the type of accommodation, but any changes would be superficial' (Glasgow University John Brown Archive UCS1/107/433 Ship No. 736 Minutes of Cunard Meetings: Diary Note of Meeting 17 December 1966).

The survey Smallpeice referred to was by the Economist Intelligence Unit, conducted mainly in America, where the majority of passengers would come from, and found that passengers would be more comfortable with no classes on board, as opposed to the three classes which Cunard had been designing for since the beginning of the company in 1840. This presented some major problems for the shipbuilders,

John Brown's, who had signed the contract to build the new Cunard in the old format in 1964.

John Brown, represented by Lord Aberconway, were not convinced by Smallpeice's reassurances, and urged Cunard to consider extending the completion deadline. John Brown emphasised: '. . . the need for a very careful examination of all changes as sometimes what appeared on the surface to be superficial involved a considerable change in design; for instance in piping.' An extension of three months was granted by Cunard and work began on converting a three class ship into a two class ship, with integration between the two. Smallpeice had discussions with the Chairman of the Council of Industrial Design, Sir Duncan Oppenheim, late in 1965, and in early January 1966 announced that 'Q4 will get the professional touch' (*Sunday Times* 2 January 1966) with James Gardner, already appointed to style the exterior of the ship, and Dennis Lennon, to co-ordinate the design of the interior.

This was a challenge, given the revision of the class segregation on board, whereby public rooms such as the dining room or library, did not have to appear in triplicate. The new approach meant that the tourist class and cabin class could be merged, giving the opportunity for a Double Room – a merging of the cabin class and tourist class lounges, previously arranged on two separate decks, one above the other, to be a double storey room with a wide sweeping staircase. Some changes in the design team also took place and were announced in February 1966. Theo Crosby and Stephan Buzas joined the existing team of eight, and Hugh Casson, then Professor of Interior Design at the Royal College of Art, was appointed, with some students to design the teenage and children's rooms, as they had done successfully on P&O's *Canberra*. This may look like 'jobs for the boys', and it is striking how the majority of women involved at various times with the interior design of the *QE2* were associated with the amateur and with the domestic. For example, John Barry in *The Sunday Times* reviewed the conflict on 28 February 1965, just after Cunard had visited the Council of Industrial Design, with the headline: 'Design men fear the Q4 will be too olde worlde' and women's involvement with the interior design of the QE2, which began as high profile, resulted in Jean Monro's resignation from the project in May 1966, possibly because she had been relegated from interior design consultant to designer of cabins with no responsibility for the public rooms. Similarly, Evelyn Pinching was charged by the new design co-ordinators to design the crew accommodation and the lower-class swimming pool, the hierarchy of gender reflecting the hierarchy which still characterized the ship's interior layout. She was replaced by Mrs Jo Pattrick. In April 1967, when work was well underway on the interiors, the *QE2* was featured in the new *Weekend Telegraph Colour Magazine*. The new model of the ship was featured, surrounded by the Cunard Board. This featured Lady Tweedsmuir, 'Cunard's first woman director who is advising on the practical aspects of the Q4 from the passenger viewpoint'.

The magazine also featured the design team. Dennis Lennon took over the design of all passageways and cabins and connecting staircases, to give the interior unity; Jon Bannenberg the public lounge, room suites and entertainment facilities; David Hicks the night club that converts to a public room by day; and Michael Inchbald the main lounge and library. The design process was tightly controlled and an internal memo by Cunard's Managing Director, Philip Bates, of May 1966 clearly set out the working arrangements whereby all decisions regarding the interior design were reported to the Chairman, Deputy Chairman and Managing Director of Cunard. As design co-ordinators, Gardner and Lennon were responsible to Cunard for 'the visual character and design treatment', and keeping the Naval Architect, Technical Director and New Project Director fully informed of progress. The approved plans were then sent to John Brown; if they had problems, then they contacted the Naval Architect at Cunard. Meetings took place in London with James Gardner and Dennis Lennon and the Naval Architect, to resolve problems. The design process was a tortuous one; the archives of the shipbuilder, John Brown in Glasgow, reveal frustration at the seemingly ever changing interior designs. For example, in December 1966 John Brown wrote to Cunard about changes to the first class Lido Lounge/Night Club and Casino: 'Reduction of the width of the doors to stairway about frame 68 is noted and we are proceeding accordingly in respect of the sliding panel fire door but it should be borne in mind that according to our present information 305 persons have to escape through the doorway which appears to be 6' 3" wide'. And in June 1967 John Brown complained to Cunard about the grill room and bar: 'Lennon's letter further advises us to assume 100 watts per table lamp. Are we to understand that the wattage will, in fact, be 100?'

Despite this clash of culture, the interior design of the *QE2* was a harmonized, British brand of modernism with acknowledgement of the pop colours and materials of Swinging London. One uniting feature was the use of Formica for most passageways and some cabin class rooms. Formica won the exclusive contract to supply all laminates, as the company had recently developed a new, textured finished to line walls and ceilings that resembled fabric or parchment, rather than the usual smooth laminate. Of the two million square feet on the ship, over half was covered in Formica in different surface patterns – for example, light blue paisley for the tourist bathrooms and brown stripes for the first class bathrooms. Wood panelling was reserved for use in the first class areas on decks 1 and 2.

Cunard were keen to publicize the ship and as part of this promotion of the *QE2* as modern there was an exhibition at the Council of Industrial Design's Headquarters in Haymarket. Entitled: 'QE2 – A First Look Inside the New Cunarder' from 21 February until 23 March 1968. The opening of the exhibition was supported by a raft of press photographs from Cunard, showing cabins inhabited by suitably swinging models. Princess Margaret opened the exhibition and enthused: '. . . this new Cunarder will show that design in Britain is not only exciting and full of vigorous common sense but is always out in front, leading the field. A great ship like *Queen Elizabeth 2*, must inevitably be looked upon as a sort of flag-ship for the nation. It just might have turned out to be a 'grandmotherly, chintzy hotel' (Potter and Frost 1969: 130). The exhibition featured the Britannia Restaurant with chairs by Robert Heritage for Race Furniture Ltd; 1,300 were required for the ship which presented immense technical challenges. The aluminium frames were stuck together with Araldite and the backs faced with Formica. There was also a model of the children's room. The media reception of the designs was positive and much in accordance with Princess Margaret's remarks. *The Daily Telegraph* commented: 'There's nothing of the old lady about the new *Queen Elizabeth 2*. She is smart, crisp and modern, using new colours and fabrics and materials'. And *The Times*, so critical of the earlier design approach, was entirely positive: 'The impression is of good 1960s hotel design compared with good 1930s design of the old Queens. Moulded wood, wrought metal, folkweave, and damask are out; plastic, tweed, leather are in; green, brown, and gold are out; oatmeal, sun yellow, dark blue, and magnolia are in' (Potter and Frost 1969 130–1).

The ship was first sailed to New York, and *Life* magazine reported 'Far better than most modern resorts, the QE2 encapsulates its customer in a comfortable world of chrome, veneer, mirror, inset brass and stainless steel . . .' (1969: 46). The first public space which passengers encountered was the circular Midships Lobby by Dennis Lennon. Traditionally this had been a grandiose space, with sweeping staircases and carved wood panelling. Here there was chrome, set off by navy hide-covered walls, apple green hide-covered seating, surrounding a trumpet-shaped, white column which spans out to meet the silver painted, segmented ceiling, illuminated by spotlights. The carpet was ink blue.

6.7
**Dennis Lennon,
First Class Cabin,
QE2, Cunard,
1969.**
Source: Brighton
University Design
Archives

The public staircases were in similar modern style. As *Design* magazine commented: 'The public stairs on the QE2 are a far cry from the extravagant sweeping steps and elaborate rococo balustrades once beloved of Hollywood musicals and ocean liners. Pure function has replaced those flights of fancy; instead of carved curlicues and ormolu nymphs, two parallel bands of coloured reinforced plastic hurtle down the stairwells in a square spiral' (1969: 51). But wasn't this one fantasy replacing another? The four sets of stairs came in four colours – red, ochre, blue and white, which was echoed in the colour schemes for the interiors of the lifts. The Double Room was by Jon Bannenberg, so called because it provided a double height room between the Upper and Boat Decks. Smoked brown glass was used to frame the dance floor and add contrast to the balustrades and aluminium planked ceiling. *Design* magazine was critical of the apparently jarring colour scheme and materials: 'But the saving feature of the room is undoubtedly its carpet, a lush herringbone of puce and damson, specially woven by Kosset . . .' (1969: 244).

One of the 'most spectacular' of the public rooms to be selected by *Architectural Review* in its special issue in 1969, was the first class lounge, or 'Queen's Room' by Michael Inchbald. This was basically square in layout, with white fibre-glass, tulip shaped columns which merge into the white fibreglass ceiling. White fibreglass troughs for plants were used to frame the sunken dance floor. The end wall was decorated in fibreglass blocks, veneered in walnut with mirror between. The chairs were designed by Inchbald, but draw heavily on Saarinen pedestal prototypes and were upholstered in beige leather. The coffee tables were polished aluminium topped with walnut, and the trumpet shape of the columns were again echoed in the form of the table pedestal.

The Lookout, by Theo Crosby, at the bow of the ship, used dark colours with cedar veneered walls and olive green carpet. Visual relief was provided by the pop art red chart reader, matched by a vermilion piano on the opposite side. The Britannia Restaurant, by Dennis Lennon, had a red, blue and white colour scheme and could seat 800. The Columbia Restaurant, by Dennis Lennon, could seat 500 first class passengers, and the first class Midships Bar by Denis Lennon, was the most opulent of the rooms, complete with gold leaf ceiling in the bar area.

Cunard successfully used modern design to express a new national identity, and moved away from chintz and embraced the world of Formica. But this was not everlasting modernism; it was fashionable modernism which did not stand the test of time. The *QE2* is still popular, now run by American owned Carnival Corporation, based in Miami. The Formica has now been stripped out to make way for more traditional wood panelling, perhaps indicating that it is the style of modernism which hasn't stood the test of time as a suitable expression of British national identity. Or perhaps in the age of globalization the nadir of national identity has passed with the demise of colonialism.

The latest cruise ship to enter the Cunard service is the *Queen Mary 2*. At 151,400 gross tons the ship is the ultimate floating hotel, the substantial increase in interior volume made possible by a huge, central six storey high atrium and a

6.8
John Bannenberg, Double Room, QE2, Cunard, 1969.
Source: Author's collection

6.9
Michael Inchbald, Queen's Room, QE2, Cunard, 1969.
Source: Author's collection

considerable air draft of 62 metres, the maximum permissible. The interiors of the ship were predominantly designed by the specialist ship architecture firm of Tilberg Design, based in Sweden. The interiors mirror current trends in global hotel design with some references to Cunard's past, with the Britannic Restaurant and mural of the original *Queen Mary* in the atrium. But this is primarily a cruise ship, designed for holidays, and is a floating, multi-storey hotel, which can transport its passengers from tourist port to port without the need to change hotel rooms. But the ship still represents a form of heterotopia, a special place which is no place, a floating fantasy world, open only to a certain section of the global population, as has been the case with all the ship interiors covered in this book. Only the constitution of the elites have changed and a new profession of ship interior architect has now emerged.

Appendix 1

Ships and their interior designers

Vessel	Line	Lead designer	Associated designers
Alsation	Allan Line	Crawley, George A.	
Amerika	Hamburg-Amerika	Mewès, Charles	Davis, Arthur E. Waring & Gillow
Andes II	Royal Mail Lines	Heaton Tabb & Co.	Hampton and Sons
Andrea Doria	Italian Line	Ponti, Gio	Longoni, Matteo
Aquitania	Cunard Line	Davis, Arthur Joseph	
Arabia	P&O-Orient Line	Collcutt, Thomas Edward	De Morgan, William
Aragon	Royal Mail Lines	Trollope & Sons	H.P. Mutters & Zn
Arcadia	P&O-Orient Line	Oakley, Barbara	
Arlanza I	Royal Mail Lines	H.P. Mutters & Zn	
Austral	Orient Line	Stevenson, J.J.	
Berengaria	Cunard Line	Mewès, Charles	
Bremen IIII	Norddeutscher Lloyd	Breuhaus de Groot, Fritz August	
Britannia	P&O-Orient Line	De Morgan, William	
Canberra	P&O-Orient Line	Casson, Hugh	Oakley, Barbara Wright, John
Carmania II	Cunard Line	Monro, Jean	Inchbald, Michael Pinching, Evelyn
Caronia II	Cunard Line	Cunard & John Brown	
China II	P&O-Orient Line	Collcutt, Thomas Edward	De Morgan, William
Columbus	Norddeutscher Lloyd	Troost, Paul Ludwig	
Conte Biancamano	Italian Line	La Casa Artistica	

Appendix 1

Vessel	Line	Lead designer	Associated designers
Conte Di Savoia	Italian Line	Pulitzer, Gustavo F.	
Conte Grande	Lloyd Sabaudo	La Casa Artistica	Ponti, Gio
Conte Rosso	Lloyd Sabaudo	La Casa Artistica	
Conte Verde	Lloyd Sabaudo	La Casa Artistica	
Cristoforo Colombo	Italian Line	Longoni, Matteo	
Egypt	P&O-Orient Line	Collcutt, Thomas Edward	De Morgan, William
Empress of Asia	Canadian Pacific Railway Company	Crawley, George A.	
Empress of Britain II	Canadian Pacific Railway Company	Staynes, P.A. and Jones, A.H.	Lavery, John Robinson, W. Heath Allom, Charles Dulac, Edmund Brangwyn, Frank
Empress of Russia	Canadian Pacific Railway Company	Crawley, George A.	
Europa	Norddeutscher Lloyd	Troost, Paul Ludwig	
Europa	Bremer Schiffsverchartungs AG, Bremen	Jochim Buchwald and Wilfred Kohnemann, with further academic advice from Prof. Arno Votteler of Akademie der Bildenen Kunste, Stuttgart	
France II	French Line	Nelson	
France III	French Line	Peynet, G.	
Franconia I	Cunard Line	Architect's drawings mentioned in Cunard PR1/48. Willink & Dod/Jacksons	
Franconia III	Cunard Line	Monro, Jean	Inchbald, Michael Pinching, Evelyn
George Washington	Norddeutscher Lloyd	Paul, Bruno	Schroder, Rudolf Vereinigte Werkstatten
Giulio Cesare	Italian Line	Ponti, Gio	
Iberia	P&O-Orient Line	Barbara Oakley	
Ile de France	French Line	Bouwens Van der Boijen, Richard	Danis, M.R. Ruhlmann, Emile-Jacques Mare, Andre Sue, Louis Patout, Pierre
Imperator	Hamburg-Amerika	Mewès, Charles	Bischoff, Alphonse
India	P&O-Orient Line	Collcutt, Thomas Edward	De Morgan, William
Ivernia II	Cunard Line	Leach, E.C.	
Kaiser Wilhelm der Grosse	Norddeutscher Lloyd	Poppe, Johannes	

Vessel	Line	Lead designer	Associated designers
Kaiser Wilhelm II	Norddeutscher Lloyd	Poppe, Johannes	
Kaiserin Auguste Victoria	Hamburg-Amerika	Mewès, Charles	Davis, Arthur E. Waring & Gillow
Kronprinzessin Cecilie	Norddeutscher Lloyd	Poppe, Johannes	Runge and Scotland Riemerschmid, Richard Paul, Bruno Olbrich. Josef
Kungsholm IIII	Swedish American Line	Tillberg Design	
La Provence	Societe Generale de Transport Maritime	Andre Arbus	
Laconia	Cunard Line	Willink & Dod/Jacksons	
Lahn	Norddeutscher Lloyd	Poppe, Johannes	
Leviathan	United States Line	Schoen, Eugene	
Liberté	French Line	Domin, Andre	
Lusitania	Cunard Line	James Miller	
Majestic II	White Star Line	Mewès, Charles	
Malta II	P&O-Orient Line	De Morgan, William	
Mauretania I	Cunard Line	Peto, Harold A.	
Michelangelo	Italian Line	Pulitzer, Gustavo F.	
Monte Sarmiento	Hamburg Sudamerika Dampfschiffahrts Gellschaft	Blohm & Voss	
Nieuw Amsterdam I	Holland America Line	H.P. Mutters & Zn	
Noordam I	Holland America Line	H.P. Mutters & Zn	
Normandie	French Line	Jean Patou/Henri Pacon and Roger-Henri Expert/Richard Bouwnes	Lalique, Rene Simon, Marc Dunand, Jean Dupas, Jean de Vilmorin, Madame Ruhlmann, Emile-Jacques
Nubia	P&O-Orient Line	De Morgan, William	
Oceana	P&O-Orient Line	De Morgan, William	
Oceanic II	White Star Line	Shaw, Richard Norman	Trollope & Sons
Olympic	White Star Line	Heaton & Co.	H.P. Mutters & Zn
Ophir	Orient Line	Stevenson, J.J.	
Orama	Orient Line	Whyte, Robert	
Orcades	P&O-Orient Line	O'Rorke, Brian	
Oriana	P&O-Orient Line	DRU	O'Rorke, Brian

Appendix 1

Vessel	Line	Lead designer	Associated designers
Oriana II	P&O-Orient Line	Tillberg Design	
Orient	Orient Line	Stevenson, J.J.	
Orion	P&O-Orient Line	O'Rorke, Brian	
Ormuz	Orient Line	Stevenson, J.J.	
Oronsay	P&O-Orient Line	O'Rorke, Brian	
Orontes	Orient Line	Stevenson, J.J.	
Orsova	P&O-Orient Line	O'Rorke, Brian	Wright, John
Orvieto	Orient Line	Prentice, Andrew N.	
Palawan	P&O-Orient Line	De Morgan, William	
Paris	French Line	Bouwens Van der Boijen, Richard	Sue, Louis Mare, Andre Follot, Paul Brandt, Edgar Lalique, Rene Remon & Fils
Pendennis Castle	Union-Castle Line	Monro, Jean	
Persia	P&O-Orient Line	Collcutt, Thomas Edward	De Morgan, William
Potsdam	Holland America Line	H.P. Mutters & Zn	
Principe di Udine	Lloyd Sabaudo	La Casa Artistica	
Prinz Friedrich Wilhelm	Norddeutscher Lloyd	Paul, Bruno	
Prinz Ludwig	Norddeutscher Lloyd	Poppe, Johannes	
Prinzessin Victoria Luise	Hamburg-Amerika	Blohm & Voss/Waring & Gillow	
QE2	Cunard Line	James Gardner and Dennis Lennon	Crosby, Theo Buzas, Stephen Bannenberg, Jon Hicks, David Inchbald, Michael Casson, Hugh Patrick, Jo Schreiber, Gaby
Queen Elizabeth	Cunard Line	Wornum, Grey	Lambert, Maurice
Queen Mary	Cunard Line	Arthur E. Davis and Benjamin Morris	Zinkeisen, Doris Lambert, Maurice
Queen Mary 2	Cunard Line	Tillberg Design	
Razmak	P&O-Orient Line	Mackay, Hon. Elsie	
Rex	Italian Line	Studio Ducrot, Palmero	
Rijndam	Holland America Line	H.P. Mutters & Zn	

Vessel	Line	Lead designer	Associated designers
Robert Ley	Deutsche Arbeitsfront	Prof. Woldenar Brinkmann	
Rotterdam III	Holland America Line	H.P. Mutters & Zn	
Rotterdam IIII	Holland America Line	H.P. Mutters & Zn	
Rotterdam IIIIII	Holland America Line	Tienhoven, J.A. van	Mutero, N.V. Bommel, Jan van Wirtz, Carl L.W. Semey, Jac F. Engelen, Cornelius J. Elffers, Cornelius
Royal Princess	Princess Cruises	Hirsch-Bedner with Njal Eide	
Saturnia	Cosulich Lines	La Casa Artistica	
Saxonia II	Cunard Line	Leach, E.C.	
St Sunniva	North of Scotland & Orkney & Shetland Steam Navigation Co., Aberdeen	Hall, Russell	
Standam I	Holland America Line	H.P. Mutters & Zn	
Standam II	Holland America Line	H.P. Mutters & Zn	
Standam III	Holland America Line	H.P. Mutters & Zn	
Star Princess	P&O-Orient Line	Welton Becket & Associates, Santa Monica	
Strathaird	P&O-Orient Line	Inchcape, Lady	Shaw, Lady Margaret
Strathnaver	P&O-Orient Line	Inchcape, Lady	Shaw, Lady Margaret
Sumatra	P&O-Orient Line	De Morgan, William	
Sutlej	P&O-Orient Line	De Morgan, William	
Titanic	White Star Line	Heaton & Co.	H.P. Mutters & Zn
Tuscania II	Anchor Line	Holden, Charles (of Adams, Holden & Pearson)	
United States	United States Line	Eggers & Higgins	Smith, Urquhart & Markwald
Vaterland	Hamburg-Amerika	Mewès, Charles	
Veendam II	Holland America Line	H.P. Mutters & Zn	
Viceroy of India	P&O-Orient Line	Mackay, Hon. Elsie	Waring & Gillow
Vulcania	Cosulich Lines	La Casa Artistica	
Wilhelm Gustloff	Deutsche Arbeitsfront	Prof. Woldenar Brinkmann	
Windsor Castle	Union-Castle Line	Monro, Jean	Inchbald, Michael

Appendix 2

Notable ships

Allan Line

Vessel	Tonnage	Builder	Built	Maiden voyage	Route	Disposed
Alsation	18,485	William Beardmore and Co.	Glasgow	1914	Britain to Canada	1934
Tunisian	10,576	Alexander Stephen & Sons Ltd	Glasgow	1917	Liverpool to St John	1928
Victorian	10,687	Workman, Clark & Co.	Belfast	1922	Glasgow to St John	1929

Anchor Line

Vessel	Tonnage	Builder	Built	Maiden voyage	Route	Disposed
Caledonia IV	17,046	Alexander Stephen & Sons Ltd	Glasgow	1925	Glasgow to New York	1940
Caledonia V	11,255	Fairfield Shipbuilding & Engineering	Glasgow	1948	New York, Mediterranean, India	1971
California III	16,792	Alexander Stephen & Sons Ltd	Glasgow	1923	Glasgow to New York	1943
Cameronia II	16,365	William Beardmore and Co.	Glasgow	1921	Liverpool to New York	1957
Cilicia	11,172	Fairfield Shipbuilding & Engineering	Glasgow	1938	New York, Mediterranean, India	1980
Circassia	11,170	Fairfield Shipbuilding & Engineering	Glasgow	1937	New York, Mediterranean, India	1966
City of Rome	11,230	Barrow Shipbuilding Co.	Barrow	1881	Liverpool to New York	1882
Columbia II	8,292	D. & W. Henderson Ltd	Glasgow	1902	Glasgow to New York	1926
Tempest	866	Sandeman & McLaurin Whiteinch	Glasgow	1856	Glasgow to New York	1857
Transylvania II	16,923	Fairfield Shipbuilding & Engineering	Glasgow	1925	Glasgow to New York	1940
Tuscania II	16,991	Fairfield Shipbuilding & Engineering	Glasgow	1922	Glasgow to New York & Mediterranean	1939

Atlantic Transport Line

Vessel	Tonnage	Builder	Built	Maiden voyage	Route	Disposed
Minnekahda	17,221	Harland & Wolff Ltd	Belfast	1921	Hamburg to New York	1936
Minnetonka II	21,988	Harland & Wolff Ltd	Belfast	1924	London to New York	1934
Minnewaska III	21,716	Harland & Wolff Ltd	Belfast	1923	London to New York	1934

Bibby Line

Vessel	Tonnage	Builder	Built	Maiden voyage	Route	Disposed
Derbyshire	10,641	Fairfield Shipbuilding & Engineering	Glasgow	1935	Port Said, Port Sudan, Aden, Colombo, Rangoon	1964
Devonshire	12,773	Fairfield Shipbuilding & Engineering	Glasgow	1939	India	1962
Leicestershire	8,922	Fairfield Shipbuilding & Engineering	Glasgow	1949	Port Said, Port Sudan, Aden, Colombo, Rangoon	1966
Warwickshire	8,917	Fairfield Shipbuilding & Engineering	Glasgow	1948	Port Said, Port Sudan, Aden, Colombo, Rangoon	1964
Worcestershire	10,329	Fairfield Shipbuilding & Engineering	Glasgow	1931	Port Said, Port Sudan, Aden, Colombo, Rangoon	1961

Blue Funnel Line

Vessel	Tonnage	Builder	Built	Maiden voyage	Route	Disposed
Centaur III	8,262	John Brown & Company Ltd	Clydebank	1963	Australia and Singapore	1985
Charon	3,964	Caledon Shipbuilding & Engineering Co	Dundee	1936	Singapore to Freemantle	1964
Gorgon	3,678	Caledon Shipbuilding & Engineering Co	Dundee	1933	Singapore to Freemantle	1964
Gunung Djati	17,891	Blohm & Voss	Hamburg	1936	Indonesia and Jeddah, Indian Ocean	1962
Hector	10,125	Harland & Wolff Ltd	Belfast	1949–50	Liverpool, Port Said, Aden, Albany, Freemantle, Adelaide, Melbourne and Sydney	1972
Helenus	10,129	Harland & Wolff Ltd	Belfast	1949–50	Liverpool, Port Said, Aden, Albany, Freemantle, Adelaide, Melbourne and Sydney	1972
Ixion	10,125	Harland & Wolff Ltd	Belfast	1949–50	Liverpool, Port Said, Aden, Albany, Freemantle, Adelaide, Melbourne and Sydney	1972

Vessel	Tonnage	Builder	Built	Maiden voyage	Route	Disposed
Jason	10,160	Swan, Hunter & Wigham Richardson Ltd.	Newcastle	1949–50	Liverpool, Port Said, Aden, Albany, Freemantle, Adelaide, Melbourne and Sydney	1972
Patroclus	10,109	Vickers Armstrong Shipbuilders Ltd	Newcastle	1950	Liverpool, Rotterdam, Port Said, Singapore, Manila, Hong Kong, Kobe and Yokohama	1973
Peleus	10,093	Cammell Laird & Co. Ltd	Birkenhead	1949	Liverpool, Rotterdam, Port Said, Singapore, Manila, Hong Kong, Kobe and Yokohama	1972
Perseus	10,109	Vickers Armstrong Shipbuilders Ltd	Newcastle	1950	Liverpool, Rotterdam, Port Said, Singapore, Manila, Hong Kong, Kobe and Yokohama	1973
Pyrrhus	10,093	Cammell Laird & Co. Ltd	Birkenhead	1949	Liverpool, Rotterdam, Port Said, Singapore, Manila, Hong Kong, Kobe and Yokohama	1972

Blue Star Line

Vessel	Tonnage	Builder	Built	Maiden voyage	Route	Disposed
Arandora Star	12,847	Cammell Laird & Co. Ltd	Birkenhead	1927	South America	1940
Argentina Star	10,716	Cammell Laird & Co. Ltd	Birkenhead	1947–8	London, Lisbon, Madeira, Las Palmas, Tenerife, Recife, Salvador, Rio de Janeiro, Santos, Montevideo, Buenos Aires	1972
Brasil Star	10,716	Cammell Laird & Co. Ltd	Birkenhead	1947–8	London, Lisbon, Madeira, Las Palmas, Tenerife, Recife, Salvador, Rio de Janeiro, Santos, Montevideo, Buenos Aires	1972
Iberia Star	10,854	John Cockerill S/A	Hoboken	1950	London, Lisbon, Las Palmas, Rio de Janeiro, Santos, Montevideo, Buenos Aires	1973
Paraguay Star	10,723	Cammell Laird & Co. Ltd	Birkenhead	1947–8	London, Lisbon, Madeira, Las Palmas, Tenerife, Recife, Salvador, Rio de Janeiro, Santos, Montevideo, Buenos Aires	1969

Vessel	Tonnage	Builder	Built	Maiden voyage	Route	Disposed
Uruguay Star	10,722	Cammell Laird & Co. Ltd	Birkenhead	1947–8	London, Lisbon, Madeira, Las Palmas, Tenerife, Recife, Salvador, Rio de Janeiro, Santos, Montevideo, Buenos Aires	1972

Booth Line

Vessel	Tonnage	Builder	Built	Maiden voyage	Route	Disposed
Anselm	10,950	John Cockerill S/A	Hoboken	1950	Liverpool to Leixoes, Lisbon, Madeira, Barbados, Trinidad, Belem and Manaus	1973
Hubert	8,062	Cammell Laird & Co. Ltd	Birkenhead	1955	Liverpool to Leixoes, Lisbon, Madeira, Barbados, Trinidad, Belem and Manaus	1984

Bremer Schiffsverchartungs AG, Bremen

Vessel	Tonnage	Builder	Built	Maiden voyage	Route	Disposed
Europa	33,819	A.G. Vulkan	Bremen	1981	Worldwide cruising	

British India Steam Navigation Company

Vessel	Tonnage	Builder	Built	Maiden voyage	Route	Disposed
Amra	8,314	Swan, Hunter & Wigham Richardson Ltd	Newcastle	1938	Bombay to Mombasa and Dar-es-Salaam	1966
Aronda	8,396	Swan, Hunter & Wigham Richardson Ltd	Newcastle	1941	Karachi to Colombo and Chittagong	1963
Dara	5,030	Barclay Curle & Co. Ltd	Glasgow	1948	Bombay and Karachi to Persian Gulf ports; Pasni, Gnadur, Muscat, Bandar Abbas, Shahjab, Dubai, Umm Said, Bahrain, Bushire, Kuwait, Adadan, Khorramshahr and Basrah	1961
Daressa	4,180	Barclay Curle & Co. Ltd	Glasgow	1950	Bombay and Karachi to Persian Gulf ports (see Dara)	1974
Devonia	12,796	Fairfield Shipbuilding & Engineering	Glasgow	1939	Educational cruising – Med, Northern Europe, Scandinavia	1967

Name	Tonnage	Builder	Place	Year	Route/Service	Year
Dumra	4,867	Barclay Curle & Co. Ltd	Glasgow	1946	Bombay and Karachi to Persian Gulf ports; Pasni, Gnadur, Muscat, Bandar Abbas, Shahjab, Dubai, Umm Said, Bahrain, Bushire, Kuwait, Adadan, Khorramshahr and Basrah	1978
Dunera	12,615	Barclay Curle & Co. Ltd	Glasgow	1937	Govt trooping – Med, Middle and Far East	1967
Dwarka	4,851	Swan, Hunter & Wigham Richardson Ltd	Newcastle	1947	Bombay and Karachi to Persian Gulf ports (see Dumra)	1982
Kampala	10,304	Alexander Stephen & Sons Ltd	Glasgow	1947	Bombay and Karachi to the Seychelles, Mombassa, Zanzibar, Dar-es-Salaam, Beira, Lourenco Marques and Durban	1971
Karanja	10,294	Alexander Stephen & Sons Ltd	Glasgow	1948	India-Pakistan-East Africa (see Kampala)	1988
Kenya	14,464	Barclay Curle & Co. Ltd	Glasgow	1951	London to Gibraltar and/or Malta, Port Said, Aden, Mombasa, Tanga, Zanzibar, Dar-es-Dalam	1969
Mombasa	2,213	Henry Robb Ltd	Leith	1950	East African coastal run between Mombasa, Tanga, Zanzibar, Dar-es-Salaam, Lindi and Mtwara	1973
Nevasa	20,527	Barclay Curle & Co. Ltd	Glasgow	1956	Govt trooping – Med, Middle and Far East	1975
Rajula	8,496	Barclay Curle & Co. Ltd	Glasgow	1926	Madras, Nagapattinam, Penang and Singapore	1975
Sangola	8,647	Barclay Curle & Co. Ltd	Glasgow	1947	Calcutta to Rangoon, Penang, Singapore, Hong Kong, Yokohama and Kobe	1963
Santhia	8,908	Barclay Curle & Co. Ltd	Glasgow	1950	Bombay and Karachi to Persian Gulf ports (see Dumra)	1977
Sirdhana	8,608	Swan, Hunter & Wigham Richardson Ltd	Newcastle	1947	Calcutta to Rangoon, Penang, Singapore, Hong Kong, Yokohama and Kobe	1972
Uganda	14,430	Barclay Curle & Co. Ltd	Glasgow	1952	London to East Africa (same ports as Kenya)	1986

Canadian Pacific Railway Company

Vessel	Tonnage	Builder	Built	Maiden voyage	Route	Disposed
Duchess of Athol	20,119	William Beardmore and Co.	Clydebank	1928	Liverpool to Montreal	1942
Duchess of Bedford	20,123	John Brown & Company Ltd	Clydebank	1928	Liverpool to Montreal	1948
Duchess of Richmond	20,022	John Brown & Company Ltd	Clydebank	1929	Liverpool to St John	1947
Duchess of York	20,021	John Brown & Company Ltd	Clydebank	1929	Liverpool to St John	1943
Empress of Asia	16,909	Fairfield Shipbuilding & Engineering	Glasgow	1912	Liverpool to Hong Kong, Nagasaki, Vancouver	1942
Empress of Australia	21,833	A.G. Vulkan	Hamburg	1927	Southampton to Quebec	1952
Empress of Britain I	14,189	Fairfield Shipbuilding & Engineering	Glasgow	1906	Liverpool to Quebec	1930
Empress of Britain II	42,348	John Brown & Company Ltd	Glasgow	1931	Southampton to Quebec	1940
Empress of Britain III	25,516	Fairfield Shipbuilding & Engineering	Glasgow	1956	Liverpool to Montreal	1964
Empress of Canada II	20,222	John Brown & Company Ltd	Clydebank	1947	Liverpool to Canada	1953
Empress of Canada III	27,284	Vickers Armstrong Shipbuilders Ltd	Newcastle	1961	Liverpool to Montreal	1972
Empress of England	25,585	Vickers Armstrong Shipbuilders Ltd	Newcastle	1957	Liverpool to Montreal	1975
Empress of France I	20,448	John Brown & Company Ltd	Clydebank	1919	Liverpool and Greenock to Quebec City and Montreal (St John, New Brunswick in Winter)	1934
Empress of Japan	26,313	Fairfield Shipbuilding & Engineering	Glasgow	1930	Transpacific service from Vancouver	1966
Empress of Russia	16,810	Fairfield Shipbuilding & Engineering	Glasgow	1913	Liverpool, Vancouver, China and Japan	1945
Melita	15,183	Harland & Wolff Ltd	Belfast	1918	Liverpool to Quebec	1950
Metagama	12,420	Barclay Curle & Co. Ltd	Glasgow	1915	Liverpool to St John	1934
Minnedosa	15,186	Harland & Wolff Ltd	Belfast	1918	Liverpool to St John	1949
Montcalm III	16,418	John Brown & Company Ltd	Clydebank	1922	Liverpool to St John	1952
Montclare	16,314	John Brown & Company Ltd	Clydebank	1922	Liverpool to Montreal	1958
Montrose II	16,402	Fairfield Shipbuilding & Engineering	Glasgow	1922	Liverpool to Montreal	1940

Collins Line

Vessel	Tonnage	Builder	Built	Maiden voyage	Route	Disposed
Artic	2,856	W.H. Brown	New York	1850	New York to Liverpool	1854
Atlantic	2,800	Brown & Bell	New York	1850	New York to Liverpool	1858

Vessel	Tonnage	Builder	Built	Maiden voyage	Route	Disposed
Baltic	2,723	Brown & Bell	New York	1850	New York to Liverpool	1856
Pacific	2,707	Jacob Bell	New York	1850	New York to Liverpool	

Cosulich Line

Vessel	Tonnage	Builder	Built	Maiden voyage	Route	Disposed
Saturnia	23,346	Cantiere Navale Triestino	Monfalcone	1928	Trieste to South America	1965
Vulcania	24,496	Cantiere Navale Triestino	Monfalcone	1928	Triest to New York	1974

Cunard Line

Vessel	Tonnage	Builder	Built	Maiden voyage	Route	Disposed
Abyssinia	3,736	J. & G. Thomson	Clydebank	1870	Liverpool to New York	1880
Acadia	1,154	John Wood	Port Glasgow	1840	Liverpool to Halifax/Boston	1858
Alaunia I	13,405	Scotts Shipbuilding & Engineering Co.	Greenock	1913	Canada	1916
Alaunia II	14,030	John Brown & Company Ltd	Clydebank	1925	Liverpool to Montreal	1957
Albania I	7,640	Swan Hunters	Newcastle	1911	London/Southampton to London	1912
Albania II	12,768	Scotts Shipbuilding & Engineering Co.	Greenock	1921	Liverpool to New York	1941
Aleppo	2,057	J. & G. Thomson	Glasgow	1865	Liverpool to New York	1909
Algeria	3,428	J. & G. Thomson	Glasgow	1870	Liverpool to New York	1903
Alps	1,440	William Denny & Bros	Dumbarton	1852	Liverpool to New York	1859
America	3,520	Robert Steele & Co.	Greenock	1848	Liverpool to Boston/New York	1875
Andania I	13,405	Scotts Shipbuilding & Engineering Co.	Greenock	1913	Canada	1918
Andania II	13,950	R. & W. Hawthorn, Leslie & Co.	Hebburn-on-Tyne	1922	Canada	1940
Andes I	1,440	William Denny & Bros	Dumbarton	1852	Mediterranean	1859
Antonia	13,867	Vickers Armstrong Shipbuilders Ltd	Barrow	1922	Canada	1948
Aquitania	45,647	John Brown & Company Ltd	Clydebank	1914	Liverpool to New York	1950
Arabia	2,402	Robert Steele & Co.	Greenock	1853	Liverpool to New York	1868
Ascania I	9,111	Swan Hunters	Newcastle	1911	Southampton to Montreal	1918
Ascania II	14,013	Armstrong Whitworth	Newcastle	1925	Southampton to Quebec/Montreal	1956
Asia I	2,226	Robert Steele & Co.	Greenock	1850	Liverpool to New York	1876
Athenia	13,465	Fairfield Shipbuilding & Engineering	Glasgow	1923	Glasgow and Liverpool to Montreal	1939
Atlas	2,393	J. & G. Thomson	Glasgow	1873	Mediterranean	1896
Aurania I	7,269	J. & G. Thomson	Glasgow	1883	Liverpool to New York	1905

Ship	Tonnage	Builder	Place	Year	Route	Year
Aurania II	13,936	Swan Hunters	Newcastle	1917	Troop ship	1918
Aurania III	13,984	Swan Hunters	Newcastle	1924	New York and Montreal	1961
Ausonia I	7,907	Swan Hunters	Newcastle	1911	Southampton to Montreal	1918
Ausonia II	13,912	Armstrong Whitworth	Newcastle	1922	Hamburg then Canada	1965
Australasian	2,902	J. & G. Thomson	Glasgow	1860	Liverpool to New York	1898
Balbec I	774	William Denny & Bros	Dumbarton	1853	Mediterranean and Atlantic Routes	1884
Batavia	2,553	William Denny & Bros	Dumbarton	1870	Liverpool to New York	1924
Berengaria	52,002	A.G.Vulkan	Hamburg	1920	Liverpool to New York	1946
Bothnia	6,530	J. & G. Thomson	Clydebank	1874	Liverpool to Boston and New York	1899
Britannia	2,370	Robert Duncan	Greenock	1840	Liverpool to Boston	1880
British Queen	772	William Denny & Bros	Dumbarton	1851	Mediterranean then Liverpool to Le Havre feeder route	1899
Caledonia I	1,138	R. Wood	Port Glasgow	1840	Liverpool to Halifax, Boston, Quebec	1851
California	8,662	D. & W. Henderson Ltd	Glasgow	1907	Liverpool to New York	1917
Cambria	1,423	Robert Steele & Co.	Greenock	1844	Liverpool to New York and Boston	1875
Cameronia I	10,963	D. & W. Henderson Ltd	Glasgow	1915	Troop ship with Anchor Line	1917
Campania	19,450	Fairfield Shipbuilding & Engineering	Glasgow	1893	Liverpool to New York	1918
Canada	1,831	Robert Steele & Co.	Greenock	1848	New York to Boston	1883
Carinthia II	20,277	Vickers Ltd	Barrow	1925	Winter cruising from New York, Atlantic run summer	1940
Carinthia III	21,947	John Brown & Company Ltd	Clydebank	1956	Liverpool and Greenock to Quebec City and Montreal; Liverpool and Cobh to Halifax and New York in winter	1968
Carmania I	19,524	John Brown & Company Ltd	Clydebank	1905	Liverpool to New York	1932
Carmania II	21,370	John Brown & Company Ltd	Clydebank	1963	Rotterdam, Southampton to Canada	1969
Caronia I	19,594	John Brown & Company Ltd	Clydebank	1905	London to Canada	1933
Caronia II	34,172	John Brown & Company Ltd	Clydebank	1949	Cruising from New York to Pacific, Africa in Jan: Med in Spring; North Cape-Sandanavia in June; Med in Autumn. S'ton, Le Havre to New York	1974
Carpathia	13,555	Swan Hunters	Wallsend	1903	Liverpool to New York	1918
Cassandra	7,396	Scotts Shipbuilding & Engineering Co.	Greenock	1924	Canadian route	1934
Catalonia	4,841	J. & G. Thomson	Clydebank	1881	New York and Boston	1901

Ship	Tonnage	Builder	Built	Year	Route	Year
Cephalonia	5,517	Laird Bros	Birkenhead	1882	Liverpool to Boston	1904
China	2,638	Robert Napier	Clydebank	1862	Liverpool to New York	1906
Columbia I	1,175	Robert Steele & Co	Greenock	1841	Liverpool to Halifax and Boston	1843
Cuba	2,668	Tod & McGregor	Glasgow	1864	Liverpool to New York	1887
Damascus	1,213	William Denny & Bros	Dumbarton	1856	Mediterranean then Atlantic routes	1912
Etna	2,215	Caird & Co.	Greenock	1855	Troop ship for Crimean War	1896
Etruria	11,381	John Elder & Co	Glasgow	1885	Liverpool to New York	1910
Europa	1,834	John Wood	Glasgow	1848	New York to Boston/New York	1867
Feltria	5,254	William Denny & Bros	Dumbarton	1916	Troop ship	1917
Flavia	9,285	Palmers Co. Ltd	Jarrow	1916	Avonmouth to Canada	1918
Franconia I	18,150	Swan Hunters	Newcastle	1911	Mediterranean and Atlantic routes, then troop ship	1916
Franconia II	20,158	John Brown & Company Ltd	Glasgow	1923	Winter cruising from New York, Atlantic run summer	1956
Franconia III	22,637	John Brown & Company Ltd	Clydebank	1963	Cruising out of New York	1973
Gallia	8,188	J. & G. Thomson	Clydebank	1879	Liverpool to Boston and New York	1900
Hecla	1,785	Robert Napier	Glasgow	1860	Liverpool to Boston	1881
Hibernia	1,422	Robert Steele & Co.	Greenock	1843	Liverpool to Halifax and Boston	1850
Ivernia I	14,058	Swan Hunters	Wallsend	1900	Liverpool to Boston	1916
Ivernia II	21,717	John Brown & Company Ltd	Clydebank	1955	Renamed Franconia – Canadian route	1963
Java	2,696	J. & G. Thomson	Glasgow	1865	Boston and New York routes	1878
Jura	2,241	J. & G. Thomson	Glasgow	1857	New York and Montreal	1864
Karnak		William Denny & Bros	Dumbarton	1855	Mediterranean service	1862
Kedar	1,783	William Denny & Bros	Dumbarton	1860	Atlantic then Mediterranean	1897
Laconia	18,099	Swan Hunters	Newcastle	1912	Emigrants from southern Europe to US	1917
Laconia II	19,680	Swan Hunters	Newcastle	1922	World's first cruise 1922 then Atlantic run	1942
Lancastria	16,243	William Beardmore and Co	Clydebank	1922	Liverpool to New York	1940
Lebanon	1,373	J. & G. Thomson	Glasgow	1855	Liverpool to New York	1859
Lucania	12,952	Fairfield Shipbuilding & Engineering	Glasgow	1893	Liverpool to New York	1909
Lusitania	30,396	John Brown & Company Ltd	Clydebank	1907	Liverpool to New York	1915
Malta	2,132	J. & G. Thomson	Glasgow	1866	New York, Boston and Mediterranean runs	1889

Marathon	1,784	Robert Napier	Clydebank	1861	Liverpool to New York and Boston	1889
Mauretania I	31,938	Swan Hunters	Wallsend	1907	Liverpool to New York	1935
Mauretania II	35,655	Cammell Laird & Co. Ltd	Birkenhead	1939	Southampton, Cherbourg and New York	1965
Media	13,345	John Brown & Company Ltd	Clydebank	1947	Liverpool direct to New York	1999
Melita	1,254	Alexander Denny	Dumbarton	1853	Mediterranean then Atlantic routes	1868
Nemesis	2,717	Tod & McGregor	Glasgow	1869	Liverpool to New York	1891
Niagara	1,824	Robert Steele & Co.	Greenock	1848	Liverpool to Boston, Halifax and New York	1875
Olympus	1,794	J. & G. Thomson	Glasgow	1860	Mediterranean then Boston	1891
Orduna	15,499	Harland & Wolff Ltd	Belfast	1914	Liverpool to New York	1920
Oregon	11,269	John Elder & Co.	Glasgow	1884	Liverpool to New York	1886
Palestine	1,800	Robert Steele & Co.	Greenock	1860	Liverpool, Halifax, Boston and New York	1872
Palmyra	2,044	Caird & Co.	Greenock	1866	Liverpool to New York	1896
Pannonia	9,851	John Brown & Company Ltd	Clydebank	1904	Emigrants from southern Europe to US	1922
Parthia I	3,167	William Denny & Bros	Dumbarton	1870	Liverpool to New York	1883
Parthia II	13,362	Harland & Wolff Ltd	Belfast	1948	Liverpool direct to New York	1969
Pavonia	5,588	J. & G. Thomson	Glasgow	1882	Liverpool and Boston	1900
Persia	3,300	Robert Napier	Clydebank	1856	Liverpool to New York	1872
QE2	65,863	John Brown & Company Ltd	Clydebank	1969	Southampton and Cherbourg to New York	
Queen Elizabeth	83,673	John Brown & Company Ltd	Clydebank	1940	Southampton. Cherbourg and New York	1972
Queen Mary	80,774	John Brown & Company Ltd	Clydebank	1936	Southampton, Cherbourg and New York	1967
Queen Mary 2	151,400	Alsthom-Chantiers de l'Atlantique	France	2004	Southampton to New York	
Royal George		Fairfield Shipbuilding & Engineering	Glasgow	1919	Atlantic routes	1922
Russia	2,960	J. & G. Thomson	Clydebank	1867	Liverpool to New York	1880
Samaria I	2,574	J. & G. Thomson	Glasgow	1869	Liverpool to Boston	1896
Samaria II	19,602	Cammell Laird & Co. Ltd	Birkenhead	1922	Liverpool to Boston	1955
Saragossa		J. & G. Thomson	Glasgow	1874	Liverpool to Mediterranean	1909
Saxonia I	14,281	John Brown & Company Ltd	Glasgow	1900	Liverpool to Boston	1925

Vessel	Tonnage	Builder	Built	Maiden voyage	Route	Disposed
Saxonia II	21,637	John Brown & Company Ltd	Clydebank	1954	Renamed Carmania – Southampton, Le Havre to Quebec City and Montreal. Winter to Halifax and New York	1963
Scotia	6,871	Robert Napier	Clydebank	1862	Liverpool to New York	1904
Scythia I	4,557	J. & G. Thomson	Glasgow	1875	Liverpool to New York.	1898
Scythia II	19,730	Vickers Ltd	Barrow	1921	Liverpool to New York	1958
Servia	14,426	J. & G. Thomson	Clydebank	1881	Liverpool to New York	1902
Siberia	2,498	J. & G. Thomson	Clydebank	1867	Liverpool to New York and Boston	1882
Sidon	1,872	William Denny & Bros	Dumbarton	1863	Mediterranean and Atlantic Routes	1885
Slavonia	10,606	Sir J. Laing & Sons	Sunderland	1904	Emigrants from southern Europe to US	1909
Sylvania II	21,947	John Brown & Company Ltd	Clydebank	1957	Liverpool to Montreal then Halifax and New York	2004
Tarifa	2,058	J. & G. Thomson	Glasgow	1865	Atlantic then Mediterranean	1898
Tenerife		William Denny & Bros	Dumbarton	1854	Mediterranean	1859
Transylvania	14,315	Scotts Shipbuilding & Engineering Co	Greenock	1914	Mediterranean and Atlantic then troop ship	1917
Tripoli	2,057	J. & G. Thomson	Glasgow	1865	Liverpool to New York	1872
Tuscania I	14,348	Alexander Stephen & Sons Ltd	Glasgow	1915	Troop ship with Anchor Line	1918
Ultonia	8,845	Swan Hunters	Newcastle	1898	Built as cattle boat then converted to emigrant trade 1904	1917
Umbria	7,718	John Elder & Co.	Glasgow	1884	Liverpool to New York	1910
Vauban		Workman, Clark & Co.	Belfast	1919	Liverpool to New York	1932

Deutsche Arbeitsfront

Vessel	Tonnage	Builder	Built	Maiden voyage	Route	Disposed
Robert Ley	38,650	Howaldts-Deutsche-Weft AG	Hamburg	1939	Worldwide cruising	1947
Wilhelm Gustloff	25,484	Blohm & Voss	Hamburg	1938	Worldwide cruising	1945

Dominion Line

Vessel	Tonnage	Builder	Built	Maiden voyage	Route	Disposed
Canada	9,413	Harland & Wolff Ltd	Belfast	1896	Liverpool to Montreal	1926
Regina	16,313	Harland & Wolff Ltd	Belfast	1922	Liverpool to Halifax	1947

Donaldson Line

Vessel	Tonnage	Builder	Built	Maiden voyage	Route	Disposed
Laurentia	8,323	California Shipbuilding Corporation	Los Angeles	1945	Glasgow to Montreal	1967
Lismoria	8,349	Permanente Shipyard No 1	Richmond, USA	1945	Glasgow to Montreal	1967

Elder Dempster Line

Vessel	Tonnage	Builder	Built	Maiden voyage	Route	Disposed
Accra	11,644	Vickers Armstrong Shipbuilders Ltd	Barrow	1947	Liverpool to Las Palmas, Freetown, Takoradi, Lagos and Apapa	1967
Apapa	11,651	Vickers Armstrong Shipbuilders Ltd	Barrow	1948	Liverpool to Las Palmas, Freetown, Takoradi, Lagos and Apapa	1975
Aureol	14,083	Alexander Stephen & Sons Ltd	Glasgow	1951	Liverpool to Las Palmas, Freetown, Takoradi, Lagos and Apapa	1974
Calabar	8,305	Swan, Hunter & Wigham Richardson Ltd.	Newcastle	1936	London to Maderia, Freetown, Takoradi, Lagos and Apapa	1963
Tamele	7,173	Cammell Laird & Co. Ltd	Birkenhead	1945	Liverpool to various West African ports	1973
Tarkwa	7,414	Caledon Shipbuilding & Engineering Co.	Dundee	1944	Liverpool to various West African ports	1971
Winneba	8,355	Swan, Hunter & Wigham Richardson Ltd	Newcastle	1938	London to Maderia, Freetown, Takoradi, Lagos and Apapa	1963

Elders & Fyffes Ltd

Vessel	Tonnage	Builder	Built	Maiden voyage	Route	Disposed
Camito	8,687	Alexander Stephen & Sons Ltd	Glasgow	1956	Southampton/Avonmouth to Barbados, Trinidad and occasionally Bermuda	1973
Golfito	8,740	Alexander Stephen & Sons Ltd	Glasgow	1941	Southampton/Avonmouth to Barbados, Trinidad and occasionally Bermuda	1971

Ellerman & Bucknall

Vessel	Tonnage	Builder	Built	Maiden voyage	Route	Disposed
City of Durham	13,345	Vickers Armstrong Shipbuilders Ltd	Newcastle	1954	London to Las Palmas, Cape Town, Port Elizabeth, East London, Durban, Lourenco Marques and Beira	1974
City of Exeter	13,345	Vickers Armstrong Shipbuilders Ltd	Newcastle	1953	London to Las Palmas, Cape Town, Port Elizabeth, East London, Durban, Lourenco Marques and Beira	1971
City of Port Elizabeth	13,363	Vickers Armstrong Shipbuilders Ltd	Newcastle	1952	London to Las Palmas, Cape Town, Port Elizabeth, East London, Durban, Lourenco Marques and Beira	1980
City of York	13,345	Vickers Armstrong Shipbuilders Ltd	Newcastle	1953	London to Las Palmas, Cape Town, Port Elizabeth, East London, Durban, Lourenco Marques and Beira	1971

Ellerman's Wilson Line

Vessel	Tonnage	Builder	Built	Maiden voyage	Route	Disposed
Borodino	3,206	Ailsa Shipbuilding Company	Troon	1950	Hull, Copenhagen and Aarhus	1966

French Line

Vessel	Tonnage	Builder	Built	Maiden voyage	Route	Disposed
France II	23,769	Chantiers de L'Atlantique	St Nazaire	1912	Le Havre to New York	1934
France III	66,348	Chantiers de L'Atlantique	St Nazaire	1962	Le Havre to New York	
Ile de France	45,153	Chantiers de L'Atlantique	St Nazaire	1927	Le Havre to New York	1959
La Provence I	13,752	Chantiers de L'Atlantique	St Nazaire	1906	Le Havre to New York	1916
Liberté	51,839	Alsthom-Chantiers de l'Atlantique	St Nazaire	1950	Le Havre to New York – refitted Europa	1962
Normandie	82,799	Chantiers de L'Atlantique	St Nazaire	1935	Le Havre to New York	1946
Paris	34,569	Chantiers de L'Atlantique	St Nazaire	1921	Le Havre to New York	1939

Furness Bermuda Line

Vessel	Tonnage	Builder	Built	Maiden voyage	Route	Disposed
Ocean Monarch	13,654	Vickers Armstrong Shipbuilders Ltd	Newcastle	1951	Weekly 6-day cruises between New York & Bermuda; occasionally extended to Nassau	1981
Queen of Bermuda	22,501	Vickers Armstrong Shipbuilders Ltd	Barrow	1933	New York to Bermuda. Later Port Everglades, Florida to Caribbean	1966

Furness Warren Line

Vessel	Tonnage	Builder	Built	Maiden voyage	Route	Disposed
Newfoundland I	6,791	Vickers Armstrong Shipbuilders Ltd	Barrow	1925	Liverpool to Boston	1943
Newfoundland II	7,437	Vickers Armstrong Shipbuilders Ltd	Newcastle	1948	Liverpool to St John's Newfoundland, Halifax & Boston	1971
Nova Scotia I	6,796	Vickers Armstrong Shipbuilders Ltd	Barrow	1926	Liverpool to Boston	1942
Nova Scotia II	7,438	Vickers Armstrong Shipbuilders Ltd	Newcastle	1947	Liverpool to St John's Newfoundland, Halifax & Boston	1971

Glen Line

Vessel	Tonnage	Builder	Built	Maiden voyage	Route	Disposed
Breonshire	9,061	Caledon Shipbuilding & Engineering Co.	Dundee	1942	GB via Suez Canal to Malaya, Hong Kong, China and Japan	1967
Denbighshire	8,983	Netherlands Shipbuilding Company	Amsterdam	1938	GB via Suez Canal to Malaya, Hong Kong, China and Japan	1969
Glenartney	8,992	Caledon Shipbuilding & Engineering Co.	Dundee	1940	GB via Suez Canal to Malaya, Hong Kong, China and Japan	1967
Glenearn	8,960	Caledon Shipbuilding & Engineering Co.	Dundee	1938	GB via Suez Canal to Malaya, Hong Kong, China and Japan	1971
Glengarry	9,144	Burmeister & Wain Shipyards	Copenhagen	1940	GB via Suez Canal to Malaya, Hong Kong, China and Japan	1971
Glengyle	8,957	Caledon Shipbuilding & Engineering Co.	Dundee	1941	GB via Suez Canal to Malaya, Hong Kong, China and Japan	1971
Glenorchy	9,324	Caledon Shipbuilding & Engineering Co	Dundee	?	GB via Suez Canal to Malaya, Hong Kong, China and Japan	1971

Vessel	Tonnage	Builder	Built	Maiden voyage	Route	Disposed
Glenroy	8,959	Scotts Shipbuilding & Engineering Co.	Greenock	1938	GB via Suez Canal to Malaya, Hong Kong, China and Japan	1966

Great Ship Company

Vessel	Tonnage	Builder	Built	Maiden voyage	Route	Disposed
Great Eastern	32,000	J. Scott Russel & Co.	London	1858	Cross Atlantic cable laying	1891

Great Western

Vessel	Tonnage	Builder	Built	Maiden voyage	Route	Disposed
Great Britain	1,016		Bristol	1845		
Great Western	1,340	Patterson	Bristol	1838	GB to New York	1857

Guion

Vessel	Tonnage	Builder	Built	Maiden voyage	Route	Disposed
Alaska	6,932	Fairfield Shipbuilding & Engineering	Clydebank	1881	Liverpool to New York	1899
Arizona	6,932	Fairfield Shipbuilding & Engineering	Clydebank	1879	Liverpool to New York	1898

Hamburg Sudamerika Dampfschiffahrts

Vessel	Tonnage	Builder	Built	Maiden voyage	Route	Disposed
Monte Sarmiento	13,625	Blohm & Voss	Hamburg	1924	Emigrant and seasonal farm labourer trade to South America, also cruising	1943

Hamburg-Amerika

Vessel	Tonnage	Builder	Built	Maiden voyage	Route	Disposed
Albert Ballin	21,131	Blohm & Voss	Hamburg	1923	Hamburg to New York	
Amerika	22,225	Harland & Wolff Ltd	Belfast	1905	Hamburg, Southampton, Cherbourg to New York	1917
Deutschland II	16,502	A.G.Vulkan	Hamburg	1900	Hamburg, Plymouth and New York	1911
Deutschland III	21,046	Blohm & Voss	Hamburg	1924	Hamburg to New York	1941

Vessel	Tonnage	Builder	Built	Maiden voyage	Route	Disposed
Imperator	51,969	A.G.Vulkan	Hamburg	1913	Hamburg, Southampton, Cherbourg to New York	1919
Kaiserin Auguste Victoria	25,037	A.G.Vulkan	Hamburg	1906	Hamburg to New York	1930
New York	22,337	Blohm & Voss	Hamburg	1927	Hamburg to New York	1948
Prinzessin Victoria Luise	4,409	Blohm & Voss	Hamburg	1900	Worldwide cruising	1906
Vaterland	54,282	Blohm & Voss	Hamburg	1914	Atlantic trade	1917

Henderson Line

Vessel	Tonnage	Builder	Built	Maiden voyage	Route	Disposed
Prome	7,043	William Denny & Bros	Dumbarton	1937	Liverpool to Port Said, Port Sudan, Aden, Colombo & Rangoon	1962
Salween	7,063	William Denny & Bros	Dumbarton	1938	Liverpool to Port Said, Port Sudan, Aden, Colombo & Rangoon	1962

Holland America Line

Vessel	Tonnage	Builder	Built	Maiden voyage	Route	Disposed
Nieuw Amsterdam I	16,913	Harland & Wolff Ltd	Belfast	1906	Rotterdam to New York	1932
Nieuw Amsterdam II	36,287	Rotterdamsche Droogdok Mij	Rotterdam	1938	Rotterdam to New York and cruising	1974
Noordam I	12,316	Harland & Wolff Ltd	Belfast	1902	Rotterdam to New York	1923
Potsdam	12,522	Blohm & Voss	Hamburg	1900	Rotterdam to New York	1947
Rijndam	12,302	Harland & Wolff Ltd	Belfast	1901	Rotterdam to New York	1929
Rotterdam I	1,684	Henderson, Coulborn & Co	Renfrew	1872	Rotterdam to Plymouth and New York	1883
Rotterdam II	3,329	Harland & Wolff Ltd	Belfast	1886	Rotterdam	1899
Rotterdam III	8,301	Harland & Wolff Ltd	Belfast	1897	Rotterdam to New York	1906
Rotterdam III	8,186	Harland & Wolff Ltd	Belfast	1897	Rotterdam to New York	1918
Rotterdam IIII	23,980	Harland & Wolff Ltd	Belfast	1908	Rotterdam to New York	1940
Rotterdam IIIII	38,650	Rotterdamsche Droogdok Mij	Rotterdam	1959	Rotterdam to New York and cruising	
Rotterdam IIIIII	62,000	Cantieri Navali Fincantieri	Venice	1997	Cruise ship for Carnival Cruises	
Standam II	32,234	Harland & Wolff Ltd	Belfast	1917	Rotterdam to New York	1918
Standam III	29,511	Harland & Wolff Ltd	Belfast	1929	Rotterdam to New York	1940

Vessel	Tonnage	Builder	Built	Maiden voyage	Route	Disposed
Standem I	10,961	Harland & Wolff Ltd	Belfast	1898	Rotterdam to New York	1928
Standem III	24,294	dok en Werf Maatschappij Wilton-Fijenoord	Rotterdam	1957	Rotterdam to New York and cruises	1982
Veendam II	15,450	Harland & Wolff Ltd	Glasgow	1923	Rotterdam to New York	1953

Inman

Vessel	Tonnage	Builder	Built	Maiden voyage	Route	Disposed
City of Berlin	5,491	Caird & Co.	Greenock	1875	Liverpool to New York	1921
City of Chester	4,566	Caird & Co.	Greenock	1873	Liverpool to New York	1893
City of Paris	14,500	J. & G. Thomson	Clydebank	1888	Liverpool to New York	1893

Italia Line

Vessel	Tonnage	Builder	Built	Maiden voyage	Route	Disposed
Andrea Doria	29,082	S.A. Ansaldo	Sestri Ponente, Genoa	1953	Genoa to New York	1956
Conte Biancamano	23,842	William Beardmore and Co.	Clydebank	1925	Genoa to New York	1960
Conte Di Savoia	48,502	Cantieri Riuniti dell'Adriatico	Monfalcone, Italy	1932	Genoa to New York	1950
Cristoforo Colombo	29,429	S.A. Ansaldo	Sestri Ponente, Genoa	1954	Genoa to New York	1982
Giulio Cesare	27,078	Cantiere Navale Triestino	Monfalcone	1951	Genoa to South America	1973
Leonardo Da Vinci	33,340	S.A. Ansaldo	Sestri Ponente, Genoa	1960	Genoa to New York	1982
Michelangelo	45,911	S.A. Ansaldo	Sestri Ponente, Genoa	1965	Genoa to New York	1976
Raffaello	45,933	Cantieri dell'Adriatico	San Marco, Italy	1965	Genoa to New York	1983
Rex	51,062	S.A. Ansaldo	Sestri Ponente, Genoa	1932	Genoa to New York	1947

Lloyd Sabaudo

Vessel	Tonnage	Builder	Built	Maiden voyage	Route	Disposed
Conte Grande	23,842	Stabilimento Tecnico	Trieste, Italy	1928	Genoa to New York	1961

Vessel	Tonnage	Builder	Built	Maiden voyage	Route	Disposed
Conte Rosso	17,048	William Beardmore and Co.	Clydebank	1922	Genoa and Naples to New York	1941
Conte Verde	18,765	William Beardmore and Co.	Clydebank	1923	Genoa and Naples to New York	1951

New Zealand Shipping Co.

Vessel	Tonnage	Builder	Built	Maiden voyage	Route	Disposed
Rangitane	21,867	John Brown & Company Ltd	Clydebank	1949	London to New Zealand via Panama (same ports as Rangitiki)	1976
Rangitata	16,969	John Brown & Company Ltd	Clydebank	1929	London to Curacao, Panama Canal, Wellington and Auckland, returning via Southampton	1962
Rangitiki	16,985	John Brown & Company Ltd	Clydebank	1929	London to Curacao, Panama Canal, Wellington and Auckland, returning via Southampton	1962
Rangitoto	21,809	Vickers Armstrong Shipbuilders Ltd	Newcastle	1949	London to New Zealand via Panama (same ports as Rangitiki)	1976
Remuera	13,619	Harland & Wolff Ltd	Belfast	1948	London to New Zealand via Panama (same ports as Rangitiki)	1970
Ruahine	17,851	John Brown & Company Ltd	Clydebank	1951	London to Curacao, Panama Canal, Wellington and Auckland, returning via Southampton	1974

Norddeutscher Lloyd

Vessel	Tonnage	Builder	Built	Maiden voyage	Route	Disposed
Bremen III	51,656	A.G. Weser	Bremen	1929	Bremen to New York	1946
Columbus	32,354	F. Schichau	Danzig	1924	Bremen, Southampton, Cherbourg to New York	1939
Europa	49,746	Blohm & Voss	Hamburg	1930	Bremen to New York	1945
George Washington	25,570	A.G. Vulkan	Hamburg	1909	Bremen, Southampton, Cherbourg to New York	1917
Kaiser Wilhelm der Grosse	14,349	A.G. Vulkan	Stettin	1897	Bremerhaven to New York	1914

Vessel	Tonnage	Builder	Built	Maiden voyage	Route	Disposed
Kaiser Wilhelm II	19,361	A.G. Vulkan	Stettin	1903	Bremen, Southampton, Cherbourg to New York	1917
Kronprinzessin Cecilie	19,400	A.G. Vulkan	Hamburg	1907	Bremen, Southampton, Cherbourg to New York	1917
Lahn	5,099	Fairfield Shipbuilding & Engineering	Glasgow	1887	Bremen to New York	1904
Prinz Friedrich Wilhelm	17,082	J. C. Tecklenborg	Geestemunde	1908	Bremen, Southampton, Cherbourg to New York	1919
Prinz Ludwig	9,630	A.G. Vulkan	Hamburg	1906	Far East service	1919

North of Scotland & Orkney & Shetland

Vessel	Tonnage	Builder	Built	Maiden voyage	Route	Disposed
St Sunniva	864	Hall Russell	Aberdeen	1887	Shetland and Orkneys Cruising	

Orient Line

Vessel	Tonnage	Builder	Built	Maiden voyage	Route	Disposed
Austral	5,524	John Elder & Co.	Glasgow	1881	London to Australia	1902
Omrah	8,130	Fairfield Shipbuilding & Engineering	Glasgow	1899	London to Australia	1918
Ophir	6,841	Robert Napier	Glasgow	1891	London to Australia	1921
Orama	12,927	John Brown & Company Ltd	Glasgow	1911	London to Australia	1917
Orient	5,386	John Elder & Co.	Glasgow	1879	London to Australia	1910
Orizaba	6,077	Barrow Shipbuilding Co.	Barrow	1886	London to Australia	1905
Ormuz	6,031	Fairfield Shipbuilding & Engineering	Glasgow	1887	London to Australia	1922
Orontes	9,028	Fairfield Shipbuilding & Engineering	Glasgow	1902	London to Australia	1926
Oroya	6,057	Barrow Shipbuilding Co.	Barrow	1887	London to Australia	1909
Ortona	7,945	Vickers Ltd	Barrow	1899	London to Australia	1906
Orvieto	12,133	Workman, Clark & Co.	Belfast	1909	London to Australia	1931
Otranto	12,124	Workman, Clark & Co.	Belfast	1909	London to Australia	1918

P&O-Orient Line

Vessel	Tonnage	Builder	Built	Maiden voyage	Route	Disposed
Arabia	7,903	Caird & Co.	Greenock	1898	London to India	1916

Ship	Tonnage	Builder	Built	Route	Withdrawn
Arcadia	29,734	John Brown & Company Ltd	1954	England to Australia & NZ via Suez, South Africa or Panama (sometimes North American Pacific coast) to Orient from North America/Australia & Circle Pacific voyages	1979
Bentick	1,974	Thomas Wilson	1843	Suez to India	1860
Britannia	6,525	Caird & Co.	1887	London to India and Australia	1909
Canberra	45,733	Harland & Wolff Ltd	1961	England to Australia & NZ via Suez, South Africa or Panama (sometimes North American Pacific coast) to Orient from North America/Australia & Circle Pacific voyages	1998
Canton	16,033	Alexander Stephen & Sons Ltd	1938	London and/or Southampton to Port Said, Aden, Bombay, Colombo, Penang, Singapore and Hong Kong	1962
Carthage	14,280	Alexander Stephen & Sons Ltd	1931	London/Southampton to Port Said, Aden, Bombay, Colombo, Penang, Singapore and Hong Kong	1961
Cathay	13,089	Cockerill-Ougree Shipyard	1957	London, Rotterdam & Southampton to Port Said, Aden, Colombo, Penang, Port Swettenham, Singapore, Hong Kong, Yokohama and Kobe. Homewards via Singapore, Port Swettenham, Penang, Colombo, Aden, Port Said, Naples and Le Havre to London	1976
China II	7,899	Harland & Wolff Ltd	1896	London to India	1928
Chitral	13,821	Chantiers de L'Atlantique	1956	London, Rotterdam & Southampton to Port Said, Aden, Colombo, Penang, Port Swettenham, Singapore, Hong Kong, Yokohama and Kobe. Homewards via Singapore, Port Swettenham, Penang, Colombo, Aden, Port Said, Naples and Le Havre to London	1976

Ship	Tonnage	Builder	Built at	Year	Route	Year
Chusan	24,215	Vickers Armstrong Shipbuilders Ltd	Barrow	1950	England to Australia & NZ via Suez, South Africa or Panama (sometimes North American Pacific coast) to Orient from North America/Australia & Circle Pacific voyages	1973
Corfu	14,280	Alexander Stephen & Sons Ltd	Glasgow	1931	London/Southampton to Port Said, Aden, Bombay, Colombo, Penang, Singapore and Hong Kong	1961
Egypt	7,912	Caird & Co.	Greenock	1897	London to India	1922
Himalaya	27,955	Vickers Armstrong Shipbuilders Ltd	Barrow	1949	London or Southampton to Australia via Suez (same ports as Stratheden)	1974
Hindostan	2,017	Thomas Wilson	Liverpool	1842	Suez to India	1879
Iberia	29,614	Harland & Wolff Ltd	Belfast	1954	England to Australia & NZ via Suez, South Africa or Panama (sometimes North American Pacific coast) to Orient from North America/Australia & Circle Pacific voyages	1972
India	7,911	Caird & Co.	Greenock	1896	London to Bombay	1915
Kaiser-I-Hind (Empress of India)	4,019	Caird & Co.	Greenock	1878	London to Bombay	1897
Malta II	6,064	Caird & Co.	Greenock	1895	London to India	1928
Nubia	5,914	Caird & Co.	Greenock	1895	London to India	1915
Oceana	6,362	Harland & Wolff Ltd	Belfast	1888	London to India	1912
Orcades	28,396	Vickers Armstrong Shipbuilders Ltd	Barrow	1948	England to Australia & NZ via Suez, South Africa or Panama (sometimes North American Pacific coast) to Orient from North America/Australia & Circle Pacific voyages	1973
Oriana	41,923	Vickers Armstrong Shipbuilders Ltd	Barrow	1960	England to Australia & NZ via Suez, South Africa or Panama (sometimes North American Pacific coast) to Orient from North America/Australia & Circle Pacific voyages	1986

Ship	Tonnage	Builder	Location	Year	Route/Service	Withdrawn
Oriana II	69,153	Meyer Werft, Papenberg	Germany	1995	Worldwide cruising	
Orion	23,696	Vickers Armstrong Shipbuilders Ltd	Barrow	1935	London to Gibraltar, Naples, Port Said, Aden, Colombo, Freemantle (and/or Adelaide), Melbourne & Sydney	1963
Oronsay	27,632	Vickers Armstrong Shipbuilders Ltd	Barrow	1951	England to Australia & NZ via Suez, South Africa or Panama (sometimes North American Pacific coast) to Orient from North America/Australia & Circle Pacific voyages	1976
Orontes II	20,186	Vickers Armstrong Shipbuilders Ltd	Barrow	1929	London to Gibraltar, Naples, Port Said, Aden, Colombo, Freemantle (and/or Adelaide), Melbourne & Sydney	1962
Orsova	28,790	Vickers Armstrong Shipbuilders Ltd	Barrow	1954	England to Australia & NZ via Suez, South Africa or Panama (sometimes North American Pacific coast) to Orient from North America/Australia & Circle Pacific voyages	1974
Palawan	4,686	Caird & Co.	Greenock	1895	London to India	1914
Persia	7,951	Caird & Co.	Greenock	1900	London to India	1915
Rawalpindi	16,618	Harland & Wolff Ltd	Belfast	1925	Far East Service	1939
Razmak	10,602	Harland & Wolff Ltd	Greenock	1925	London to Bombay	1930
Rome	5,013	Caird & Co.	Greenock	1881	London to Bombay and Sydney	1912
Sea Princess	27,670	John Brown & Company Ltd	Clydebank	1966	Sydney to Pacific ports. Thereafter Southampton to Mediterranean, West Africa, Caribbean, Scandinavia	
Star Princess	63,524	Alsthom-Chantiers de l'Atlantique	St Nazaire	1989	Worldwide cruising	
Strathaird	22,568	Vickers Armstrong Shipbuilders Ltd	Barrow	1932	London to Australia via Suez (same ports as for Strathnaver)	1961

Vessel	Tonnage	Builder	Built	Maiden voyage	Route	Disposed
Stratheden	23,372	Vickers Armstrong Shipbuilders Ltd	Barrow	1937	London to Gibraltar, Aden, occasionally Bombay, Colombo, Adelaide, Freemantle, Melbourne and Sydney. Home via Marseille	1969
Strathmore	23,580	Vickers Armstrong Shipbuilders Ltd	Barrow	1935	London to Australia via Suez (same ports as for Strathnaver)	1969
Strathnaver	22,270	Vickers Armstrong Shipbuilders Ltd	Barrow	1931	London to Gibraltar, Aden, occasionally Bombay, Colombo, Adelaide, Freemantle, Melbourne and Sydney. Home via Marseille	1962
Sumatra	4,607	Alexander Stephen & Sons Ltd	Glasgow	1895	London to India	1914
Sutlej		Barrow Shipbuilding Co	Barrow	1882	London to India	1902
Viceroy of India	19,648	Alexander Stephen & Sons Ltd	Glasgow	1929	London to India and cruise ship	1942

Pacific Steam Navigation

Vessel	Tonnage	Builder	Built	Maiden voyage	Route	Disposed
Reina Del Mar	20,334	Harland & Wolff Ltd	Belfast	1956	Liverpool to La Rochelle, Santander, Coruna, Bermuda, Nassau, Havana, Kingston, La Guaira, Curacao, Cartegena, Cristobel, La Libertad, Callao, Arica, Antofagasta and Valparaiso. Homewards via Vigo and Plymouth	1969

Princess Cruises

Vessel	Tonnage	Builder	Built	Maiden voyage	Route	Disposed
Island Princess	19,907	Nordseewerke Shipyard	Rheinstahl	1972	Los Angeles to Panama Canal, Caribbean and return. LA to Mexico	
Pacific Princess	19,904	Nordseewerke Shipyard	Rheinstahl	1971	Los Angeles to Panama Canal, Caribbean and return. LA to Mexico	
Royal Princess	44,348	Oy Wartsila Ab Helsinki Shipyard	Helsinki	1984	Los Angeles to Panama Canal, Caribbean and return. LA to Mexico	
Spirit of London	17,370	Cantieri Riuniti del Tirreno e Riuniti Spa	Genoa	1972	Summer Vancouver to Alaska; winter San Juan to Caribbean	

Red Star Line

Vessel	Tonnage	Builder	Built	Maiden voyage	Route	Disposed
Belgenland	27,132	Harland & Wolff Ltd	Belfast	1923	Antwerp to New York	1936
Lapland	17,540	Harland & Wolff Ltd	Belfast	1909	Antwerp to New York	1934
Pennland	16,322	Harland & Wolff Ltd	Belfast	1922	Antwerp to New York	1941
Zeeland	11,905	John Brown & Company Ltd	Clydebank	1902	Antwerp to New York	1930

Royal Mail Lines

Vessel	Tonnage	Builder	Built	Maiden voyage	Route	Disposed
Amazon	20,348	Harland & Wolff Ltd	Belfast	1959	London to Cherbourg, Vigo, Lisbon, Las Palmas, Rio de Janeiro, Santos, Montevideo and Buenos Aires. Homewards Boulogne	1968
Andes II	26,860	Harland & Wolff Ltd	Belfast	1939	Southampton to North Cape, Baltic, Mediterranean, West Africa, the Canaries, Caribbean and long cruises to South Africa, South America and US	1971
Aragon	9,441	Harland & Wolff Ltd	Belfast	1905	Southampton to South America	1917
Aragon II	20,362	Harland & Wolff Ltd	Belfast	1960	London to Cherbourg, Vigo, Lisbon, Las Palmas, Rio de Janeiro, Santos, Montevideo and Buenos Aires. Homewards Boulogne	1969
Arlanza I	15,043	Harland & Wolff Ltd	Belfast	1912	Armed merchant cruiser	1938
Arlanza II	20,362	Harland & Wolff Ltd	Belfast	1960	London to Cherbourg, Vigo, Lisbon, Las Palmas, Rio de Janeiro, Santos, Montevideo and Buenos Aires. Homewards Boulogne	?
Asturias I	12,001	Harland & Wolff Ltd	Belfast	1908	London to Australia, Southampton to Buenos Aires and cruising	1933

Savannah Ship Company

Vessel	Tonnage	Builder	Built	Maiden voyage	Route	Disposed
Savannah	320	Samuel Fickett & William Crockett	New York	1819	From USA to Liverpool	1821

Shaw Savill Line

Vessel	Tonnage	Builder	Built	Maiden voyage	Route	Disposed
Akaroa	20,348	Harland & Wolff Ltd	Belfast	1959	London to Azores, Barbados, Trinidad, Curacao, Panama Canal, Tahiti, Auckland, Wellington, Sydney, Melbourne, Freemantle, Durban, Cape Town, Las Palmas and return to London	1981
Aranda	20,362	Harland & Wolff Ltd	Belfast	1960	London to Azores, Barbados, Trinidad, Curacao, Panama Canal, Tahiti, Auckland, Wellington, Sydney, Melbourne, Freemantle, Durban, Cape Town, Las Palmas and return to London	1981
Arawa	20,362	Harland & Wolff Ltd	Belfast	1960	London to Azores, Barbados, Trinidad, Curacao, Panama Canal, Tahiti, Auckland, Wellington, Sydney, Melbourne, Freemantle, Durban, Cape Town, Las Palmas and return to London	1981
Athenic	15,187	Harland & Wolff Ltd	Belfast	1947	London to Curacao, Panama Canal, Auckland and Wellington	1969
Ceramic	15,896	Cammell Laird & Co Ltd	Birkenhead	1948	London to Curacao, Panama Canal, Auckland and Wellington	1972
Corinthic	15,682	Cammell Laird & Co Ltd	Birkenhead	1947	London to Curacao, Panama Canal, Auckland and Wellington	1969
Dominion Monarch	26,463	Swan, Hunter & Wigham Richardson Ltd.	Newcastle	1939	London & Southampton to Las Palmas, Cape Town, Freemantle, Melbourne, Sydney, Wellington	1962

Vessel	Tonnage	Builder	Built	Maiden voyage	Route	Disposed
Gothic	15,911	Swan, Hunter & Wigham Richardson Ltd.	Newcastle	1948	London to Curacao, Panama Canal, Auckland and Wellington	1969
Northern Star	24,731	Vickers Armstrong Shipbuilders Ltd	Newcastle	1962	76 day round world – Southampton to Bermuda, Port Everglades, Trinidad, Curacao, Panama Canal, Tahiti, Fiji, Wellington, Auckland, Sydney, Melbourne, Freemantle, Durban, Cape Town, Las Palmas and return Southampton	1976
Southern Cross	20,204	Harland & Wolff Ltd	Belfast	1955	76 day round world – Southampton to Bermuda, Port Everglades, Trinidad, Curacao, Panama Canal, Tahiti, Fiji, Wellington, Auckland, Sydney, Melbourne, Freemantle, Durban, Cape Town, Las Palmas and return Southampton	1973

Societe Generale de Transport Maritime

Vessel	Tonnage	Builder	Built	Maiden voyage	Route	Disposed
La Provence	15,719	Swan, Hunter & Wigham Richardson Ltd	Newcastle	1951	Marseilles to South America	

Swedish American Line

Vessel	Tonnage	Builder	Built	Maiden voyage	Route	Disposed
Gripsholm	18,815	Armstrong Whitworth	Newcastle	1925	Gothenburg to New York	1955
Gripsholm II	23,216	S.A. Ansaldo	Sestri Ponente, Genoa	1957	Gothenburg to New York	1974
Kungsholm II	21,532	Blohm & Voss	Hamburg	1928	Gothenburg to New York	1941
Kungsholm III	21,164	De Schelde Koninklijke Maaatschappij	Flushing, Belgium	1953	Gothenburg to New York	1965
Kungsholm IIII	26,677	John Brown & Company Ltd	Clydebank	1966	Gothenburg to New York	1975
Stockholm IIII	12,396	Gotaverken	Gothenburg	1948	Gothenburg to New York	1960

Union-Castle Line

Vessel	Tonnage	Builder	Built	Maiden voyage	Route	Disposed
Athlone Castle	25,567	Harland & Wolff Ltd	Belfast	1936	Mailship from Southampton via Madeira or Las Palmas to Cape Town, Port Elizabeth, East London and Durban	1965
Braemar Castle	17,029	Harland & Wolff Ltd	Belfast	1952	Around Africa – London and Rotterdam to Las Palmas, Ascension, St Helena, Walvis Bay, Cape Town, Port Elizabeth, Durban, Lourenco Marques, Beira, Dar-es-Salaam, Zanaibar, Tange, Mombasa, Aden, Suez, Port Said, Genoa, Marseilles, Gibraltar and return to London	1965
Capetown Castle	27,002	Harland & Wolff Ltd	Belfast	1938	Mailship from Southampton via Madeira or Las Palmas to Cape Town, Port Elizabeth, East London and Durban	1967
Carnarvon Castle	20,148	Harland & Wolff Ltd	Belfast	1926	Mailship from Southampton to Madeira or Las Palmas, Cape Town, Port Elizabeth, East London and Durban	1962
Durban Castle	17,382	Harland & Wolff Ltd	Belfast	1938	Around Africa – London and Rotterdam to Las Palmas, Ascension, St Helena, Walvis Bay, Cape Town, Port Elizabeth, Durban, Lourenco Marques, Beira, Dar-es-Salaam, Zanaibar, Tange, Mombasa, Aden, Suez, Port Said, Genoa, Marseilles, Gibraltar and return to London	1962
Edinburgh Castle	28,705	Harland & Wolff Ltd	Belfast	1948	Mailship express – Southampton via Madeira or Los Palmas to Cape Town, Port Elizabeth, East London & Durban	1976

Name	Tonnage	Builder	Location	Year	Route	Year
Kenya Castle	17,041	Harland & Wolff Ltd	Belfast	1952	Around Africa – London and Rotterdam to Las Palmas, Ascension, St Helena, Walvis Bay, Cape Town, Port Elizabeth, Durban, Lourenco Marques, Beira, Dar-es-Salaam, Zanaibar, Tange, Mombasa, Aden, Suez, Port Said, Genoa, Marseilles, Gibraltar and return to London	1967
Pendennis Castle	28,582	Harland & Wolff Ltd	Belfast	1958	Mailship from Southampton via Madeira or Las Palmas to Cape Town, Port Elizabeth, East London and Durban	1980
Pretoria Castle	28,705	Harland & Wolff Ltd	Belfast	1948	Mailship express – Southampton via Madeira or Los Palmas to Cape Town, Port Elizabeth, East London and Durban	1975
Rhodesia Castle	17,041	Harland & Wolff Ltd	Belfast	1951	Around Africa – London and Rotterdam to Las Palmas, Ascension, St Helena, Walvis Bay, Cape Town, Port Elizabeth, Durban, Lourenco Marques, Beira, Dar-es-Salaam, Zanzibar, Tange, Mombasa, Aden, Suez, Port Said, Genoa, Marseilles, Gibraltar and return to London	1967
Stirling Castle	25,554	Harland & Wolff Ltd	Belfast	1936	Mailship from Southampton via Madeira or Las Palmas to Cape Town, Port Elizabeth, East London and Durban	1966
Transvaal Castle	32,697	John Brown & Company Ltd	Clydebank	1961	Mailship from Southampton via Madeira or Las Palmas to Cape Town, Port Elizabeth, East London and Durban	1977

Vessel	Tonnage	Builder	Built	Maiden voyage	Route	Disposed
Warwick Castle	17,387	Harland & Wolff Ltd	Belfast	1939	Around Africa – London and Rotterdam to Las Palmas, Ascension, St Helena, Walvis Bay, Cape Town, Port Elizabeth, Durban, Lourenco Marques, Beira, Dar-es-Salaam, Zanzibar, Tange, Mombasa, Aden, Suez, Port Said, Genoa, Marseilles, Gibraltar and return to London	1962
Winchester Castle	20,001	Harland & Wolff Ltd	Belfast	1930	Mailship from Southampton to Madeira or Las Palmas, Cape Town, Port Elizabeth, East London and Durban	1960
Windsor Castle	37,640	Cammell Laird & Co. Ltd	Birkenhead	1960	Mailship from Southampton via Madeira or Las Palmas to Cape Town, Port Elizabeth, East London and Durban	1977

United States Line

Vessel	Tonnage	Builder	Built	Maiden voyage	Route	Disposed
Leviathan	54,282	Newport News Shipbuilders	Virginia, USA	1923	Southampton to New York – refurbished Vaterland	1938
United States	53,329	Newport News Shipbuilders	Virginia, USA	1952	New York to Southampton	1969

White Star Line

Vessel	Tonnage	Builder	Built	Maiden voyage	Route	Disposed
Adriatic	3,868	Harland & Wolff Ltd	Belfast	1872	Liverpool to New York	1899
Adriatic II	24,541	Harland & Wolff Ltd	Belfast	1907	Liverpool to New York	1935
Albertic	18,940	A.G. Weser	Bremen	1920	(Formerly Royal Mail Line) Liverpool to Montreal	1934
Arabic III	16,786	A.G. Weser	Bremen	1921	Southampton to New York	1931
Atlantic I	3,708	Harland & Wolff Ltd	Belfast	1872	Liverpool to New York	1873
Baltic I	3,708	Harland & Wolff Ltd	Belfast	1871	Liverpool to New York	1898
Baltic II	23,876	Harland & Wolff Ltd	Belfast	1904	Liverpool to New York	1933

Ship	Tonnage	Builder	Place	Built	Route	Year
Britannic I	5,004	Harland & Wolff Ltd	Belfast	1874	Liverpool to New York	1903
Britannic II	48,158	Harland & Wolff Ltd	Belfast	1915	Hospital ship	1917
Britannic III	27,778	Harland & Wolff Ltd	Belfast	1930	Liverpool to New York	1961
Calgaric	16,063	Harland & Wolff Ltd	Belfast	1917	(Formerly Royal Mail Line) Liverpool to Montreal	1935
Canopic	12,097	Harland & Wolff Ltd	Belfast	1903	Liverpool to Boston	1925
Cedric	21,035	Harland & Wolff Ltd	Belfast	1903	Liverpool to New York	1932
Celtic I	3,867	Harland & Wolff Ltd	Belfast	1872	Liverpool to New York	1893
Celtic II	20,904	Harland & Wolff Ltd	Belfast	1901	Liverpool to New York	1928
Doric	16,484	Harland & Wolff Ltd	Belfast	1923	Liverpool to Montreal then cruising	1935
Georgic	27,759	Harland & Wolff Ltd	Belfast	1932	Liverpool to New York	1956
Homeric	34,351	F. Schichau	Danzig	1922	Southampton to New York then cruising	1936
Laurentic	18,724	Harland & Wolff Ltd	Belfast	1927	Liverpool to New York	1940
Majestic I	13,500	Harland & Wolff Ltd	Belfast	1890	Liverpool to New York	1914
Majestic II	56,551	Blohm & Voss	Hamburg	1922	Southampton to New York	1936
Megantic	14,878	Harland & Wolff Ltd	Belfast	1909	Liverpool to Montreal	1933
Oceanic I	3,707	Harland & Wolff Ltd	Belfast	1871	Liverpool to New York	1895
Oceanic II	17,274	Harland & Wolff Ltd	Belfast	1899	Liverpool to New York	1914
Olympic	46,439	Harland & Wolff Ltd	Belfast	1911	Southampton to New York	1937
Republic I	3,708	Harland & Wolff Ltd	Belfast	1872	Liverpool to New York	1889
Teutonic	9,984	Harland & Wolff Ltd	Belfast	1889	Liverpool to New York	1921
Titanic	46,328	Harland & Wolff Ltd	Belfast	1911	Southampton to New York	1912

Glossary

Aft   The rear of the ship.

Amidship   In the centre of the ship.

Boat   A small vessel for travel on the water, compared to the larger ship.

Bow(s)   The front of the ship.

Bulkhead   The inside, vertical partitions of the ship.

Cruise Ship   A ship destined for holidays only, rather than ocean travel as under-taken on a liner.

Forecastle   The space at the front end of a ship below the main deck. The crew's quarters were traditionally located here.

Gross Tonnage   This has nothing to do with weight, but is a measurement of the volume of the accommodation of the ship. One ton represents one hundred cubic feet. This figure has been given for all ships in Appendix 2, and is an invaluable aid to comparing the sizes of ships. The measurement may change during the career of the ship, as changes to its superstructure are made.

Launch   The year in which the hull of the ship, or the main structure, was launched into the water. This was usually celebrated as an important event by the ship-builder. Very little of the interior would be finished at this point.

Liner   An ocean-going vessel able to carry a significant number of passengers, rather than cargo, on specific lines between major international ports. Liners were superseded by aircraft in the 1960s.

Maiden Voyage   Usually at least one year after the launch, the maiden voyage would follow the fitting out of the ship and sea trials. This would be the first major voyage for the vessel, and gave some indication of its routes for subsequent journies. Wherever possible, this route has been indicated in Appendix 2.

Port   The left hand side of the ship when facing the bows.

Scuppers   The holes around the main deck of the ship which allow water to drain away.

Starboard   The right hand side of the ship when facing the bows.

Stem   The curved upright beam at the front of a ship into which the hull timbers are shaped to form the prow.

Stern   The back of the ship.

Bibliography

Unpublished sources

Anchor Line, *Directors' Minute Book*, UGD255/1/2/1, University of Glasgow Archives.

Anderson, C. (1967/9) *Unpublished Memoirs/Biography of Sir Colin Skelton Anderson, KBE, 1969?*

Cornelius, A. (1993) *Dromen Tussen Europa en de VS: een cultuurhistorische studie van 100 jaar luxt-vervoer aan boord van de transatlantische passagiersschepen (1840–1940)*. Unpublished thesis for Proefschrift, Rijksuniversiteit te Leiden.

Grainger, H. (1985) *The Architecture of Sir Ernest George and his Partners, c.1860–1922*. Unpublished Ph.D. thesis, University of Leeds.

Harland & Wolff (1961) PRONI Ref: D/2805/CPS/A/2/25 Heaton & Tabb & Co. Ltd papers, letter dated 5.12.1961

Longworth, H. (2002) 'From Plain to Posh: The Interior Design of Steam Powered Passenger Liners in the Victorian Period'. Unpublished thesis, Royal College of Art/Victoria and Albert Museum.

OSN/15/6 TSS Orion, 'Bills of Quantities and Decorations First Class Saloons forward and After Staircases', MS72/114, National Maritime Museum.

OSN/15/7 'Presscuttings File: Orion', National Maritime Museum.

P&O65/157 ms 'Passenger Accommodation in 1844'.

Rabson, S. 'All at sea with P&O', paper presented at National Maritime Museum study day on passengers, Greenwich, March 2001.

Ricardo to De Morgan, 28 February 1895, Coll. John Catleugh.

Union Castle Line (1960) Press Information *Windsor Castle*, National Maritime Museum.

Walmsley, F. (1991) 'Pragmatism and Pluralism: The Design of the Queen Mary, 1928–1939'. Unpublished thesis, Royal College of Art/Victoria and Albert Museum.

Primary Published Sources

Books and Pamphlets

Anchor Line (1923) *California*, UGD255/1/23/23

Breuhaus de Groot, Fritz August (1930) *Der Ozean-Express Bremen*, Munich: F. Bruckmann.

Burrow, J. (1932) *The Book of the Anchor Line: An Outline of the Company's Activities from Its Inception in 1852 until the end of 1931*.

C.G.T. (1935) *Decoration Interieure de Normandie: Locaux Communs des Premiere Classes*, Paris.

Casson, Hugh (1968) Inscape, the Design of Interiors, London, Architectural Press.

Chatterton, E.K. (1910) *Steamships and Their Story*, Cassell & Co., London.

Cunard White Star Line (1937) *The Queen Mary: World's Newest and Fastest Liner*, USA: Unz & Co.

Dickens, C. (1842; this edition 1972) *American Notes for General Circulation*, edited Whiteley, J.S. and Goldman, A., Harmondsworth: Penguin.

Fletcher, R.A. (1913) *Travelling Palaces: Luxury in Passenger Steamships*, Pitman, London.

Fry, H. (1896) *The History of North Atlantic Steam Navigation with Some Account of Early Ships and Shipowners*, London, Sampson Low, Marston.

Holland-Amerika Line, (c.1938) *Nieuw Amsterdam: Facts and Figures*, Haarlem: Jon Enschede en Zonen.

Holland-America Line (1959a) *Facts and Figures: S.S. Rotterdam*.

Holland-America Line (1959b) *S.S. Rotterdam.*

Holmes, G.V.C. (1906) *Ancient and Modern Ships,* Part I, Wooden Sailing Ships, and Part II, The Era of Steam, Iron and Steel, Victoria and Albert Museum Science Handbook. Printed for His Majesty's Stationery Office by Wyman and Sons Ltd, London, 1906.

Hughes-Stanton, C. (nd) *Transport Design*, Studio Vista, London.

Hughes-Stanton, C. (nd) *Transport Design*, London: Studio Vista.

Loftie, W.J. (1908) *Orient-Pacific Guide*, London: Orient-Pacific, sixth edition.

Monro, J. (1988) *11 Montpelier Street: Memoirs of an Interior Decorator*, Weidenfeld & Nicholson, London.

Orient Line (c.1949) *Orama, Orion, Oronsay, Orontes, Otranto*, London.

Paul, B. (1914) 'Passagierdampfer und ihre Einrichtungen', *Der Verkehr*, 3rd Year book of the German Werkbund, Jena.

P&O (1935) *Happy Event: The New Strathmore*, London.

P&O-Orient Lines (1961) *Canberra*, London.

Reilly, C.H. (1931) *Representative British Architects of the Present Day*, London, Batsford.

Schip en Werf, Nieuw Amsterdam special issue, 1938.

Veblen, T. (1899) *The Theory of the Leisure Class: An Economic Study of Institutions*, New York.

Waring & Gillow Ltd, (c.1907) *Decorative Contracts by Warings (Waring & Gillow Ltd)*, no publisher, City of Westminster Archives Centre: Waring & Gillow Ltd company records, Ref: 2233/101.

Warren, M.D. (1987) *The Cunard Turbine-Driven Quadruple-Screw Atlantic Liner 'Mauretania': Authentically Reproduced From a Rare 1907 Commemorative Edition of 'Engineering', with Additional New Material Selected by Mark D. Warren and with the Assistance of Swan Hunter*, Wellingborough, Patrick Stephens.

White Star Line, (1911) *Royal Mail Triple-Screw Steamers 'Olympic' and 'Titanic'*, Liverpool: The Liverpool Printing & Stationery Co. Ltd.

Articles

Anderson, C. (1966) 'The Interior Design of Passenger Ships', *Journal of the Royal Society of the Arts*, May, pp. 477–493.

Anderson, C. (1967) 'Ship Interiors: When the Breakthrough Came', *Architectural Review*, Vol. 141, June, pp. 449–52.

Architect & Building News (1936) 'R.M.S. "Queen Mary" ', 29 May, pp. 240–5.

Architect's Journal (1936) 'Notes and Topics: 'Queen Mary" ', April, p. 649.

Architect's Journal (1969) 'QE2: Design for Future Trends in World Travel', 149, pp. 985–96.

Architectural Review (1969) 'Queen Elizabeth 2, a special issue edited by Sherban Cantacuzino', Vol. 145 No. 868, pp. 396–462.

Art Digest (1936) ' "Queen Mary", a floating gallery of art', 1 May, p. 20.

Baschet, J. (1935) 'The Decorative Work in the "Normandie"', *L'Illustration,* 1 June, pp. 3–4.

Beaton, C. (1936) '??' *Vogue*, June ??

Bernard, O.P. (1935) 'Once Aboard the "Normandie" ', *Shipbuilding and Shipping Record*, 12 September, pp. 287–8.

The Blue Peter (1929) 'The New Turbo-Electric S.S.Viceroy of India', Special Supplement, May, pp. a–k.

Byron, R. (1935) 'A New Orient Boat', *Country Life*, 31 August, p. XXIV.

Churchill, W. (1936) 'Queen of the Seas', *The Strand Magazine*, May, pp. 42–53.

Clonmore, Lord (1931) 'The Architecture of the Liner', *Architectural Review*, October, pp. 61–3.

Davis, A.J. (1914) 'The Architecture of the Liner', *Architectural Review,* Volume 35, pp. 87–110.

De la Valette, J. (1936) 'The Fitment and Decoration of Ships: From the "Great Eastern" to the "Queen Mary"', *Journal of the Royal Society of Arts*, 22 May, pp. 705–26.

Design (1969) 'Queen Elizabeth 2', 244, April, pp. 399–409.

Design for Living (1937) 'The New Orient Liner "Orcades", 23,500 tons', 1st August 1937, pp. 596–9.

Design For To-Day (1935a) 'Design in Ships: R.M.S. Orion', October, pp. 381–6.

Design For To-Day (1935b) 'S.S. *Normandie* – the magnificent', October, pp. 387–9.

Diard, A. (1930) 'La Décoration Moderne a Bord des Navires', *Echos d'Art*, Mars, pp. 20–3.

Garrett, S. (1961) 'Amid-ships', *Architectural Review*, 130, No. 775, September, pp. 155–8.

Interior Design and Decoration (1940) 'Interior Design Aboard the S.S. *America*, September, 30, pp. 133–40.

McCallum, I. (1956) 'Ship Interiors', *Architectural Review*, Vol. 119, No. 710, February 1956, pp. 133–40.

Mourey, G. (1927) 'S.S. "ILE DE FRANCE": A FLOATING MUSEUM OF FRENCH DECORATIVE ART', *The Studio*, 1927, pp. 242–9.

Pulitzer, G.F. (1930) 'Nuovi Arredamenti Navali', *Casabella*, September, pp. 29/40.

Rambosson, Y. (1935) 'Le Paquebot Normandie: Héraut de France', *Mobilier & Decoration* July, No. 7, pp. 255–97.

Robertson, H. (1935) 'What I Think of the ORION', *Shipbuilding and Shipping Record*, 22 August, pp. 197–200.

The Cabinet Maker and Complete Home Furnisher (1935) 'R.M.S. "Orion": Contemporary Style in Ship Furnishing', 17 August, pp. 214–15.

The Shipbuilder (1929) 'The P&O Liner "Viceroy of India": The First Large Liner Employing High-pressure Steam and Electric Transmission', April, pp. 260–75.

The Shipbuilder and Marine Engine-Builder (1938) 'The Holland-America Liner "Nieuw Amsterdam": The Largest Vessel yet built in Holland', June 1938, Vol. XLV, No. 344, pp. 354–8.

The Shipbuilder and Marine Engine-Builder (1938) 'The Holland-America Liner "Nieuw Amsterdam": The largest vessel yet built in Holland', July 1938, Vol. XLV, No. 345, pp. 409–24.

The Shipbuilder and Marine Engine-Builder (1960) 'Dutch Liner "Rotterdam", January, Vol. 64, No. 624, pp. 23–30.

Shipbuilding and Shipping Record (1935) 'Strathmore, the Largest and Fastest of the P&O Fleet', 19 September, pp. 315–28.

Shipbuilding and Shipping Record (1935) 'Informality in Ship Furnishing', 26 December, pp. 709–14.

Shipbuilding and Shipping Record (1935) 'The Traveller and His Stateroom', 26 December 1935, pp. 715–22.

Shipbuilding and Shipping Record (1954) 'The "Saxonia" enters service', 9 September, pp. 335–42.

The Studio: An Illustrated Magazine of Fine and Applied Art (1931) 'Empress of Britain: The Decoration of a Liner', Vol. 102, pp. 20–43.

The Studio: An Illustrated Magazine of Fine and Applied Art (1938) 'The Nieuw Amsterdam: A Floating Palace of Art', July, pp. 3–17.

The Studio: An Illustrated Magazine of Fine Art, Home Decoration, and Design (1937) 'Ship Decoration Simplified', pp. 284–5.

Tatton-Brown, W. (1935) 'Architecture Afloat: The "Orion" Sets a New Course', *Architectural Review*, October, pp. 131–9.

The Textile Manufacturer (1935) 'Modern Ships' Textiles', September, p. 14.

Secondary Sources

Books

Anderson, B. (1991) *Imagined Communities: Reflections on the Origin and Spread of Nationalism*, London, Verso. Revised edition, originally published 1983.

Ball, A. and Wright, D. (1981) *SS Great Britain*, Adrian Charles.

Banham, R. (1966) *Theory and Design in the First Machine Age*, London: Architectural Press.

Barker, R. (1978) *Great Mysteries of the Air*, London: Pan Books.

Barthes, R. (1973) *Mythologies*, London: Paladin. First published 1957.

Battersby, M. (1969) *The Decorative Twenties*, London: Studio Vista.

Battersby, M. (1971) *The Decorative Thirties*, London: Studio Vista.

Bayer, P. (1988) *Art Deco Sourcebook*, London: Phaidon.

Bayer, P. (1990) *Art Deco Interiors: Decoration and Design Classics of the 1920s and 1930s*, London: Thames & Hudson.

Baynes, K. and Pugh, F. (1981) *The Art of the Engineer*, Guildford: Lutterworth Press.

Benton, C., Benton, T. and Scharf, A. (1975) *Design 1920s*, Milton Keynes: The Open University Press.

Black, P. (1994) *Geoffrey Clarke*, London: Lund Humphries.

Booker, F. (1985) *The Great Western Railway: A New History*, second edition, London: David St John Thomas.

Black, P. (1994) *Symbols for Man: Geoffrey Clarke, Sculpture and Graphic Work, 1949–94*, London: Ipswich Borough Council Museum and Galleries in association with Lund Humphries Publishers.

Bourdieu, P. (1984) *Distinction: A Social Critique on the Judgment of Taste*, London, Routledge & Kegan Paul.

Brinnin, J.M. (1972) *The Sway of the Grand Saloon: A Social History of the North Atlantic*, second edition, London: Macmillan.

Brinnin, J.M. (1982) *Beau Voyage: Life Aboard the Last Great Ships*, Thames & Hudson: London.

Brinnin, J.M. and Gaulin, K. (1988) *Grande Luxe*. New York: Henry Holt and Company Inc.

Cannadine, D. (2005) *The Decline and Fall of the British Aristocracy*, London: Penguin.

Casarino, C. (ed.) (2002) *Modernity at Sea: Melville, Marx, Conrad in Crisis*, University of Minnesota Press.

Catleugh, J. (1983) *William De Morgan Tiles*, Trefoil Books: London.

Claxton, C. (1845) *A Description of the Great Britain Steam Ship, built at Bristol, for the proprietors of the Great Western Steam Ship Company with remarks on the comparative merits of iron and wood as materials for ship building*. Bristol, printed at the Mirros Office by John Taylor (courtesy of SS Great Britain Trust).

Colomino, B. (1994) *Privacy and Publicity. Modern Architecture as Mass Media,* Cambridge (MA): MIT Press.

Crellin, S. 'Infrastructures: Formation and Networks: 1925–50' in Henry Moore Institute, *Sculpture of the Twentieth Century*.

Dalkmann, H.A. and Schoonderbeek, A.J. (1998) *One Hundred and Twenty-Five Years of Holland America Line*, The Pentland Press, Durham.

Dawson, P. (2000) *Cruise Ships: An Evolution in Design*, London: Conway Maritime Press.

Dawson, P. (2005) *The Liner: Retrospective & Renaissance*, London: Conway Maritime Press.

Dean, D. (1983) *The Thirties: Recalling the English Architectural Scene*, London: Trefoil Books Ltd.

Dickens, C. (1842; this edition 1972) *American Notes for General Circulation*, edited Whiteley, J.S. and Goldman, A., Harmondsworth: Penguin.

Dougan, D. (1968) *The History of North East Shipbuilding*, London: George Allen and Unwin Ltd.

Dugan, J. (1953: second edition 2003) *The Great Iron Ship*, Stroud: Sutton Publishing Ltd.

Ellery, D. (1994) *RMS Queen Mary: The World's Favourite Liner*, Blandford Forum: Waterfront Publications.

Emmons, F. (1972) *The Atlantic Liners 1925–70*, New York: Bonanza Books.

Emmons, F.E. (1985) *American Passenger Ships: The Ocean Lines and Liners, 1873–1983*, London: University of Delaware Press.

Farley, F. (1843) *Felix Farley's Bristol Journal*, 22 July, 1843, p. 2. (Courtesy of SS Great Britain Trust).

Fogg, N. (2002) *The Voyages of the Great Britain: Life at Sea in the World's First Liner*, London: Chatham Publishing.

Forty, A. (1986) *Objects of Desire: Design and Society 1750–1980*, London: Thames & Hudson.

Gardner, J. (1993) *James Gardner: The ARTful designer*, London: Centurion Press.

Greenhill, B. and Giffard, A. (1972) *Travelling by Sea in the Nineteenth Century: Interior Design in Victorian Passenger Ships*, London: Adam and Charles Black.

Grigson, G. (1935) 'Design of the Temporary Home', *The Studio*, October 1935, pp. 191–202.

Gronberg, T. (1998) *Designs on Modernity: Exhibiting the city in 1920s Paris*, Manchester: Manchester University Press.

Gronberg, T. (1999) 'The *Titanic*: an Object Manufactured for Exhibition at the Bottom of the Sea' in Kwint, M., Breward, C. and Aynsley, J. (eds) *Material Memories: Design and Evocation*, Oxford: Berg.

Guns, N. (2004) *Holland America Line: Short History of a Shipping Company*, Zutphen: Walburg Pers.

Hammond, M. and Massey, A. (1999) '". . . it was true! How can you laugh?": The Conflation of History and Memory in the Reception of *Titanic* in Britain and Southampton' in Sandler, K. and Studlar, G. (eds) *Titanic: Anatomy of a Blockbuster*, Rutgers University Press, Rutgers.

Harvey, C. (2004) *RMS Empress of Britain: Britain's Finest Liner*, Stroud: Tempus.

Harvey, D. (1989) *The Condition of Postmodernity: An Enquiry into the Origins of Cultural Change*, Oxford: Basil Blackwell Ltd.

Heskett, J. (1986) *Design in Germany, 1870–1918*, London: Trefoil Books Ltd.

Heynen, H. (1999) *Architecture and Modernity: A Critique*, MIT Press.

Bibliography

Hillier, B. (2003) *Young Betjeman*, London: John Murray, first published 1988.

Horn, P. (1995) *Women in the 1920s*, Stroud, Allan Sutton.

Hyde, F.E. (1975) *Cunard and the North Atlantic 1840–1973*, London: Macmillan.

Jackson, L. (1998) *'Contemporary': Architecture and Interiors of the 1950s*, Phaidon.

Johnson, H. (1987) *The Cunard Story*, London: Whittet Books.

Johnston, I. (2000) *Ships For A Nation 1847–1971: John Brown & Company, Clydebank:* Glasgow, West Dumbartonshire Libraries & Museums.

Jones, S. (1986) *Two Centuries of Overseas Trading: the Origins and Growth of the Inchcape Group*, London: Macmillan.

Jones, S. (1989) *Trade and Shipping: Lord Inchcape 1852–1932*, Manchester: Manchester University Press.

Kirkham, P. (ed) (2000) *Women Designers in the USA, 1900–2000: Diversity and Difference*, New Haven and London: Yale University Press.

Lacey, R. (1973) *The Queens of the North Atlantic*, London: Sidgwick & Jackson.

Le Corbusier, (1987) *Toward a New Architecture*, The Architectural Press, London, first published in French 1923.

Loudmer, G. (1983) *Oeuvres d'Art du 'France' Tableux de Marine: Collections de la Compagnie Generale Maritime*, Paris.

Lynch, J. (2004) *Forgotten Shipbuilders of Belfast: Workman, Clark, 1880–1935*, Belfast: Friar's Bush Press.

Marcilhac, F. (1991) *Jean Dunand: His Life and Works*, London: Thames & Hudson.

Massey, A. (1997) (ed.) *Romancing Hollywood: The Construction and Reception of Glamour*, Southampton: Millais Gallery.

Massey, A. (2000) *Hollywood Beyond the Screen: Design and Material Culture*, Oxford: Berg.

Massey, A. (2001) *Interior Design of the Twentieth Century*, London: Thames & Hudson.

Maxtone-Graham, J. (1972) *The Only Way To Cross*, New York: Macmillan.

McCaughan, M. (1998) *The Birth of the Titanic*, Belfast: The Blackstaff Press.

McCluskie, T. (1998) *Anatomy of the Titanic*, PRC Publishing.

McConkey, K. (1993) *Sir John Lavery*, Edinburgh: Canongate Press.

Miller, B.S. (1977) *Sail, Steam and Splendour: A Picture History of Life Aboard the Transatlantic Liners*, New York: Times Books.

Miller, W.H. (1985) *The Fabulous Interiors of the Great Ocean Liners in Historic Photographs*, New York: Dover Publications.

Miller, W.H. (1986) *British Ocean Liners: A Twilight Era, 1960–1985*, London and New York: W.W. Norton & Co.

Miller, W.H. (1987) *Famous Ocean Liners*, Wellingborough: Patrick Stephens.

Miller, W.H. (2001) *Picture History of British Ocean Liners, 1900 to the Present*, New York: Dover Publications, Inc.

Miller, W.H. and Correia, M. (1997) *SS Canberra of 1961*, Lisbon, Liner Books.

Miller, W.H. and Correia, M. (2002) *SS France of 1961, SS Norway of 1979*, Lisbon, Liner Books.

Morris, C.F (1980) *Origins, Orient and Oriana*, Brighton: Teredo Books Ltd.

Moss, M. and Hume, J.R. (1986) *Shipbuilders to the World: 125 Years of Harland and Wolff, Belfast, 1861–1986*, Belfast: Blackstaff.

The National Trust (2003) *Cragside*, National Trust Enterprises Ltd.

Nicholson, V. and Panourigias K.K. (2002) *The Sculpture of Maurice Lambert*, Aldershot: The Henry Moore Foundation in Association with Lund Humphries.

Ottewill, D. (1989) *The Edwardian Garden*, Yale University Press, New Haven and London.

Padwell, P. (1981) *Beneath the Houseflag of the P&O*, London: Hutchinson.

Parry, L. (1983) *William Morris Textiles*, London: Weidenfeld & Nicolson.

Parry, L. (1988) *Textiles of the Arts and Crafts Movement*, London: Thames & Hudson.

Peck, J. (2001) *Maritime Fiction: Sailors and the Sea in British and American Novels, 1719–1917*, Basingstoke: Palgrave.

Pevsner, N. (1991) *Pioneers of Modern Design From William Morris to Walter Gropius*, Harmondsworth: Penguin.

Phillips-Birt, D. (1971) *When Luxury Went to Sea*, Newton Abbot: David & Charles.

Potter, N. and Frost, J. (1961) *The Queen Mary, Her Inception and History*, London: George G. Harrap & Co.

Potter, N. and Frost, J. (1969) *QE2: Queen Elizabeth 2, The Authorised Story*, London: Harrrap.

Prior, R. (1993) *Ocean Liners: The Golden Years*, London: Tiger Books International.

Quartermaine, P. (1996) *Building on the Sea: Form and Meaning in Modern Ship Architecture*, London: Academy Editions.

Said, E.W. (2003) *Orientalism*, London: Penguin (originally published 1978).

Saint, A. (1983) *Richard Norman Shaw*, Yale: Yale University Press.

Service, A. (ed.) (1975) *Edwardian Architecture and Its Origins*, London: Architectural Press.

Schaefer, K. (1907) 'Die moderne Raumkunst im Dienste des Norddeuteschen Lloyd', *Innendekoration*, p. 296.

Smallpeice, Sir B. (1981) *Of Comets and Queens: An Autobiography*, Shrewsbury: Airlife Publishing Ltd.

Smith, K. (1997) *Mauretania: Pride of the Tyne*, Newcastle Libraries & Information Service, Newcastle.

Southampton City Art Gallery (1986) *Art on the Liners: A Celebration of Elegance at Sea*, Southampton.

Sparke, P. (1988) *Italian Design: 1870 to the Present*, London: Thames & Hudson.

Sparke, P. (1995) *As Long As Its Pink: The Sexual Politics of Taste*, London: Harper Collins.

Sparke, P. (2004) 'Introduction' in McKellar, S. and Sparke, P. (eds) *Interior Design and Identity*, Manchester: Manchester University Press.

Sparke, P. (2005) *Elsie de Wolfe: The Birth of Modern Interior Design*, New York: Acanthus Press.

Steele, J. (1995) *Queen Mary*, London: Phaidon Press.

Urry, J. (1995) *Consuming Places*, London: Routledge.

Vernon Gibbs, C.R. (1970) *Western Ocean Passenger Lines and Liners 1934–1969*, Glasgow: Brown, Son & Ferguson.

Vian, L.R. (1992) *Arts Decoratifs a Bord des Paquebots Francais 1880–1960*, Editions Fonmare, Paris.

Walmsley, F. (2004) 'Pragmatism and Pluralism: the interior decoration of the *Queen Mary*', in McKellar, S. and Sparke, P. (eds) *Interior Design and Identity*, Manchester: Manchester University Press.

Ward, D. (2005) *Berlitz Ocean Cruising and Cruise Ships 2005*, London: Berlitz Publishing.

Whale, D.M. (1986) *The Liners of Liverpool: Part 1*, Merseyside: Countryvise Ltd.

White, S.G. and Wallen, J. (1998) *The Houses of McKim, Mead and White*, New York: Rizzoli.

White, S.G. and White, E. (2003) *McKim, Mead and White: The Masterworks*, New York: Rizzoli.

Willett, J. (1978) *The New Sobriety 1917–33: Art and Politics in the Weimar Period*, London: Thames & Hudson.

Articles

Atkinson, P. (2005) 'Man in a Briefcase: The Social Construction of the Laptop Computer', *Journal of Design History*, Vol. 18, 191–205.

Buxton, I. (1996) '*Mauretania* and Her Builders', *The Mariner's Mirror*, 82, pp. 55–73.

Forsyth, A. (1985) 'The Grand Hotel Afloat: Cunard's Maritime Masterpiece', 26 December, 2034–6.

Foucault, M. (1967) 'Of Other Spaces, Heterotopias', http://foucault.info/documents/heteroTopia/foucault. heteroTopia.en.html accessed 1.9.2005.

Journal of the RIBA (1947) 'The Creator of the Modern Luxury Hotel: Charles Mewès, Architect, 1860–1914', Vol. 54, No. 13, October, pp. 603–4.

Potvin, J. (2005) 'Vapour and Steam: The Victorian Turkish Bath, Homosexual Health, and Male Bodies on Display', *Journal of Design History*, Vol. 18, pp. 319–33.

Rassegna (1990) Special Issue: Ocean Liners, Vol. 44, pp. 4–88.

Robichon, F. (1985) '*Normandie*, Palais Flottant', *Architectes Architecture*, 162, pp. 32–3.

Sekules, V. (1985–6) 'The Ship-owner as an Art Patron: Sir Colin Anderson and the Orient Line 1930–1960', *Journal of the Decorative Arts Society*, No. 10, pp. 22–9.

Van der Merwe, P. (2001) 'Views of the Royal Naval Exhibition', *Journal of Maritime Research*, September, www.jmr.nmm.ac.uk, (accessed 24 March 2005).

Bibliography

Videos

The Liners: A Voyage of Discovery – The Great Duel, Australian Film Finance Corporation, 1997.
The Liners: A Voyage of Discovery – Ships of War, Australian Film Finance Corporation, 1997.

Websites

http://www.cunard.com/AboutCunard/default.asp?Active=Heritage&Sub=Fleet
www.frenchlines.com
www.dkb.nl/mutters/mutters-UShtm
http://www.clydesite.co.uk/clydebuilt/index.asp
http://www.lascars.co.uk
http://www.theshipslist.com/index.html

Archives and Collections Consulted

Design History Collection, Brighton University
www.brighton.ac.uk/designarchives
Houses the Design Council Archive and the James Gardener archive, both of which contain material relating to the *QE2*.

French Line Archives
www.frenchlines.com
Located at Le Havre, a fabulous collection of papers and photographs relating to the design and operation of the French Line ships.

Liverpool Maritime Museum
www.liverpoolmuseums.org.uk/maritime/archives
Collection of Cunard material, mainly technical, including ship plans and photographs.

Mariners' Museum, Newport News, Virginia, USA
www.mariner.org
Holds a useful library and also the Steamship Ephemera Collection, currently undergoing digitization.

Maritime Museum Rotterdam
www.maritiemmuseum.nl
Collection of material, including photographs, relating to Holland America Line. The business records of the line are located at the Rotterdam Municipal Archives.

National Maritime Museum, Greenwich
www.nmm.ac.uk
The Caird Library holds the collections of P&O, the Orient Line and Union-Castle, plus a wealth of other material. The photographic collection is also useful and is located at Woolwich Arsenal. The Museum also holds sample books containing fabrics swatches and drawings of P&O ships from the 1920s.

Public Record Office of Northern Ireland (PRONI)

www.proni.gov.uk

The Harland & Wolff company records are lodged with PRONI. The entire collection is labelled D/2805, and the majority of files are closed to the public, but access may be granted by Harland & Wolff if a plausible case is made in writing. D/2805/A contains records relating to work for the Admiralty. Section D/2805/AGC consists of agreements and contracts, which are not open to the public and only date from 1934, so really after their heyday. Section D/2805/AGM contain official minutes etc, but these only date from 1953 onwards. Files such as D/2805/CPS/A/1 contain the early correspondence of F.E. Rebbeck mainly about business arrangements, for example, the Scottish plant, the take-over of Union-Castle, which are well documented in Moss and Hume (1986). D.2805/CPS/A/2/25 is a file containing the agenda, and general correspondence concerning the business of Heaton Tabb & Co. Ltd., Ship Decorators and Furnishers, London. However, this is only a collection of agenda for the Annual General Meetings in London, which Rebbeck never attended. The correspondence consists of his apologies for not attending.

Tyne & Wear Archives Service

www.thenortheast.com/archives

Collection featuring aspects of the north east's industrial heritage. Features the archive of shipbuilders Swan Hunter and Wigham Richardson Ltd, including photographs of ship interiors, in the process of being catalogued.

Ulster Folk and Transport Museum

www.uftm.org.uk

An invaluable photographic source for ships built by Harland & Wolff, particularly the ships of the late nineteenth and early twentieth centuries. Covers interiors of important ships such as the *Oceanic* (1899), *Amerika* (1905), *Nieuw Amsterdam* (1906) *Olympic* (1911) and the *Canberra* (1961) all well organized and easy to consult.

University of Glasgow Archive Services

www.archives.gla.ac.uk

Collection includes archives of Wylie & Lochhead, John Brown and the Anchor Line. Note that photographs of the ship interiors taken for John Brown are located in Edinburgh, at the Public Records Office there.

University of Liverpool Cunard Steam-Ship Company Archives

www.liv.ac.uk

A tremendous source for background information on the interior design of liners, of particular value are the Chairmen's correspondence, particularly C3 Sir Percy Bates papers, Chairman of Cunard 1930–4 and then Chairman of the Cunard Steam-Ship Company before its merger with White Star in October 1934. He was the first Chairman of the newly inaugurated Cunard White Star until he died in1946. *Mauretaina II, Queen Elizabeth, Queen Mary* are included in this section. The Company Secretary files include the S7 files on particular ships – the *Mauretania, Lusitania* and *Aquitania*. The Public Relations Department files, include photographs of many of the exteriors and some interiors of Cunard liners, posters, press cuttings, and printed ephemera.

Index